LEARNING TO TEACH, TEACHING TO LEARN

LEARNING TO TEACH, TEACHING TO LEARN

A Guide for Social Work Field Education

Carmen Ortiz Hendricks

Jeanne Bertrand Finch

Cheryl L. Franks

COUNCIL ON SOCIAL WORK EDUCATION
ALEXANDRIA, VIRGINIA

Library of Congress Cataloguing-in-Publication Data

Hendricks, Carmen Ortiz.
    Learning to teach, teaching to learn : a guide for social work field
education / Carment Ortiz Hendricks, Jeanne Bertrand Finch, Cheryl L.
        Franks.—1st ed.
            p. cm.
    Includes bibliographical references.
    ISBN 0-87293-117-X
    1. Social work education.   2. Social service—Field work.   3. Field work
(Educational method)   I. Finch, Jeanne Bertrand.   II. Franks, Cheryl L.
III. Title.

    HV11.H43 2005
    361.3'071'55—dc22   2005000897

Printed in the United States of America on acid-free paper that meets the American National Standards Institute Z39-48 Standard.

Council on Social Work Education, Inc.
1725 Duke Street, Suite 500
Alexandria, VA 22314-3457
www.cswe.org

CONTENTS

ACKNOWLEDGMENTS

The authors would like to acknowledge the seminal work of Naomi Pines Gitterman for her role in chairing the original *Seminar in Field Instruction Subcommittee* (SIFI) of the greater New York area directors of field education (see p. 263) and leading the development of the NYS field instruction curriculum in the late 1970s. We also owe a debt of gratitude to Dee Livingston for her leadership and involvement with the subcommittee for over 25 years. Their work created a structure that is evident in SIFIs today.

We would like to acknowledge the directors and subcommittee members over the last 30 years who have inspired our work. They include: Sidney Berengarten, Martha Bial, Ethel Catlin, Dan Gottlieb, Helen Graber, Alisa Hammerman, John Haynes, Reinhold Heckeler, Reva Fine Holtzman, Theodora Kaplan, Catherine Faith Kappenberg, Judith Lemberger, Eve Lodge, Maxine Lynn, Elaine Marshack, Jackie Mondros, Murray Raim, Cristy Ramirez, Michele Sarracco, Georgiana Shephard, Bea Seitzman, Selma Stevens, Carol Sturtz, Carlos Vidal, and Sylvia Weiss. We also acknowledge Betty-Jean Wrase of Stony Brook University, Barbara Stoker of Rutgers University, and Alice K. Wolson of New York University for their contributions in the early stages of the development of this text.

We would like to recognize and thank the current Greater New York Metropolitan Area directors of field education for their support and guidance throughout the development of this text. They are: Peter Chernack, Adelphi University; Kathryn Conroy, Columbia University; Jeanne Bertrand Finch, Stony Brook University/SUNY; Urania Glassman, Yeshiva University; Minou Minchlip, Southern Connecticut State University; Catherine Medina, New York University; Jan Miner, Fordham University; Glynn Rudich, Hunter College/CUNY; Bonita Sanchez, University of Albany/SUNY, and Marjorie Talbot, Rutgers University. The authors extend a special thank you to Elaine Marshack, Dee Livingston, and Beverly Feigelman for their time and careful attention to a review of this text. We also wish to acknowledge Tanya

Manvelidze, assistant librarian at Hunter College School of Social Work Library, for her help with references.

Finally, we would like to thank our SIFI teachers for their important contribution to field education and for their feedback on this text.

Current or past members of the SIFI Subcommittee who made contributions to this book in its earlier stages include:

Beverly Feigelman, MSW, LCSW, CASAC, adjunct professor, Adelphi University School of Social Work, private practitioner and former assistant director, Field Education Department, Adelphi University School of Social Work. She has been a field instructor and continues to be a faculty liaison and SIFI instructor.

Esther Howe, DSW, LCSW, associate professor, Department of Social Work, Southern Connecticut State University, former director of field education. She continues to teach the SIFI and courses on diversity and oppression and social work in educational settings.

Ruth Bigman, MSW, LCSW, is the director of admissions at Yeshiva University, Wurzweiler School of Social Work. Previously she served as assistant director of field instruction, faculty liaison, and SIFI teacher at Wurzweiler. She has worked in child preventive services in New York City working with children and families at risk and as a field instructor.

Patricia M. O'Dell, MSW, LCSW, is the clinical supervisor of the Adult and Family Treatment Program at Family Service of Morris County in Morristown, NJ, and maintains a private practice, where she specializes in chronic and life-threatening illness. Previously she worked at Rutgers University, School of Social Work, where she taught numerous graduate-level courses and served as assistant dean and director of field work.

Mary E. Remito, MSW, LCSW, is currently director of Adelphi University's social work program in Manhattan. She participated on the SIFI subcommittee when she was assistant director of field instruction for Fordham University. She has many years of experience as a field instructor, faculty liaison, and SIFI instructor.

PREFACE

This book brings together the collected experiences, ideas, and knowledge of a group of very competent and talented scholars in field education. It contains a rich selection of ideas generated from the experience of social workers who bring into focus and combine what they have learned as practitioners and field instructors. As teachers of Seminars in Field Instruction (SIFIs) they are now sharing their ideas and expertise with an audience of students and teachers. The contributions of many experts to the content of this book are readily apparent in a strong and clear voice, bringing comprehensiveness and thoroughness to its discussions. From preparing for the arrival of students to identifying learning styles, managing problematic situations, and evaluating learning, this book offers detailed and explicit suggestions and tools for excellence in field education.

Social work practice, as the term implies, is composed of professional actions. To learn which actions work well, whether in helping clients and communities make necessary changes and improvements, or in helping them respond to personal or organizational challenges, social work students need to combine theory (derived primarily from the classroom and reading) with practice (derived mostly in the field). Because we value the field placement component in social work education, we pay attention not only to content to be learned, but also how to best learn and teach that material. Yet, despite our long history of field education, we have few books that guide the learning and teaching in the field that is recognized as critical in the development of competent social work practitioners. This book offers state-of-the-art guidelines to students and teachers for the vital tasks of field education. It pulls together ideas from a rich and broad range of books and articles related to field education, to develop a marvelous compendium of what we know and hope for in field education. It is in many ways a fine tribute to the extraordinary work undertaken by field educators.

Just as we have to learn how to practice as social workers, we have to learn how to teach others how to practice within the profession. While we depend on field instructors being expert practitioners themselves with the extensive knowledge base of theory and skills that needs to be transmitted to students, their high level of competence as practitioners does not necessarily translate automatically to readiness and expertise as teachers. The Seminar in Field Instruction offered by most schools helps to translate field instructors' knowledge and experience into transferable knowledge and skills. Similarly, this book helps field instructors reconsider the many ideas and concepts that are so deeply ingrained in daily practice and that seem automatic, and to reconceptualize practice wisdom that many have taken for granted. In this way, field instructors arrive at notions and connections of theory to practice that can be demonstrated, discussed, and made explicit in such terms that the student can take hold of them actively and put them to use.

Field instructors are busy as advanced practitioners and, from time to time, they may resist the idea of making time to attend a seminar, or they may assume that they will not need assistance to take their knowledge and skills and make them readily teachable and available to their students. At times, they may hold unrealistic views of the student as an empty vessel, waiting to be filled with the practice wisdom that they enthusiastically offer, based on their years of experience and success. It is often at the beginning of the seminar meetings that the new field instructor first stops to think about the importance of creating an active learning environment and avoiding the pitfall of overteaching. This book is a rich source of ideas for how to make that learning environment a reality and how to engage students as adult, active learners. Adult learners need to learn to identify the knowledge, skills, and values that they bring to the field while raising questions about new knowledge, skills, and values posed by their classroom and field instructors. An active learner will find more questions arising as more is learned and, sometimes, as prior patterns and understanding are given up or "unlearned."

This book is a perfect opportunity for field instructors to recognize and manage their own anxiety or concerns, whether about knowing what is needed by students or being able to assess whether the intended learning is taking place. It helps new and experienced field instructors, eager to prepare students for professional practice, with the tools to understand the ups and downs of the field education experience. Students, field instructors, faculty liaisons, educational coordinators, and SIFI teachers will find throughout this book rich illustrations, many practical guidelines, and models to apply to their part in field education.

I am proud to introduce this book, as it promotes excellence in field education and is one that I would have been proud to write. It offers all social work teachers thorough discussions of the learning and teaching process that can lead to practice excellence. Those educators who use this book as a guide, taking its collected wisdom to heart and putting its many suggestions into practice, will be very well prepared to teach social work practice. Their students will be very fortunate!

Kay Davidson, Dean & SIFI Teacher
University of Connecticut
School of Social Work

INTRODUCTION

*T*he traditional image is one where the field instructor is viewed as belonging to one domain, typically the organization...The second image recognizes there are competing interests and views the field instructor as being in a precarious position pivoting on a point where work, school, occupation and home intersects, consequently pulling the individual in many directions. A third more collaborative image views the field instructor as being at the heartland, a vital and solid place, balanced at the nexus of practice, education, profession and personhood. It is the pursuit of this collaborative image, the image of choice, which will lead us to the confluence of quality and competence in field education and into the 21st century. (Rogers, 1995, p. 34)

In *Social Work Field Education: Views and Visions*, Rogers draws an ideal image of field instructors as partners and collaborators in the education of social work students. Her view and vision are clear. It is through collaboration with field instructors that "quality and competence" in field education will emerge. This text starts with Rogers's premise by offering a guide that strengthens the pivotal position field instructors hold in the education of future social workers.

The significant role that field education plays in the development of social work professionals is well documented in social work literature (Berg-Weger & Birkenmaier, 2000; Bogo & Vayda, 1991; Goldstein, 1993; Kadushin, 1992; Reisch & Jarman-Rohde, 2000; Schneck, Grossman, & Glassman, 1991). Most field education texts emphasize the centrality of field education to social work education and the reciprocal and interactive quality of field instruction while conceptualizing the content and process of field education. These include Sheafor and Jenkins (1982), *Quality Field Instruction in Social Work: Program Development and Maintenance*; Bogo and Vayda (1987, 1993), *The Practice of Field Instruction in Social Work: Theory and Process* and *The Practice of Field Instruction: A Teaching Guide*; Urbanowski and Dwyer (1988), *Learning*

Through Field Instruction: A Guide for Teachers and Students; Schneck, Grossman, and Glassman (1991), *Field Education in Social Work: Contemporary Issues and Trends*; Shulman (1983, 1994), *Teaching the Helping Skills: A Field Instructor's Guide*; and Rogers (1995), *Social Work Field Education: Views and Visions*. This text is an effort to build on this body of work and advance the knowledge, skills, and values of field education.

Field education is referred to as the laboratory or testing ground for undergraduate and graduate social work education. From the very beginning of its origins

> field work provided an opportunity for both paid and volunteer workers to obtain intimate knowledge of the poor and of actual social and economic conditions. It was believed that only through continuing contact, as a representative of an agency under expert guidance over an extended period of time, could a charity worker develop. (Sikkema, 1966, p. 3)

Field education is the playing field where the knowledge, skills, and values of a profession are transmitted. It is the place to understand, apply, and integrate theory and practice, and where fundamentals of practice, policy, human behavior, and research taught in the classroom are tested and consolidated. It is in this context that educational principles are balanced with the reality of agency-based and community-based practice and the demands of service delivery to a range of diverse client systems. However, the relationship between classroom and field teaching is not always compatible or a comfortable fit.

> Since the establishment of the first formal training program in social work in 1898, practice and education have remained uneasily interdependent. Initiated by the Charity Organization Society of New York, classroom teaching of social work was originally intended to support and extend the practice in the field.... But by the 1960's field instruction seemed to have come full circle from its original conception. It was viewed by many as a 'laboratory extension and support of class experiences' with 'the flow of content heavily from class to specially devised field experiences' rather than being reciprocal and interactive. (Marshack & Rosenfeld, 1986, pp. 2–3)

The *Journal of Social Work Education* dedicated a special section to field education in social work. In the editorial, Lager and Robbins (2004) summarize the thinking of field education scholars on the need for an expanded vision

for field education. This expanded vision includes the realization of field education's potential for shaping both social work education and social work practice.

> In the field, students have the opportunity to test what they learn in the classroom;
> integrate theory with practice; evaluate the effectiveness of interventions; contend
> with the realities of social, political and economic injustice; strive for cultural sen-
> sitivity and competence; deliberate on the choices posed by ethical dilemmas;
> develop a sense of self in practice; and build a connection to and identity with
> the profession. (Lager & Robbins, 2004, p. 3)

However, there is a major gap between a call for an expanded vision, and
the "eclectic" or often unstructured approaches to the training and support
provided to field instructors. This inconsistency may reflect the current challenges to social work practice, the lack of attention to field instruction models,
tasks and procedures, and the general lack of support for the role of field
instructor in today's agency-based environments for practice. This text aims to
bridge that gap. It is a book for field instructors and students. It offers an
expanded vision of field education that supports field instructors in their role.
This book attempts to lay out the steps for achieving a quality field education
experience for both students and field instructors by placing the field instruc-
tor/student relationship as central to achieving learning goals and objectives.
It emphasizes the best way to teach adult learners and highlights the student
and field instructor as active participants in a mutual, collaborative process.
This book is intended to be a good "how to" in field education. It lays out in
detail the tasks of field instruction—developing assignments, teaching agency-
based practice, evaluating students' abilities to learn social work practice
skills and achieve learning goals—but it offers more than that. The authors
seek to "re-image" field education as an interactional approach, a "sacred
space" (Gray & Gray, 1999), an interconnected experience in which students
learn/teach and field instructors teach/learn in the Freirian (1993) tradition.

> Through dialogue, the teacher-of-the-students and the students-of-the-teacher cease
> to exist and a new term emerges: teacher-student with students-teachers. The
> teacher is no longer merely the-one-who-teaches, but one who is himself taught in
> dialogue with the students. (Freire, 1993, p. 80)

Another way of saying this, "No longer can we tell whether it is the student
offering himself to the teacher or the teacher offering herself to the student. We

see each of the two beings mirroring the other in pure reflection" (Huang & Lynch, 1995, p. 4). In this kind of "connected teaching" the teacher welcomes diversity of opinions as the truth inside students is uncovered in an objective manner, which is seeing students in their own terms. "Connected teachers are believers. They trust their students' thinking and encourage them to expand it" (Belenky, Clinchy, Goldberger, & Tarule, 1986, p. 227). The spirit behind this text draws the reader to focus on the process as much as the content of field education.

This book has integrated a wide range of knowledge and information available on field education and presents it in a systematic manner that guides field instructors from the beginning orientation stage through to the final evaluation process and termination of the placement. Field instructors can choose from the models presented freely creating their own field instruction style and approach. The text presents content in what appears to be a linear fashion; however, real life does not always fit the linear design. For example, field instructors are often faced with teaching issues of termination long before this content is presented in the classroom. Field instructors may need to provide students with special knowledge about diverse populations, needs, situations, or settings that may not be covered in curricula. As a consequence, field instructors are often the students' primary source of information and support. This book is a guide to generic aspects of field education, and it can be adapted to specific geographic locations, communities served, and placement settings. The book addresses the role transition from practitioner to educator of social work students and how best to adapt teaching styles and practice preferences to student learning needs, learning patterns, and learning styles. Like the practice of social work itself, this book is rooted in time and will require revisions as the profession continues to evolve in response to the current social, political, cultural, and economic landscape. For instance, the use of the language "client" or "client system" does not sufficiently capture the complexity of units of attention represented in service delivery, which include the environmental systems in which clients interact with the interdependent systems of the individual, family, group, community, and organizations. Throughout this book, the term "client" or "client system" is used in this broader context.

It is also clear that field instructors increasingly face challenges in creating organizational environments that protect student learning needs. Providing appropriate learning opportunities for students despite these challenges can be a daunting task (Carlson et al., 2000; Jarman-Rohde, McFall, Kolar, & Strom, 1997; Lager & Robbins, 2004; Raskin & Bloome, 1998; Reisch & Jarman-Rohde, 2000). The intent of this book is to highlight the knowledge and skills needed to pass on the art and science of professional social work practice in the face of current and future challenges. Challenges include preparing the agency for students in the midst of reduced agency resources, pressures on staff time, and the demands for productivity; preparing students for self-directed and self-reflective learning within an increasingly technological era; meeting the demands of diversity and culturally competent practice; instilling an international, global lens on practice for the 21st century; responding to the impact of managed care on service delivery and professional education; providing reasonable accommodation for the special needs of students; and teaching advocacy skills in an increasingly conservative political environment. Each of these challenges requires creating space for reflection and for crafting innovative practice approaches to increasingly complex social problems and situations.

Chapter 1, "Learning to Teach, Teaching to Learn," examines field instructor/ student relationships as the cornerstone of field education. This chapter emphasizes the field instructor as educator and the responsibilities associated with this role—teacher of adult learners with a range of learning needs.

Chapter 2, "Beginning Processes in Field Instruction: Setting the Stage," considers what is involved in orienting students to field instruction and preparing the agency for students. It describes how the beginning phase sets the stage for teaching and learning throughout field placement experiences.

Chapter 3 introduces "The Range of Student Assignments: Micro to Macro Practice" by presenting many of the factors involved in choosing and developing assignments that meet student learning needs in foundation and advanced concentrations of study.

Chapter 4, "Adult Learning, Learning Styles, Learning Stages," describes the ways in which field instructors create an environment for adult learners that accommodates different learning styles and stages of learning.

Chapter 5 explores "Teaching Methods," including the differences between didactic and experiential teaching, the benefits of individual, peer, and group supervision, and how to teach critical thinking skills. This chapter includes a self-evaluation instrument for field instructors to select teaching methods and adapt different learning styles.

Chapter 6, "Process Recordings, Logs, and Journals," presents a range of recording methods to enhance student learning experiences. It discusses various ways to construct recordings, how to use these recordings in teaching, and how to prioritize the learning focus from the material presented in recordings.

Chapter 7, "Educational Assessment and Learning Plans," discusses the purpose and structure of educational assessment, how to assess what students know and need to know, and how to develop learning plans to address learning needs.

Chapter 8, "Evaluation of Field Performance," tackles the evaluative role and gate-keeping function for field instructors. It addresses the importance of ongoing feedback to students about their performance through mid-semester verbal evaluations and the end-of-semester written evaluations.

Chapter 9 explores the important arena of "Professional Ethics and Values" and how field instructors can support students as they navigate through value conflicts and conflicts of interest, the parameters of confidentiality, and the challenges of dual relationships. This chapter stresses the importance of raising confidentiality and other ethical issues as an integral part of social work practice and field education experiences.

Because social workers have an ethical responsibility to be culturally competent practitioners, chapter 10 focuses on "Cultural Competence and Diversity." The *NASW Standards for Cultural Competence in Social Work Practice* is introduced, and a range of diversity dimensions and their impact on teaching and learning in field education are discussed. This chapter also gives special attention to working with gay, lesbian, bisexual, and transgender students and ends with a series of diversity scenarios that are useful discussion triggers for field instructors and students.

Chapter 11 examines the "Teaching Challenges in Field Instruction" by looking at the different skills needed to teach gifted, experienced, or "challenging" students. It offers a perspective on understanding and dealing with resistance to learning and how to accommodate the special needs of students with disabilities. This chapter also looks at sexual harassment situations and boundary violations that may arise in agency life or in field instruction relationships.

Chapter 12 supports field instructors in teaching about "Transitions and Termination" when it is time for students to end working relationships with clients and client systems, field instructors, and field placement agencies. It explores this unique phase of learning how to end relationships well; the value of review, evaluation, and assessment in the end phase; and how field instructors help students to plan for their future careers.

And, finally, chapter 13, "Concluding Thoughts," provides some ideas about the future directions of field education. It is followed by an appendix that includes guidelines for how to use this text in seminars in field instruction (SIFIs). SIFIs are places where new field instructors, supervising their first students, are brought together by social work programs for training and support. The appendix contains a sample SIFI course outline and assignments.

This text emphasizes the following important aspects of field education:

- Beginning, middle, and end phases of field instructor/student relationships and parallel student/client system experiences. *Parallel process* is present and active throughout field instruction.

- The emphasis in field education is on developing professional, generic knowledge, skills, and values rather than on technical or vocational skills. Field instructors teach *professional social work practice*, not just agency-based practice.

- Although generic aspects of field education apply to all social work programs, each school has a range of specific requirements for field education. Field instructors should become familiar with these requirements by reviewing the program's *Field Education Manual*, an essential resource to the task of field instruction.

- Unlike supervision that tends to emphasize a "getting-the-job-done" attitude, field education is first and foremost about *teaching and learning* social work practice.

- Creation of conducive learning environments requires a *partnership* between the agency and the social work program and a relationship with field instructors based on collaboration and mutual respect.

- Field education operates from a *strengths-based approach* to teaching adult learners, which fosters a collaborative and egalitarian relationship between field instructors and students.

- Taking on the responsibility of becoming a field instructor requires an interest in broadening one's *professional expertise* and participating in the development of future social work professionals.

There are many intrinsic rewards that evolve from the work of field instruction, including "teaching and sharpening practice skills; learning new ideas;

contributing to the profession; and relieving the boredom of the job" (Rosenfeld, 1989, p. 187). This book is designed as a "gift" for field instructors (Fishbein & Glassman, 1991) who seek to become skillful field teachers. It also provides students with a clear exposition of what they might expect from field instruction. New field instructors will find in this book the needed support for the assumption of the roles and responsibilities of field education. Experienced field instructors will find substantive guidelines and encouragement over the course of their field education careers. In addition to being a gift to field instructors, this book is intended to reinforce the centrality of field education in social work education. "Only in the transition of knowledge into practice, acquired in the field, does social work education achieve professional justification" (Kadushin, 1991, p. 11).

Chapter 1

LEARNING TO TEACH, TEACHING TO LEARN

*W*e do not have to reinvent the wheel in order to meet some of the challenges [of teaching students] before us, but we do need to know what we value, to value what we know, to recommit ourselves to the teaching-learning process, and to try to create a better fit between our teaching techniques and our students. (Goldstein, 1989, p. 20)

Possessing a clear rationale for teaching that is rooted in our professional mission guides the practice of field instruction. It provides a framework from which to begin and provides support to answering questions regarding why we do what we do and why we choose to teach a specific point in any particular format. Likewise, understanding the goals of field instruction provides direction and purpose. Abramson and Fortune (1990, p. 274) discuss the five elements that constitute a competence base for field instructors:

1. A common body of social work knowledge shared by field instructors;

2. The capacity of field instructors to conceptualize this knowledge to communicate it effectively;

3. The creation of an appropriate climate for learning;

4. Clarity regarding the standards for student performance; and

5. The ability to evaluate student performance in light of these standards.

A central goal in social work education is aiding students to achieve a professional sense of identity, "the integration of knowledge, skills, and values into a concept of oneself as a professional and into a style of practice consistent with the knowledge, skills, and values that define the social work profession" (Hamilton & Else, 1983, p. 19). The following steps (Hamilton & Else, 1983; Council on Social Work Education, 2001) are involved in the achievement of this goal:

- Helping students to develop a critically attentive frame of mind and curiosity that is self-directed, autonomous, and creative. This means promoting a questioning stance to theories and interventive strategies by looking at the context of practice, and by asking such questions as, "Why might this be so?" "Who says?" "Under what circumstances?" and "Who has been advantaged by it?" (Hartman, 1997);

- Helping students to apply knowledge in a purposeful, planned, problem-solving manner; acquiring a repertoire of specific practice strategies and techniques; promoting the development of professional relationships with other professionals and client systems; and

- Helping students to promote the values of the profession which includes respect for individual orientations and different world views.

The task for us as field instructors is more than enabling students to turn knowledge into action. It requires the development of "reflection-in-action" (Schon, 1983, 1987), an acceptance that uncertainty is part of the natural process of the work, that critical thinking aids knowing, and that each intervention provides a rich resource for questioning and enhancing knowledge (Papell & Skolnik, 1992). "To 'become what one knows' is to be able to participate in the social world of our clients and requires the learner to develop the ability to use critical reasoning or reflective thinking.... A single correct or objective solution does not exist for the human problems encountered in the field by social workers" (Goldstein, 1993, p. 173). We need to help students move from concrete absolutism to a more reflective style that is comfortable with ambiguity. Enabling students to transfer knowledge and to apply it differentially involves making the information real, making it understood, and making it meaningful to the individual while also transmitting substantive content and promoting the attainment of skills (Gitterman & Miller, 1977).

Unless we teach our students to question and to maintain an inquiring and gentle skepticism, they will be exposed to persistent frustrations and disappointments. Yet, to question and to be inquiring or curious is not a simple thing to do;

the habit must be acquired over a lifetime. Professional socialization formalizes our work and stiffens our approach. Ambiguity threatens us; it ought to challenge us. . . . Our task therefore is to help students break through theoretical and personal boundaries, and cultivate their natural curiosity and spontaneity. (Gitterman, 1988, p. 37)

These aims form the basis of a vision for our teaching style and agenda. They shape the credibility from which students begin to trust that their learning goals will be achieved. The establishment of a trusting learner/teacher relationship is essential (Bogo & Vayda, 1993; Cohen, 2004; Fox, 1989; Kadushin & Harkness, 2002; Munson, 2001; Siporin, 1982). It is within the field instructor/student relationship that students begin to examine their assumptions and to expand their knowledge, skills, and values. The degree to which we can be genuine and authentic determines, to a large extent, the likely establishment of a positive learning environment. The construction of a conducive environment requires the creation of a space where it is possible to be creative, to engage in the risk-taking implicit in new learning, and to examine efforts that fail (Bogo & Vayda, 1987; Drisko, 2000). Our ability to model professional behavior provides a guide for our students to follow.

In addition to modeling, Shulman (1994) delineates four skills associated with effective teaching: (1) having knowledge, (2) having the ability to transmit this knowledge, (3) having the ability to empathize with students, and (4) presenting ideas so that these ideas are open to challenge. Akin and Weil (1981) identify seven processes that foster the development of learning how to supervise others. These processes include: (1) learning by doing or embracing the role and enacting the responsibilities of being a supervisor; (2) following the model of others and enacting the role according to how one has experienced it; (3) adapting the skills one possesses to the new task; (4) acquiring new skills required; (5) participating in formal education regarding the task; (6) following prescribed behaviors; and (7) being selected to the task by being seen as possessing the needed qualities.

Dearnley (1985) suggests that these processes may occur step-wise in the development of supervisory skills. She suggests that we often begin by being thrown into the role with little preparation, that in this situation, we rely on models we have experienced or observed. As the role begins to fit more comfortably and confidence builds, we draw on our repertoire of skills and apply these to the supervisory relationship. As competence develops further, seeking support from colleagues and seeking additional knowledge are common. Finally, there is "the development of a sense of credibility...a freedom 'not to know' and to be more open, by imaginative association, to the worker's [student's] explicit and implicit material . . . one discovers one's own style, becomes more comfortable with it, and creates and refines a framework of knowledge in which to operate" (Dearnley, 1985, p. 62).

Learning how to become an effective teacher may be assumed to improve over time with experience and exposure to a variety of students with varying learning needs and cultural backgrounds. Effective teaching is not unidirectional. As we progress in our work with students we influence and are influenced through the interaction over time. Competence is achieved, yet new challenges emerge. Field education, much like social work practice, is an ever-evolving search for increased competence and effectiveness in our work. In this framework, the student–field instructor relationship is crucial to the learning that takes place. Of course, so much of this depends on the authenticity of the relationship which respects differing value orientations and worldviews. Whether we have participated in formal supervisory training, or we are modeling supervisory behaviors of our previous supervisors or field instructors, eventually we face the implications of assuming the responsibilities of this role.

Our Changing Roles

Becoming a field instructor requires several different types of role changes that create expected stresses and possible tensions, but these role changes also involve professional growth and expansion of our professional responsibilities. The role of field instructor is different from the role of agency supervisor, yet field instruction entails the components of staff supervision—administrative, supportive, and educative functions. The difference resides in the field instructors' educative functions and the need to become "critically reflective about their practice as social workers and field instructors, so that they, in turn, [can] both demonstrate and describe this process to their students" (Rogers & McDonald, 1992, p. 167). In Schon's (1987) terms the facilitation of reflective practice requires "coaching," that is, providing expertise through mentorship and guidance while promoting the acquisition of needed skills.

Field instructors undergo several role changes (Perlman as quoted in Aptaker, 1966) that include making the transitions from:

1. Helper of those in need of support (clients) to teacher and mentor of future colleagues (students)

2. Supervisee or supervisor to educator

3. Doer to explainer

4. Member of an agency hierarchy (worker) to a colleague and collaborator with a social work student

5. Service giver to service critic and analyst

6. Empiricist to theoretician—or at least to competent conveyer and interpreter of theory and practice principles

7. Employee to advocate for organizational change to secure a conducive learning environment

8. Consumer of professional education to educator, colleague, and collaborator with other social work educators

One of the important shifts from supporter of those in need to educator and advocate for the student's learning, entails moving away from the direct line of service provision or administration to the management of service delivery one step removed with an eye on the organization as a training site, not just as a service site. Provision of services performed through the eyes and voices of students calls for the acquisition of authority in the role of mentor. In fact, Reynolds (1985) advises that working through students to meet clients' needs involves learning to sharpen our focus on the student while maintaining a balance that keeps the client system and task in mind. Our lens must be adjusted to include the student's focus as well as the client's focus. This is accomplished by "starting where the student is" and by being prepared to individualize the assessment of each student's capacities so that these capacities can be channeled to serve the client system's needs.

The task facing us is being ready to teach another individual what we do as social workers. Garnering confidence and recognizing that we know something about social work that we are eager to impart to students is essential. Anticipation of barriers or blocks to our effectiveness is an important part of this preparation. Some hints toward achieving this needed mindset are:

- Being realistic about our limitations, areas of strength and weakness, and what is possible to achieve

- Identifying aspects of what it was like being supervised that may be drawn upon as we assume the role of field instructor

- Identifying what makes us anxious

- Respecting the student's desire to learn

- Expanding the notion of success from student satisfaction to a more significant evaluation of the student's demonstrated progress

- Learning how to tell others what to do and how to do it, but also being prepared to listen carefully and provide a structure that supports listening

- Recognizing and handling resistance and the reality that people do not always do what is asked of them

- Building an alliance based on trust, confidence, and fairness

- Developing a frame of reference that promotes critical thinking in ourselves as well as others and developing a sense of when is the right time to push or pull back

- Examining our agencies from the perspective of what learning opportunities are available that support the development of new professionals

- Understanding that coming from a particular world view requires that we develop the capacity to move beyond this comfort zone and open ourselves to other ways of knowing and learning

Our credibility as field instructors is rooted in knowledge, theoretical familiarity, and experience. Basic skills such as understanding the elements involved in the establishment of a trusting, authentic relationship, neutral methods of exploration and clarification, the importance of probing, and the power of initiating change by posing questions that challenge assumptions are directly applicable to methods of teaching students. However, the application of these clinical skills in field instruction is applied to our role as teachers, not counselors.

Differences Between Treating and Teaching

The primary field instruction relationship is that of teacher–student, yet relationships of therapist, employer, or friend can also develop (Congress, 1996). Field instruction is about teaching not treating, but because of the sensitive nature of client material and the powerful feelings that are often evoked in discussions with clients it is frequently necessary for us to explore students' innermost thoughts and feelings. The skill is in establishing a trusting relationship that enables students to disclose feelings related to their work with clients while maintaining clear boundaries. Student self-disclosures are primarily important as they relate to the work. Walking this delicate line between treating and teaching entails emphasizing the difference between developing practitioner self-awareness and learning more about oneself through a therapeutic relationship (Grossman, Levine-Jordano, & Shearer, 1990).

Self-development and growth are part and parcel of the learning goals for students and are integral to the development of the professional self. Ambivalence, regression, and resistance are normal and to be expected when adult learners confront new ways of looking at familiar situations. Taking on new roles can be threatening to the adult self. Learning requires risk, like the risk of admitting that one does not know something or the risk of exposing oneself as vulnerable and dependent. These are natural outcomes and must be understood from this perspective (Grossman et al., 1990). If students need more help in dealing with feelings evoked by their practice, we should not take it upon ourselves to take on a therapeutic role or to refer a student for counseling, but instead to sensitively refer students to their faculty liaisons who know of school resources for student counseling (Bonosky, 1995; Plaut, 1993).

Towle (1954) reminds us that the "practice of social work is inextricably related to the life-experience of the learner, so that it is impossible to isolate the learning experience for study of its effects" (p. 24). This "emotional learning experience" presents a challenge to how we facilitate the learning without crossing the boundary into therapy or treatment. Keeping this balance involves creating a safe environment and setting a framework and structure that permits discussions of personal feelings and experiences as they relate to the work and the learning at hand and respects how this may be manifested cross-culturally. For example, students engaged in new learning often become preoccupied with themselves or their lack of skill. Their energies become directed toward their discomfort rather than toward the issues and questions of their clients. In these expected situations, we re-establish a focus on the reality of clients' needs, the facts of their situations, and methods and techniques that further the work, instead of focusing solely on the student's discomfort. This often shifts the student back into a more stable state and provides a return to a client-centered agenda for greater learning. Maintaining this balance is a challenge. The aim is to avoid delving into a student's internal conflicts or problems. Some teaching does involve helping and some helping does involve teaching, but our focus is on the work with individuals, families, groups, communities, or organizations, and what students need to learn about social work practice. This does not mean a total avoidance of attention to personal discussions or to personal issues that affect the progress of the work. Boyd Webb (1988) addresses the importance of this balance and suggests that attending to aspects of a student's personality or work style, both when things are going well and when work falters, is an essential part of field instruction. She encourages attention to these issues and warns against delay in addressing them:

> Becoming a social worker involves the integration of professional and personal identity via the various formal and informal socialization experiences that comprise social work education. ...one learns to use aspects of one's personality and style in a conscious deliberate way, according to the needs of a given client or situation. This conscious use of self is the mark of a true professional; the field instructor has a pivotal role in modeling [and balancing] this aspect of professional identity. (p. 40)

Pursuing personal issues within field instruction is never an end in itself. The aim is always to advance the learning and the work. "Furthermore [in a co-constructed, mutually derived relationship] the supervisee [student] has the power to limit the focus on his or her issues, whereas the supervisor [field instructor] ensures that the supervisee's personal issues, aside from the treatment of the client, do not co-opt the supervision. In otherwords, the degree and level with which the exploration of personal issues are discussed with the supervisee is negotiated between the participants and authorized by the supervisee." (Ganzer & Ornstein, 2004, p. 439)

As the boundaries between therapy and education are sometimes vague and permeable, the following guidelines are offered:

- Establish professional boundaries by consciously and appropriately using physical space, work environment, body language, proper attire, communication skills, time, attitude, respect for diversity, and observing confidentiality.

- Respect students' reluctance to disclose personal material, set appropriate boundaries to this disclosure, and be mindful to connect students' personal experiences to teaching points and the work.

- Move the focus back to students' learning needs and do not allow the focus on personal material to take over field instruction.

- Be conscious and purposeful in what personal experiences are disclosed to students, why we are doing so, and who is benefiting from the self-disclosure.

- Consider if there is another way to make the same point without using self-disclosure as a teaching method or practice technique.

- Know ourselves, our own areas of sensitivity, and predispositions.

The Field Instruction Journal

Keeping a journal of our teaching, including the challenges, satisfactions, and dilemmas of this role, is recommended (Brookfield, 1990; Rogers & McDonald, 1992). Included in this journal could be an assessment of our strengths and limitations as teachers. Over time, the journals can reflect how we develop as teachers and how our students respond to our teaching. Using reflective journals to monitor our own growth parallels teaching our students to use recordings as a self-reflective tool in field instruction. Not only are we modeling professionalism by our receptiveness, honesty, and openness, but we are also creating an environment for learning, self-reflection, and professional growth. Journals aid reflection on the process of learning by keeping track of critical episodes and events in learning and by recording the actions and processes that enhance or hinder us (Brookfield, 1990). Rogers and McDonald (1992) use video taping of supervisory sessions in training seminars for field instructors and recommend editing those sequences that represent "excellence, a specific skill, a problematic situation, a phase or stage in the learning process, or . . . an issue or concern" (p. 171). Although the experience of seeing oneself in action adds a rich perspective to the task, the exercise of writing a reflective journal also provides a useful vehicle toward achieving this goal.

Being Role Models for Our Students

Practice principles are "as often caught as taught" (Shulman, 2004). As field instructors we are role models for our students across the broad spectrum of professional values and behaviors. When they enter this phase of their careers, students will refer back to how we provided field instruction and supervision and will use us as models for how to provide field instruction to their students. Consider the following ways we directly influence our students through the modeling we provide (Bertrand Finch, Bacon, Klassen, & Wrase, 2003; Hartman, 1997; Solomon, 1982):

- Listening, conveying a nonjudgmental attitude, and being open to students' thinking processes. For instance, responding to questions and not being afraid to say, "I don't know!" or "Let's find out!"

- Accepting criticism

- Taking our responsibilities seriously

- Demonstrating that differences related to culture, race, ethnicity, language, geographical region, gender, age, religions, abilities, class, or sexual orientations and value orientations are important in the development of social work practice and need to be discussed openly in field instruction

- Demonstrating that similarities with regard to race, ethnicity, gender, age, sexual orientation, or other dimensions of diversity need not imply similar world views or experiences

- Having the same expectations for ourselves as for our students. For example, making certain that process recordings are reviewed in a timely manner when telling students to hand in process recordings on time, and being timely in submission of written materials required by the social work program such as educational plans or end-of-semester written evaluations.

- Demonstrating the importance of consistency and structure by ensuring a regular field instruction conference time

- Finally, managing the power differentials between ourselves and our students with respect and mutuality. The power we hold over students resembles that held by students in relation to clients and communities. We control access to learning opportunities, feedback on student progress, and the final evaluation of student performance in the same way that students hold power over clients with respect to access to resources and other forms of help. The manner in which we manage the field instruction relationship is a model for students' practice with client systems.

Setting the Stage for Field Instruction: Before Students Arrive

Specialized readings that will help students acclimate to the agency, its service delivery goals, and the populations served can be gathered before the student arrives. It is a good idea to plan how to explain issues and policies of the agency, particularly as they relate to students' anticipated roles and functions and limitations on confidentiality. It is also a good time to review field placement requirements by reviewing the social work program's Field Work Manual.

Schools have different procedures covering agency–student contacts before field instruction begins. However, there are some general guidelines that, when followed, will ease the beginning phase. Many field instructors want to arrange preplacement interviews with students and an increasing number of schools require that preplacement visits occur. If it is not possible to meet with students, it is helpful to arrange a telephone contact prior to the first day of field instruction. This first conversation aims to ease the tension for students regarding beginnings in field placement by addressing:

- Any initial questions students may have regarding workload and field instruction expectations

- The specific location and directions to the placement

- Date and time of expected arrival on the first day of field instruction

- Agency requirements prior to placement, such as fingerprinting, copies of health exams, etc.

- A description of what students can expect during the first day

- Any organizational norms and rules such as those about appropriate dress

The following are some important cautions for new field instructors:

- Anticipate the demands of teaching, including learning to teach across a range of learning styles. Identify and anticipate ways to adapt these approaches to teaching for a better fit with students' particular learning styles. This is the focus of chapter 4, Adult Learning, Learning Styles, Learning Stages.

• Identify barriers or blocks to effectiveness on our part, including potential career moves, life situations or personal stresses, planned vacations, or issues in agency environments that may affect field instruction. We are responsible to arrange for qualified "temporary" field instruction in any of the above situations, or for unanticipated situations such as illness, jury duty, or strikes. It is good practice to have a plan in place for unanticipated emergencies, and to have ways of informing students and field liaisons of any significant changes.

• Be alert to a tendency to overprotect students, or the opposite tendency to overestimate students' abilities. This involves being prepared to create possibilities for risk-taking that are manageable and yet not too premature for students.

• Expect to work with students of different regional, linguistic, racial/ethnic, religious, and class backgrounds. Additionally, anticipate encountering situations in which students require special accommodations in the placement such as those needed by hearing or visually impaired, learning-disabled students, or those who use a wheelchair or other assistive device.

• Students represent a range of world view perspectives. Appreciating personal or cultural identities and developing cultural sensitivity is an ongoing and evolving process. We create a climate where these discussions can take place from the beginning of the teacher–learner relationship. This provides encouragement to students to develop comfort in these aspects of their professional identities and aids the development of a trusting authentic relationship.

• Establishing rapport with students happens over time. We need to strive to be aware of our own biases, prejudices, perceptions, and defenses as they relate to a range of human behaviors. We also need to help students to become aware of what unique qualities they bring to field instruction and to their practice. There should be a good give and take between us and our students about what each brings to field instruction and social work practice.

• We need to anticipate that we are models for developing self-awareness and sensitivity, and that we must be comfortable in directly addressing differences and similarities that we share with our students that may contribute to the teacher–learner relationship.

• Conflicts between educational expectations and the realities of agency-based practice may emerge. For example, some schools may require group assignments for students, but the agency may not offer group experiences; or an agency may prefer a long period of observation prior to independent assignments, whereas the school may prefer assignments be undertaken in the first week of placement. Additionally, we need to understand how to train for the profession, not only for agency-based practice. A student, for example, may start an after-school group program even if this is not a regular agency service, or a student may have the opportunity to do family work in an agency even if the agency is not reimbursed for this service.

• Negotiating and securing assignments for students within the organization takes time and planning. Initial assignments should be ready for students in the first few weeks of the placement. The potential struggle, including increased demands on our time, to find appropriate assignments for students should be anticipated. If arranging assignments is not directly under our control as field instructors, problem solving around this issue should be considered to insure the appropriate pacing and range of assignments for students.

• Acknowledge with students the power implicit in the field instruction relationship and explore the meaning of power within the student's culture and value orientation. Acknowledging this dynamic is essential as a first step toward understanding its place in the field instruction relationship and in students' assumption of their personal authority and power (Bertrand Finch et al., 2003; Solomon, 1982).

• Anticipate inevitable questions regarding the context of practice within the setting. Gathering examples around potential conflicts and difficult practice situations can be helpful learning tools. It is helpful to be proactive in this regard.

• Mistakes will be made; it is part of the learning process. Keeping a field instructor journal can be very helpful in understanding this process.

Establishing a Reflective Stance in Field Education

The following brief process recording of a field instructor's reflection on a supervisory interchange early in the academic year provides a glimpse into a developing field instructor–student relationship.

THE SETTING

The individuals served in this medical outreach program are either ill themselves or have a member of their family who is being seen at the clinic attached to this program. Clients are also experiencing difficulties in their relationships with their partners or families. This recording describes a supervisory session after the third contact between a 2nd-year student and a widower with heart disease who is experiencing difficulties with his new live-in partner. The student has not worked with adults before; her previous placement was working with young children in a residential group home setting.

SUPERVISION OF A STUDENT SESSION

The student reported finding her client upset upon her home visit. When she asked what had upset him, he reported that no one was helping him although he had been asking for months. He and his live-in partner had another fight. The student acknowledged the client's frustration and his desire to find a solution to his problems. She reminded him of the steps they had begun to take together over the past few weeks and recounted what had been achieved as well as what had been identified and agreed on as next steps that could be taken. The client continued to express his irritation and expressed that he had to do everything himself.

The student expressed her disappointment as she had assessed that they were working well together and she was somewhat annoyed by the client's dismissal of her efforts and of the work they had achieved together. Before discussing the nature of the fight between the client and his live-in partner, the field instructor stated that she would like to understand the interchange better and asked the student to describe in greater detail what it was like being with this client while he was expressing his anger and frustration. The student replied that she was taken off guard, but that she knew she had done all that she could and that she had worked hard to go at his pace, not hers. She expressed frustration in not being clear how to respond next. The field instructor acknowledged that there are often no "good" solutions. Clients sometimes feel frustrated, and we sometimes do, too. The field instructor and student continued to process the student's contact with the client, and they spent time considering the client's situation and medical condition—"What was it like being older, sick, and facing life alone, as this client is?" The field instructor then asked the student to contrast her work with this client with that of another client. The other client, a middle-aged female client whose sick son lives with her, is seeking support because of the challenges this son's care presents to her. The student's work with this woman has involved the identification of alternative resources and the introduction of additional supports to aid the mother in her efforts to manage her son. The comparison of the work with these two clients enabled the student to consider levels of support not yet explored with the first more emotionally distant client and the challenges in the work related to his very different expectations of service and responses to receiving help. Questions posed included, what was he experiencing in the face of difficulties in this new relationship and the possibility of living on his own once again? Was he feeling that the student had let him down, like others? What worries and concerns might underlie his anger and frustration? How might she better understand his frustration and the implications for their work together? What thoughts did the student have regarding the ease of her relationship with the mother of the invalid son compared to the challenges in working with this somewhat rejecting male client?

The student successfully engaged with her field instructor in considering alternative ways to look at her beginning work with these clients. She felt heard by her field instructor and not rejected for the frustration she experienced and expressed. Instead, these factors were taken as related to the work and used to further the student's thinking regarding how to better approach both of her clients' situations. The supervisory session ended with the field instructor providing a reading that was relevant to further the student's thinking about her clients and the work ahead.

Although this interchange is brief and early in the year, it demonstrates that the field instructor is able to create a reflective posture within their supervisory time that allows the student to consider her work from different perspectives. The student responds by attempting to look at her clients' needs and her differential responses to them. The beginning of trust, acceptance, and the student's entry into new realms of thinking is evident. The tone is set for a relationship in which an honest appraisal of the potential blocks in the work and answers to complex questions can be explored together. The student is given adequate practical information and is channeled to readings that will increase her knowledge and confidence, while a model for problem solving and risk taking is provided.

Summary Points

- Field instruction can be demanding and time consuming.

- Barriers or blocks to effectiveness will emerge.

- Be alert to a tendency to overprotect students or overestimate their abilities.

- Expect to work with a diverse group of students.

- Establishing rapport with students happens over time.

- The "fit" of personal style and professional style provides a helpful foundation for discussion.

- Conflicts between educational expectations and the realities of agency-based practice may emerge.

- Securing possible assignments for students and negotiating assignments within the organization takes time and planning.

- Power and authority are inherent components of the field instruction relationship.

- Anticipate questions that challenge protocols and the context of practice within the setting.

- Mistakes will be made; this is a natural part of the learning process.

Chapter 2

BEGINNING PROCESSES IN FIELD INSTRUCTION: SETTING THE STAGE

*T*he educational task…[involves] balancing giving and demanding, taking care not to give too much at once in too great detail. This entails giving first things first, with a realistic expectancy that they be mastered. It also implies helping the learner put them to use and holding him [or her] accountable for doing so. (Towle, 1954, p. 33)

Preparing for the Arrival of Students

Setting the stage for learning entails pairing and balancing expectations with realistic goals. The manner in which the placement starts sets the tone and affects how next steps are taken (Dettlaff, 2003; Nelson, 1990; Nisivoccia, 1974). How we prepare ourselves and our agencies for students has a far-reaching impact on students and a direct effect on how students understand what is involved in beginning with assigned tasks and responsibilities. As the teacher/learner relationship develops, engagement of clients in professional working relationships is modeled. This parallels the student's work with clients and client systems (Dore, 1993). Just as some clients have limited understanding of the helping process and unrealistic expectations of social work students, social work students may be unclear about the process of field instruction and have unrealistic expectations of us as field instructors (Kahn, 1979; Mattinson, 1975; Searles, 1955). It stands to reason that just as it is good social work practice to teach students to tune into beginning processes, there are similar positive effects on learning when we prepare ourselves for educating students using this same technique.

Reynolds refers to this entry period of field instruction as "the vestibule to learning" (1985, p. 214). She proposes that beginning the field instruction relationship requires different skills and attitudes from later on in the field instruction relationship when the foundation has been established. Initially students come with understandable uncertainties, fears, and concerns. These may not be dissimilar to our own concerns as field instructors. Anxiety is a shared, necessary, and natural part of the process—the anxiety of being a student and the anxiety of being a field instructor. More specifically, being an evaluator and being evaluated emerge as issues. Students worry about being evaluated—and about assessing client systems. Unsurprisingly, questions surface from these varying perspectives such as: *"What will be expected of me?" "Will I be able to meet the demands of this setting, this field instructor, or these clients?" "How will I be evaluated?" "Will I meet my own expectations and achieve my goals?"*

Since these dynamics are inherent and are expected to arise (Gelman, 2004), it is possible to manage them through anticipatory planning and preparation. One mechanism that achieves containment of this anxiety is an agency orientation. This is not to recommend a fixed approach to this beginning phase. On the contrary, field instruction should move at an appropriate pace to allow the process to unfold. Each student will require a somewhat different approach, yet the beginning phase can be enhanced by paying attention to some basic factors. Understanding the differing expectations of the agency, of the social work program, and of students is a critical aspect that affects decisions about what form the formal and informal orientation will take.

In summary, before students arrive in the agency, we can best prepare by planning ways to orient our students about the:

- Agency, from its physical layout to its policies, procedures, and place in the continuum of services to the population and community served;

- Clientele served by the agency and needs of the community; and

- Purpose of social work in the setting, including the student's expected role and function.

Preparing the Agency for the Student's Arrival

Students are assigned to an agency/organization, not just to an individual field instructor. Everyone in the setting has a role to play in the overall educational experience. Some agencies assign staff to work as educational coordinators responsible for organizing student assignments within the agency and student orientation programs. However, preparing the agency/organization for students is frequently our responsibility as field instructors. Drawing on our own experiences and recalling what it was like when we began field placements or started new jobs is a helpful way to tune into the issues involved. However, it often happens that we can only fully appreciate what is required of the agency and ourselves after the first experience of working with a student. Discussions with other, more experienced field instructors within the agency are a useful way to pool expertise.

The structure of students' time in the placement—specific days, location, and length of field instruction meetings—needs to be considered. For example, it is important to determine what staff meetings or discussion groups are essential for student participation and which need to be built into students' field instruction experiences. In this way, answering the question, "What are the necessary components for a healthy and stimulating learning experience within this setting?" initiates consideration of the practicalities of the placement and provides a foundation for what else needs to be incorporated into the agency orientation. In addition, the following factors can assist us in preparing for students' arrival.

- What has been the experience of this agency with students in the past? What is the agency's attitude toward students? Is there a commitment to provide professional training?

- Does the agency provide a culturally competent workplace environment, or is the student culturally isolated? For example, is the student the only person of color among an all-White agency staff serving a culturally diverse client population?

- What special accommodations are needed to facilitate students' entry into the work environment?

- What are the agency's attitudes or responsibilities toward field instructors? Does the agency provide support and flexibility to field instructors, or are increased demands anticipated? Who can be relied on to support field instructors within the agency?

• If students are employees of the agency doing work/study internships, what special considerations are needed to support their transition to new roles as students versus employees? Are there written educational plans in place authorized by the school and the agency administrator that address field assignments and field instruction? Are all parties (students, job supervisors, field instructors, administrators, and the school) in agreement regarding the placement expectations and field instructors' roles and responsibilities?

• If the agency has been experiencing difficulties, consideration as to how to create meaningful learning experiences is needed. This presents special challenges in the current climate of fiscal cutbacks facing many social service agencies. When staff turnover is high and staff morale is low, poor administrative choices or oppressive policies or procedures may exist. Discussions with the social work program's field education department may be useful in determining a plan in these situations. Any concerns that emerge about the agency as a placement site should be discussed with the faculty liaison or field education department.

• When considering schedules, a time for orienting students and providing ongoing regular field instruction conferences needs to be secured. It often occurs that in some fast-paced agencies, securing a regular uninterrupted hour for supervision seems an unrealistic goal. In these situations, it may be possible to arrange less than one 1-hour periods more frequently than the traditional hour or hour and a half per week. Interspersing longer sessions throughout the academic year on a regular basis protects time for the development of thoughtful reflection rather than providing only short spurts of supervision that too frequently model a quick-fix focus on practice concerns.

• If there will be task supervision, collaborative relationships need to be established. Task supervisors are experts in the agency who will teach the student some particular task or aspect about social work practice or impart a special expertise (e.g., grant writing, lobbying activities, group work, family therapy, or welfare rights information). Three-way meetings with task supervisors should occur periodically to review how students are doing and to incorporate this aspect of the learning experience into the student's overall performance and learning goals.

• Establish what arrangements need to be made to ensure an adequate flow and balance of work for students well before the student arrives.

• Consider the implications of the work in the agency and whether students will be exposed to such issues as vicarious traumatization or compassion fatigue. These issues are discussed in chapter 11, Teaching Challenges in Field Instruction.

What Are the Agency's Expectations?

It sometimes happens that the idea and anticipation of having a student differs from the realities of this added responsibility. Therefore, assessing how the field instruction site will react to students is an important factor. Will students be accepted as professional staff in training, as free labor, or as outsiders? Given this knowledge, we play an important role in the protection and creation of conducive learning environments for our students. We can mitigate against some of the problems that arise by alerting agency staff to the following expectations:

• Students will be present at staff meetings and should assume more than an observational role;

• Students need space and the resources to do their work;

• Students need assignments that reflect their methods of study and program year;

• Students need orientation to the agency and its policies and procedures; and

• Students need assignments that extend their capacities. This may involve extending agency service and cooperation from agency staff.

What Are the Student's Expectations?

Stepping into our students' shoes helps our understanding of their fears and worries regarding field education (Gelman, 2004; Grossman et al., 1990). Remembering how it felt to be a student, who was instrumental in the facilitation of our learning, identifying anything special about the experience that is important now, and bearing in mind what assumptions underlie this information and how it aids or blocks the tasks ahead are all important factors. In addition, providing time to appreciate students' expectations is an important part of beginning.

Students expect us to be available to them, frequently in the beginning and less frequently as the placement proceeds. During this initial phase, the examination of strengths and learning needs that students bring to the field placement experience should be the focus of discussions. This is usually not an easy dialogue, and students may need help to give voice to the many concerns and uncertainties they experience in this early phase. Expressing interest in their work and life experiences gives reassurance that they will not be assessed separately from their achievements and abilities. Providing links from their previous experience to this new situation eases anxiety and provides encouragement to move ahead. These discussions naturally relate to field performance expectations, such as attendance, placement hours, assignments, recordings, learning goals, and our role in helping students meet these expectations.

Normalizing and validating the anxiety and nervousness that students experience at the start of a new placement requires a direct and supportive response. We may try a variety of ways to reduce anxiety, but we simply need to give students time before assessing their apprehension as excessive. Anxiety generally subsides gradually before being replaced with more comfort and growing confidence. However, anxiety that remains high over a number of weeks takes on a different dimension and will need to be examined as part of the educational assessment.

What Are the Social Work Education Program's Expectations?

The initial requirements of social work education programs revolve around hours and workload, selection of assignments, written recordings for field instruction, initial assessments of learning needs, oral evaluations, and collaboration with faculty liaisons. These issues are generally spelled out in the program's Field Education Manual, and students and field instructors should review these issues together. Understanding the social work program's philosophy and mission includes examination of the following factors:

- Organization of the curriculum and its relationship to field teaching and expectations. Elective and specialization or concentration choices in the curriculum often reflect the program's emphasis and practice orientation.

- Programmatic structures and expectations that affect student assignments (advanced standing, work/study, second year, specializations, or double-method students).

- Administration of field instruction as expressed through the organization of the field education department.

- Defined roles and responsibilities of faculty liaisons as central to balancing the agency's and field instructors' needs with educational requirements.

- School policies regarding accountability, collaboration, and grading of students. Faculty liaisons generally give the field work grade in consultation with the field instructor.

- Rights and responsibilities of the social work program, students, field instructors, and agencies.

- The social work education program's calendar and holidays, religious holidays, sick leave policy, end-of-semester evaluation due dates, and relevant policies as they affect field placements, such as days and number of field work hours, and home visiting expectations.

Orienting Students to the Agency and Organizational Life

Introducing students to the hierarchical structures and the formal and informal communication patterns existing within the agency is an important teaching component, as it aids understanding of agency systems and their impact on service delivery. Agency orientations also help students to develop a sense of belonging and identification with the agency and their new role. Although this may begin through an orientation program that takes many forms, the orientation is an ongoing process that begins during the first few weeks in placement and continues throughout the placement as the student is introduced to different aspects of organizational life. Some orientation programs are agency-wide, formal programs that are organized by a group of field instructors and agency administrators. Some include a welcoming breakfast, structured lectures, tours, meetings with key personnel, and handouts and literature. Still other orientation programs are less formal and consist of the field instructor and student walking through the agency, going to a staff meeting together, or having the student shadow a worker for an afternoon.

The balance of how much information to provide and in what form requires careful thought. During the first few days of placement, students mostly want to know, *"What will I be doing here?"* *"What will be expected of me?"* *"Will I fit in?"* *"Are there people who look like me here?"* Addressing these questions translates agency functions and procedures into the kind of work students will be doing. Instructing students to read the agency policy manual without including other activities is not recommended. Policy manuals are often written in formal tones that may, more than likely, alienate students rather than acclimate them to the agency.

Orientation to the agency runs concurrent with beginning first assignments. In the beginning it is best not to overburden students with too much information too quickly, as it may increase anxiety. The aim is to give enough information so students can feel included and clued into the agency's environment and culture, so that they can start with a sense of direction. This can be achieved by selecting what information is most important for students to have on the first day of placement, in the first week of placement, the second week, and so on. Students need to understand the agency they will be working in, but much of this understanding comes with incremental time and exposure. Partializing and developing specific, understandable explanations about the social work role, purpose, focus, and goals in the agency and in the profession gives a step-by-step method that gradually introduces students to the agency and the work. In this way, the information is broken up into what is needed to manage the placement from what is needed to manage the role students will be playing in the setting from what is needed to manage assignments. The following are some pointers about orientations for us to keep in mind as the work with students begins.

Components of Student Orientation to a Field Placement

- Introduce students to agency staff, from maintenance workers to the executive director. If there is an agency reception area or main telephone receptionist, make sure students' names, office locations, and schedules of placement hours are known.

- A tour of the agency with students helps them achieve a sense of the physical layout and how clients are accommodated in the agency. A tour of the community with students, or arranging such a tour for students, gives them a broader view of the external environment and provides a context for understanding accessibility of resources, the culture of the community, and the organization's place within the community, where it is located. For these reasons, community tours are strongly encouraged. Tours can come later in the placement depending on the nature of the student's beginning, timing, and agency constraints. Following these activities, students can be asked to expand on their perceptions, observations, and feelings about the agency and community. This exercise introduces the student to the framework that all activities within the placement are sources of learning. Arranging for students to sit in and observe the waiting room of the agency is another orienting possibility.

- Brief descriptions of agency staffing patterns, services offered, populations served, the role of the social worker, funding sources, agency rules and regulations, and how to answer the telephone are all helpful pieces of information. Deciding which pieces of information are usefully discussed as opposed to given in prepared handouts is another way of breaking up the flow of information to be absorbed. Available agency brochures, organizational charts, and mission statements are useful guides.

- Understanding the organizational culture, significant agency procedures that the student will need to know, such as rules and norms, formal and informal communication systems, dress codes, and lunch break details, are important. Do not forget such essentials as bathroom keys, supplies, mailboxes, identification or name tags, and safety precautions.

Orientation to a student's role within the agency includes:

- Gathering information in a folder that helps the student understand the agency and provides references to pertinent information that will facilitate adjustment to social work practice in the agency setting. A glossary of terms, agency telephone extensions, examples of completed agency forms, an organization chart, and articles regarding practice considerations regarding the population served are several examples of items to be included.

- Regarding safety issues, students appreciate information presented in a sensitive, clear, and caring manner. Students need to know discretionary practice protocols as they relate to safety, both in the agency and in the community. Discussing the realities of practice and the specific implications this places on work in this setting provides students with necessary information with which they can protect themselves and exercise appropriate discretion.

- Reaching for students' reactions and expectations of field placement helps them take one day at a time and trust that they will be listened to and that understanding comes with time and exposure.

- Providing direction and helping students practice how to introduce themselves as social work students or interns immediately connects them to the professional code of ethics regarding honesty and the prohibition against misrepresentation of skills (Feiner & Couch, 1985; Miller & Rodwell, 1997). Helping students practice their introductions to clients is a useful exercise to see how well they can articulate their understanding of their role and function within the agency. Ideally, the function of the agency should be stated in non-jargonized, operational terms, e.g., "We provide help to drug-addicted individuals who have been recently discharged from an in-patient psychiatric hospital and are in need of housing, psychiatric clinic follow-ups, and counseling" versus "We provide intensive case management to MICA patients."

- Introduction to the types of agency records students will need to complete as part of agency requirements provides structure to what is expected. This discussion should include the uses of these recordings, amount of time allocated for recording in the agency, and field instructors' plans for their review.

- It is never too early to discuss "worst case scenarios" or special situations that may arise in the course of agency work. This gives students permission to voice their fears and devise problem-solving skills in crisis situations. For example, do the agency and social work education program have policies on home visits? What safety measures are taken into consideration for home visits? What is the procedure to be followed when

clients threaten to hurt themselves or others? Plans should also be discussed around how students should handle illnesses or emergencies of
their own. Lines of communication should be clarified, as well as to
whom students should turn in the absence of their field instructors. Above
all, we should provide an atmosphere where it is permissible to consider
a balanced discussion of all these circumstances.

There is a great deal for students to absorb in the beginning, and we should
take a moment to consider the first day for students in its totality. How long
will it be? How balanced will it be between didactic material and activity or student participation? What provisions will you make to meet with students individually? Even if briefly, and even if a group field instruction meeting of students is planned, meeting individually with students goes a long way toward
establishing the student/field instructor relationship. This meeting confirms
that field instruction is a place of containment in the midst of all that students
are trying to manage.

Evaluation of orientation programs introduces students to evaluation
processes from the very start of placement. Legitimate questions include: *"How
did the orientation go?" "What worked?" "What was useful? ?" "What did
not work?" "What might be done differently?" "How did the first day go?"
"How did the first individual meeting or group meeting with students go?"
"Did anything unanticipated occur?" "What needs have not been met?"* and
"What questions remain unanswered?" Such specific questions address whether
students have the information they need to begin their assignments and whether
there are aspects of their assignments that remain unclear and they yield important information for the progression of the work and learning ahead. These
questions provide useful information for future orientation programs. These
early opportunities for review and feedback also establish a model of field
instruction in which mutual feedback and collaboration is an expectation.

The education of students in the field provides a different lens from which
to view the agency, and this new lens yields new information. In this regard,
gaining information on how students are experiencing the orientation provides
information on which to base understanding of their learning needs as well as
what type of information is required, and in what form, to facilitate adaptation

to the agency and to the student role. As students become more familiar with the agency—its culture, its services, and its philosophy toward service delivery—we should ask them to comment on the strengths and gaps in service delivery, and how different or similar they experience this agency in comparison to other agency experiences. These formulations help students develop their ability to move from one agency perspective to a professional stance regarding service provision.

Orientation and Planning for Advanced Students

Not all students are beginning-level students. The orientations for more experienced students may be handled differently and adapted to their needs. In addition, attention needs to be paid to the special circumstances of students who use their place of employment as a placement and the tendency to assume that because they work in the agency, orientation is not vital. For example, work/study students may have considerable experience but will require assistance making the transition from employee to student. It cannot be assumed that these students will not benefit from orientation.

Students currently employed in the agency may not need an orientation to the agency's structure but will need an orientation to their new role of student and to their role within a new department or assignment. Students who have had other careers, or developed skills and knowledge over time, need support to translate this knowledge into their new social work role and function. This requires attention to bridging or transferring learning from one situation to another. Drawing attention to the nature of the learning task ahead in relation to previous life and work experiences gives students reassurance that they will not be viewed as a blank slate but valued for what they already possess and bring with them into this new field instruction experience.

Open discussions of students' previous paid or volunteer work or placement experiences encourages the development of an individualized learning plan. In addition, the social work education program's transfer summaries, placement planning forms, or any other written materials received on students shape educational assessments and ideas about possible assignments. Directly discussing this information with students provides a foundation on which students understand that learning needs will be mutually discussed and assignments will be shaped in relation to their learning needs and interests.

Orienting Students to Field Instruction

As mentioned above, it is important to meet individually with each student on the first day of placement even if only briefly and even if there are multiple students in the placement. At this meeting parameters are set for the field instructor/student relationship. A first step in establishing this relationship is to involve students in developing an educational plan that includes an assessment of the student's present level of skill, identification of learning objectives, and design of appropriate learning experiences. Ways to initiate and clarify this task include:

- •Establishing the contract for work, including purpose, expectations, and formats and procedures for field instruction conferences and process recordings, journals, or logs.

- •Spelling out the social work education program's criteria regarding weekly supervision time, recording requirements as distinguished from agency recording procedures, types of recordings, the number and format of recordings expected, and the use of agendas in field instruction conferences.

- •Clarifying lines of communication and responsibilities, particularly if other supervisors or task supervisors are involved. Discuss the availability of back-up staff for emergency questions or issues that arise between field instruction conferences. We should remember that we are not the only source of learning for students, and they should be encouraged to use as many resources within the agency as possible.

- •And, finally, eliciting students' reactions and expectations of field instruction thus far.

In summary, setting the stage for field instruction involves understanding the respective expectations of students, agencies, field instructors, and social work education programs. It involves welcoming and orienting students to their new setting and prearranging appropriate assignments. It involves preparing for students, paving the way ahead in the agency, and anticipating potential obstacles. The orientation process begins with the establishment of initial learning contracts and engages students in learning relationships that entail mutual exchanges.

Orientation for a First Assignment

Background information. A 1st-year, Hispanic, 37-year-old, male student. His field placement is in a large urban hospital on a medical service. He is placed with a new field instructor who is in her early 30s, is a French Caribbean Black woman with 6 years' post-master's experience.

Conference. The field instructor gave a first assignment to her student the second day in placement. He had a tour of the hospital and the floor on which he was to work and was given an orientation to the medical charts, chart materials, a medical dictionary, and a tour of the patients' rooms. He was introduced to some medical and nursing staff and shown how to locate the doctors and nurses caring for the patients. The field instructor told him she would go over the above information again with him, as she knew it could be overwhelming. The student was also briefed about the role of the social worker in hospital, the sources of referrals, and what to expect when interviewing in a patient's room.

The patient, Ms. B., was referred by her doctor to the field instructor for help with financial problems. The patient had been in the hospital 3 days because of renal failure, secondary to systemic lupus. The doctor told Ms. B. that the field instructor would be seeing her. After reading the chart, it was decided that this would be an appropriate assignment for the student. The field instructor informed the patient that a social work intern would speak with her that afternoon.

The student was given the referral information and it was explained that, although the referral was being made for financial problems, there may be other problems presented by the patient or picked up during the interview, and that it was necessary to get an understanding of what the patient's medical problems and limitations are. The student was told that the medical chart would tell him about her medical condition.

This was the student's first experience in a hospital. He was given some literature that explained the patient's disease in simple language, including its symptoms and prognosis. He asked questions about the illness, some of which the field instructor was able to answer, but he was told that medical and nursing questions could be answered directly by the doctor and nurse caring for the patient or by using the medical dictionary.

The field instructor and student went together to the patient's floor so that they could read the medical chart together and discuss what there was to do.

The field instructor started off by showing him where to obtain data from the chart. He was then asked to comment on what information he identified as pertinent. He reported the patient's age, address, and marital status. He was shown other information that was important and why.

He was shown how to read the progress reports on the patient. From his body movements, the field instructor noted that he was anxious. This was not commented upon; instead she pointed out that they would go over what he did not understand and again stated that he could ask the nurse or doctor for clarification of chart notes if needed. The student asked whether she understood the scribbled notes. The field instructor replied that sometimes they are difficult to decipher. He asked if all the charts are similar. The field instructor responded that most are. He was reassured that after reading the same doctor's notes it is possible to get the gist of what is being said. He continued with several questions about the notes, especially abbreviations and medical jargon. He read the chart on his own, and other medical information regarding the patient's condition was discussed.

He was asked what he thought the next steps might be. He answered that he would see the patient to find out what financial problems she had. He was asked if he had any other questions. Silence. He was asked what he thought someone in the patient's condition might be experiencing. He mentioned that the nurse's admission sheet noted that the patient had young children; he commented that it must be hard for her to be away from them. The field instructor said that was a good observation and helped him focus on the children. He was asked if he would ask the patient about her children. He replied: "I don't know." The field instructor explained that since the patient had young children, their ages would be important to know as was how these children were being cared for while their mother was in the hospital. The state laws regarding child neglect and our obligations as social workers to make sure that the home situation was safe for the children were reviewed. It was suggested that he may want to find out what it is like for the patient and children to be separated during the hospitalization. He was asked to consider what he thought the patient might be going through. He was silent and did not seem to know. Again he seemed to be getting anxious and he began to shift in his seat. The field instructor shifted the conversation to the identifying data sheet, which noted that the mother is disabled and on Medicare. This means she was out of work for some time, and that it may be helpful to find out how being disabled and unable to work was affecting her.

The student added that she was separated from her husband and that may be why she is having financial problems.

What was known for certain was summarized. What was important to consider for discussion during his first contact was reviewed—her children, her medical condition, her physical functioning, her role as a mother, what assistance she gets from family, what support systems she has for herself, and her financial situation—and that it might not be possible to do everything in one interview. He was told to focus on what the patient saw as her problems and what she feels she needs.

The student asked if he should just walk into the room and start asking questions. He shared that he felt uncomfortable going in and asking questions of the patient. He questioned how he should introduce the topics. He asked what he should do if the patient refused to talk with him, or if she had nothing to say about her financial problems. What was involved was reviewed again. The student wanted to know what was required of him in writing a process recording on this interaction. This was discussed, and the field instructor explained that she would be available after the interview for supervision that afternoon.

DISCUSSION

This example demonstrates that much is expected of students and they frequently have to hit the ground running. It also depicts the tendency to overload a student with practical information in the beginning of a placement. The flavor of the interchange results in a task-oriented atmosphere in which the field instructor attempts to prepare the student with every eventuality but provides little space for reflection. Let us consider how the orientation of this student could be handled differently. We have the dual task of orienting students to the setting while simultaneously preparing them for a first assignment. Addressing the student's anxiety with support could help prepare the student for success in this new role. We could join the student in conducting his first intake and case assessment, or we could allow the student to observe us complete the assessment. We need to be creative in thinking about methods and techniques that support students in assuming their tasks and roles. We should also pay attention to cultural and gender factors that should be addressed from the beginning of the field instructor/student relationship. Giving students adequate information to start with and ample time to consider the expectations of the role and function within the setting is necessary. Sometimes students ask appropriate questions, but their need to know gets lost amid the many different demands of the agency. Sometimes we respond to student questions with concrete answers rather than taking the opportunity to develop their ability to search for possible answers or to develop confidence in their own sense of how to proceed. We need to take a *questioning* stance rather than an *answering* stance in order to stimulate critical thinking skills in students.

Summary Points on Beginning Processes in Field Education

BEFORE THE STUDENT STARTS PLACEMENT: PRE-PLACEMENT CONTACT

- Initial questions regarding workload and field instruction expectations

- The specific location and directions to the placement

- Date and time of expected arrival on the first day of field instruction; a description of what can be expected during the first day

- Overview of a typical day/workload

- Organizational norms and rules such as those about appropriate dress, hours of agency operation, etc.

GETTING STARTED

- Brief explanation of agency, its services, goals, population being served

- Brief discussion about expectations and responsibilities: the student's, the field instructor's and the agency's

- Beginning of the educational contract and identification of student's objectives and goals

- Brief clarification of field instructor's style of supervision

- General discussion of agency culture, general questions and answers

FORMAL ORIENTATION

- Agency overview—work-related policies, procedures, staffing hierarchy, roles, community resources

- Agency required tasks, responsibilities, and knowledge needed:

  - documentation and record keeping

  - protocols for and lines of communication both written and verbal, ongoing and in crisis

  - tone of facility and organizational culture (dress code, appropriate behavior, do's and don'ts)

  - introductions

- Field instructor/student/school tasks and responsibilities:

  - review of student's educational objectives and school performance expectations

  - requirements of process recordings, logs, or both

  - process for review, feedback, and evaluation

  - practical expectations: hours, absences, lateness, time off, supervisory times and other required meetings

  - expectations of field instructor and field instructor's responsibilities

  - communication protocols with school, field instructor, and faculty field liaison

ONGOING ORIENTATION NEEDS

- Agency overview continued:

  - workload-specific requirements

  - identification of advocacy needs

  - role of agency within the community

  - funding patterns, gaps in services, and implications for service delivery

- Field instructor/student/school tasks and responsibilities continued:
  - identification of student's learning needs
  - ongoing bridging communication among field instructor, student, and school
  - preparing for review, evaluation, and liaison contact
- Orientation to assignments:
  - role and function
  - case-specific information
  - anticipation of possible obstacles
  - information and identification of resources that are case specific

Tips

- Express interest in students' previous experiences, cultural backgrounds, world views, and motivation to enter the profession.

- Explore areas of specific interest, expectations of field instruction, and any difficulties or disappointments with supervision in the past.

- Accept a student's need to shadow a worker as part of orientation. This can be a helpful tool for anxious students, observational learners, or beginning students with no previous social service experience.

- Clarify possible conflicts between educational expectations and the realities of agency-based practice. For example, the student may express specific interest in developing a community assignment, but the agency may not be able to provide this experience.

- Listen carefully; create a structure that supports listening through the provision of a protected, regular time for supervision.

- Provide support and reassurance that taking one day at a time will produce understanding and adjustment.

- Set the stage by early provision of balanced feedback that includes praise, reinforcement, and encouragement as well as constructive criticism that points to the growth and development of professional social workers.

Chapter 3

THE RANGE OF STUDENT ASSIGNMENTS: MICRO TO MACRO PRACTICE

*L*earning activities are all those experiences and tasks undertaken in order to achieve learning objectives. (Hamilton & Else, 1983, p. 109)

Thus far, we have looked at the beginning stage of field instruction in which: (1) students learn about the placement agency—its physical layout, staff, policies and procedures, and populations served; (2) students are oriented to the role and function of social workers and other disciplines in the placement setting; and (3) students are introduced to the field instructor/student relationship as central to field learning. It is now time for students and field instructors to collaborate in the development of an educational plan or learning contract, which includes an assessment of students' present level of skill, identifying learning goals and objectives, and designing appropriate learning activities and experiences. Educational assessment and learning plans are discussed in chapter 7, but we want to focus this chapter on how to design optimum learning assignments for students that include work with individuals, families, groups, communities, and organizations. To this end, each level of practice is identified in this chapter, and a list of possible assignments is suggested to elucidate the varied roles students may engage in as they develop and expand their skills and knowledge base. The examples set forth are not intended to represent an exhaustive list of assignments; rather, they are presented to stimulate ideas for additional, innovative assignments. Some assignments are specific to particular levels of practice, while others are appropriate for all levels of practice.

Well-crafted assignments early in the field placement are essential even before we understand and assess who our students are and what they can do. As the experience unfolds, students can have greater input into designing their assignments, but it is important to anticipate and prepare a range of activities that will help students get started working with people from a micro-, mezzo-, and macro-system perspective.

Social workers practice in highly complex organizations with diverse staff and clients. The agency context frequently determines the kinds of assignments and activities available to students. But despite the vast range of social problems agencies address, student roles and activities generally fall within three interrelated areas of intervention, each of which is united by a core of common values and ethics, skills, and knowledge. The three areas involve micro (work with individuals), mezzo (work with families and small groups), and macro (work with communities and organizations).

This chapter presupposes that student assignments are shaped by the realities of agency-based practice. These realities demand that over the course of training, students have exposure to as many of the following components as possible:

- *Diversity*—Exposure to a diversity of client populations, problems, and needs and a diversity of resources to meet those needs;

- *Timing and pacing*—Work with different time dimensions and foci, e.g., crisis intervention, intakes, short- and long-term contacts, case management, interdisciplinary collaboration, collateral contacts, information and referral, assessment and multi-axial diagnosis, intervention planning, advocacy and empowerment, substance abuse monitoring, etc.;

- *Environments*—Experiences that enable students to interface with clients and their environments, e.g., community and home visits, community board meetings, case conferencing, interagency collaboration, community resources and referrals, etc.;

- *Settings*—Assignments may also include opportunities to experience different settings, such as hospitals, prisons, schools, employee assistance programs, preventive services, and other community-based agencies.

It is important to consider the multi-method orientations represented within our settings. Begin by assessing the range of methodologies employed by the agency, including individual counseling or casework, family work, group work, administration, community organizing, research, policy analysis, and advocacy. For example, what methods does the agency generally employ or prefer? Is one method used more than others? Are some methods ignored by the agency? Does the agency have an ideology about the use of certain methods? Are there unmet needs among the client populations that the agency can best address through the use of different methods?

Next, become familiar with the curriculum of each student's social work education program. Each social work education program has an individualized curriculum that reflects the program's mission and objectives. These distinctions reflect historical, philosophical, and theoretical positions that emphasize certain curriculum content or approaches over others. As a result, it is important to refer back to the social work program's curriculum and Field Education Manual for additional information or for clarification when selecting students assignments.

The challenge is to identify student assignments that meet both educational and service delivery goals. Assignments need to be developed that are balanced to meet: (a) students' learning needs and their educational levels of study, i.e., 1st year, advanced standing, or work/study students; (b) coursework requirements and the demands of the students' chosen methods of practice, i.e., generalist practice, direct practice, administration, or policy analysis; and (c) the needs of the agency, clientele, and community served.

Regardless of the social work program's focus, it is increasingly clear that social work practitioners are expected to move in and out of a variety of roles and activities that require a repertoire of skills and knowledge ranging from micro to macro practice. Without question, the majority of social workers choose to focus on developing clinical skills to help individuals on a one-to-one basis, as well as the skills to work with families and small groups. However, it is also evident in today's practice environment that social workers are required to intervene within organizations and communities and to influence policy in order to effect change (Kirst-Ashman & Hull, 2001; Netting, Kettner, & McNurtry, 1998).

Identifying a broad range of assignments to prepare students for today's practice presents special challenges when we are immersed in one aspect of practice over others, or when our agencies are limited in the range of modalities used. We can begin the process of identifying what types of assignments to allocate to students by considering the following questions:

- What skills will students learn through these assignments?

- What explicit learning objectives are associated with the assignments?

- How will students understand the assignments and their role in them?

- How do students' educational level and work or life experiences affect the choice of assignments?

- To what extent do assignments meet students' learning needs?

- To what extent do they help students learn about diversity and cultural competence?

- To what extent do assignments fit into the field instructors' expertise?

- To what extent do assignments have agency support and sanction?

- How does the social work education program's curriculum support the assignments?

Micro Practice Assignments

The majority of social work students need assignments that expose them to work with individuals, pairs or dyads, and families in order for them to experience themselves responding to these client systems through the helping process. This work focuses on an assessment of the bio-psycho-social needs of people and includes the direct influence the worker has in working with people, problem-solving skills, and the strengths people bring to the work at hand (Barker, 1999).

> Clinical social work shares with all social work practice the goals of enhancement and maintenance of psychosocial functioning of individuals, families, and small groups. Clinical social work practice is the professional application of social work theory and methods to the treatment and prevention of psychosocial dysfunction, disability, or impairment including emotional and mental disorders. It is based on knowledge of one or more theories of human development within a psychosocial context. The perspective of person-in-situation is central to clinical social work practice. Clinical social work includes interventions directed to interpersonal interactions, intrapsychic dynamics, and life-support and management issues. Clinical social work services consist of assessment; diagnosis; treatment, including psy-

chotherapy and counseling; client-centered advocacy; consultation; and evaluation. The process of clinical social work is undertaken within the objectives of social work and the principles and values contained in the NASW Code of Ethics. (NASW, 1984, p.1)

The range of problems that may fall into this broad definition include:

- *Personal problems*, e.g., mental or physical illness (or both), substance abuse, financial problems, developmental crises, friendship/peer relationships, work/education problems, etc.

- *Family-centered problems*, e.g., marital conflict, divorce, addiction, parent-child conflict, illness of family members, etc.

- *Environmental problems*, e.g., unemployment, discrimination, inadequate housing and education, and the personal impact of other limited societal resources, etc.

Micro practice requires workers to move freely among these three interrelated categories and to use different modalities of intervention. In addition to cases that require ongoing concrete services, case management, and clinical services, students benefit from a range of client interactions that expand their perceptions of their roles and interventions with people. These include:

- Outreaching to clients by telephone or in writing to set up appointments for interviews.

- Preparing for first contacts with a new client population by seeking out and using existing sources of data, including case records, anticipating clients' perceptions of their needs or situation, and their feelings about seeking help.

- Gathering data, preparing assessments, and developing intervention plans for clients, including data on:

    Individual functioning

    Family relationships and roles

    Cultural background

    Language abilities and preferences

    Spiritual beliefs and practices

Financial status and economic conditions

Education and employment history

Medical history/health status

History of victimization and survival (trauma, violence, abuse, oppression)

The presence or absence of support networks and activities

- Distinguishing between external and internal stresses on clients such as discrimination, oppression, unemployment, homelessness, and institutional inadequacies versus intrapsychic, interpersonal, physiological, or psychological challenges.

- Identifying clients' strengths and vulnerabilities, coping and adaptation skills, resiliency, capacities, opportunities, and motivation for change.

- Drawing eco-maps to identify the major systems clients are involved in, including the transactions among these systems.

- Preparing genograms to assess family patterns, intergenerational transmission, and cross-cultural experiences.

- Helping clients apply for government benefits and needed services, like public assistance, medicaid, public housing, food stamps, or day care. This involves finding out about eligibility requirements, helping clients locate needed documentation, assisting and accompanying clients to apply for services.

- Understanding the differences between contracting with mandated/involuntary clients and contracting with voluntary/self-referred clients.

- Providing culturally competent services to clients who are different from or similar to students' cultural backgrounds.

- Writing process recordings that describe the process of working with individuals, the feelings associated with helping, transference and counter-transference reactions, self-awareness, brief summaries of work done together and plans for the future. (Refer to chapter 6 on Process Recordings, Logs, and Journals.)

- Learning about the broad range of community services that exists or evaluating the lack of community services for populations served.

- Working with clients in crisis, learning the skills of crisis intervention, and using good judgment when working under pressure in emergency situations.

- Advocating for clients and implementing steps to social change.

- Collaborating with collateral contacts and learning to work within multidisciplinary environments.

- Planning for the termination of assignments or transfer and referral of clients.

Mezzo Practice With Families

A family is far more than a collection of individuals sharing a specific physical and psychological space . . . [a family] is a natural social system . . . one that has evolved a set of rules, is replete with assigned and ascribed roles for its members, has an organized power structure, has developed intricate overt and covert forms of communication, has elaborated ways of negotiating and problem solving that permit various tasks to be performed effectively. (Goldenberg & Goldenberg, 2000, p. 3)

Social work students are frequently exposed to families in a variety of settings and from different perspectives. In some cases, we may teach students about the centrality of family systems as the unit of attention or encourage them to develop a family-centered approach to practice (Hartman & Laird, 1983). Sometimes we have the opportunity or the agency has the expertise to introduce students to specific models of family treatment—psychodynamic, experiential, transgenerational, structural, strategic, systemic, cognitive-behavioral, postmodernist and constructionist, or psycho educational (Goldenberg & Goldenberg, 2000). Since the early days of family treatment in the late 1950s, numerous schools of thought have evolved and influenced the way social workers work with families. Much has been written about the different pioneers of family therapy—Bowen, Jackson, Ackerman, Bell, Haley, Satir, Whitaker, and Minuchin to name a few, and the many models of family therapy that have evolved over time—Psychoanalytic, Systems, Structural, Cognitive-Behavioral, Object-Relations, Strategic, Solution-Focused, and Narrative (Hartman, 1995). Today, work with families is considered so important that family treatment is often a major priority and focus for social work education programs in particular during the advanced or 2nd-year curriculum.

Students sometimes feel overwhelmed by so many different models of working with families and may be tempted to use one model with every family, whether it is appropriate or not. Kilpatrick and Holland (1995) suggest the use of an integrative model for practice that is based on assessing the level of functioning in families within the context of the broader ecosystem. Although the skills necessary for family-centered practice encompass the core skills applicable for social work practice (Hartman & Laird, 1983), these skills take on greater complexity when applied to work with families. For example, what was an assessment of a client's readiness to discuss feelings, now becomes an assessment of the client's readiness to reveal feelings in the presence of other family members, and it is important to assess the role this may have in the dynamics of family intervention.

Over the years the focus of work with families has shifted from a pathological perspective to a strengths perspective, from dysfunction to resilience, and from remediation to prevention and early intervention. Today's family therapist needs to attend to issues related to changing family life cycles (Carter & McGoldrick, 1999) and other factors affecting the family. These include members moving in and out of the family because of divorce or immigration patterns, single parenthood, remarried or blended families, gay/lesbian families, families with adopted or foster children, families with young children, and families with older family members. There are also many stresses on families, including poverty, unemployment, and homelessness; the need for two or more wage earners to support a family; the intersectionality of family violence, substance abuse, and child abuse and neglect; catastrophic illness, medical insurance, and health care costs, to name a few. The emotional and financial toll experienced by caregivers as a result of increasing needs of all family members must also be factored into work with families.

SAMPLE FAMILY PRACTICE ASSIGNMENTS

- Preparing genograms for each family the student is working with.

- Planning an interview with a family; taking into consideration different roles, ages, and developmental levels of family members; thinking about ways of differentially engaging the family in family therapy; assessing the impact of authority issues, boundary structures, and communication patterns.

- Contracting with families in clear, specific terms and eliciting from members their perceptions of the problems/issues to work on and the conditions needed for solutions.

- Writing process recordings of family sessions providing both verbal and nonverbal communication patterns among members.

- Selecting a family and assessing family system dynamics, including the family's history, culture, structure and roles, resources, physical environment, and economic and social supports.

- Examining different family therapy approaches and determining which models are best suited to particular families and the rationale for the selection.

Mezzo Practice With Groups

Group work theory and practice is not always well conceptualized in the field and the classroom despite the demand for group work services (Birnbaum, Middleman, & Huber, 1989). "Students, underexposed to group content in the classroom, are often supervised in their group work by field instructors lacking solid group work education" (Cohen & Garrett, 1995, p. 136). Steinberg (1993) found that social workers without group work education were more controlling as group facilitators, less aware of the functions of group conflict, and more focused on individual group members than on the group as a whole. This suggests the need for "a carefully executed, multi-pronged approach aimed at strengthening academic, field, and continuing education curricula in group work" (Cohen & Garrett, 1995, p. 137).

Most placements have the opportunity or potential for work with a variety of groups, including: educational, socialization, recreational, self-help, problem-solving, milieu, discussion, mutual-aid, and task-centered groups. Garvin, Gutierrez, and Galinsky (2004) provide an overview of group practice models that serves as a useful resource to field instructors and students. Groups also vary in structure from open-ended to closed membership and have different time frames, from a single session to long-term, ongoing treatment. Although the type and character of intervention in these groups may differ, field instructors should focus on the engagement of students in the process of the group as a system. Students should have the opportunity to appreciate the power of "effective group work, in which people interact personally to support and challenge one another as they consider, understand, appreciate, respect and build upon each other's experiences, situations, problems, dilemmas and points of view" (Northern & Kurland, 2001, p. vii).

Certain core skills and knowledge are essential for students to learn as they begin to study and work with groups, including: the facilitator's role, stages of group development, group process, roles of members, dealing with conflicts and silence, promotion of mutual aid, use of activity, and assessment and evaluation. To the greatest extent possible, opportunities for student group work assignments should be available in the placement even if groups are not a general modality of service in the agency.

Creating group work assignments requires sensitivity to the fact that students often fear taking on a group. Shulman (1999) identifies the "fear-of-groups-syndrome that relates to generalized worries about performance. These worries are connected to the complexity of groups—"After all, there are more of them than me!"—and a fear that whatever acting out occurs among members, the group will become uncontrollable and it will be impossible to maintain any semblance of competence. Lack of exposure to groups may account for some of this fear, but even if the student has some experience with groups, the next group is different. Students must learn to be comfortable with different personalities in each group, the vast array of information that emerges, and how to begin groups that sets the climate for the work ahead (Wayne & Cohen, 2001).

Our task as field instructors is to convey the essential dynamics of groups and to focus on the following elements:

Group formation. There are several variables that may influence the educational experience of suitable group assignments for students. For instance, students may be assigned to a new group, an existing group, or a student-developed group, or they may begin their exposure to groups through co-leadership experiences. The experience of planning and developing a group provides students with a very rich, oftentimes neglected, aspect of group work practice (Wayne & Cohen, 2001). Planning a group allows students to learn about group purpose, composition, duration and meeting patterns, membership norms, physical environment, and use of group activities. However, it may be preferable that students be assigned to groups that are formed in response to a real need experienced by clients rather than to develop groups solely to meet students' interests or the social work program's requirements. Although the student has an interest that motivates the development of a group, there may be insufficient client response unless the group focus meets a real need. (See Outline for Planning a Group in chapter 6, Process Recordings, Logs and Journals.)

Group development. This refers to the process of growth that groups experience over time, the predictable stages that occur, and the challenges groups must address in order to continue to grow and move forward. The role in assessing developmental stages and facilitating growth is critical to progress and increasing group maturity over time. There is general agreement that "the stages of group development are orientation, dissatisfaction, resolution, production, and termination" (Berman-Rossi, 1992, p. 244).

Group workers' roles. Students may be co-facilitators or the primary worker. Co-leadership may involve field instructors, other staff, or other students. The issue of co-leadership has assumed increasing interest in social work practice with groups. Co-leadership may be valuable for beginning-level students with little or no group work practice experience. However, co-leadership is not easy and requires mutual honesty, considerable planning efforts, and frequent evaluation of group sessions. Frequently what is defined as co-leadership is in reality not a situation of "equals" working together, but rather one where students function as observers, or as assistants to staff members with greater power and authority. The reluctance to provide genuine hands-on experiences for students is sometimes rationalized by field instructors who believe the client group is too difficult or the student is not experienced enough (Glassman & Kates, 1988; Toseland & Rivas, 1984). However, the reality is that practice skills are acquired through the actual "doing" of the work, and students need to transform knowledge into action by forming, running, and evaluating their facilitation of groups.

Group process. This refers to changes that take place in groups from session to session and over the life span of the group. Group work students need to identify and monitor the following interrelated characteristics of effective group facilitation: (1) goal determination and pursuit, (2) values and norms, (3) roles, (4) communication, (5) conflict resolution, and (6) attraction/cohesion (Garrett, 1993).

Group work supervision. As field instructors, we need to discuss group processes as regular parts of weekly field instruction conferences with students. If we do not feel as competent with group assignments as with other assignments, we can ask someone else in the agency to supervise or supplement students' supervision around groups or we can arrange for special group work seminars to be offered to students and staff. Students are expected to process-record selected group processes as part of their learning experience, and we need to give explicit instructions about how they gather information and present group interactions in an organized and logical manner. (See Group Process Recording Outline in chapter 6.)

SAMPLE GROUP WORK ASSIGNMENTS

- Observe a group, prepare a process recording on the group that focuses on group dynamics within the group, leadership patterns, and interventions that facilitate group process.

- Co-lead a support group and discuss in field instruction the differences in leadership styles between the co-leaders and the strengths and limitations of each style. Also discuss how conflict in leadership styles can be addressed.

- Prepare a needs assessment questionnaire to determine client interest in a group.

- Prepare an outline on a specialized topic area to present to a group that is currently running.

- Prepare an outline for planning a group.

- Discuss the types of communication patterns that exist in a group and ways to promote mutual aid environments.

- Describe the skills required to sustain the resiliency of members once the group comes to an end. Anticipate the kinds of reactions to ending that members will have and what techniques are needed to facilitate the group ending well.

Macro Practice With Organizations

Social administration or management of organizations is a domain that provides students with macro experiences around organizational dynamics. The issues that concern social work administrators include internal as well as external management of organizations. *Internal management* refers to work with program structures and design, employee supervision and leadership development, motivation and control, and resource acquisition. *External management* pertains to "interactions and exchanges with funding sources, political relationships, bureaucratic requirements, dependencies on suppliers, regulators and cooperating agencies for clients, money and materials" (Fauri, Wernet, & Netting, 2000, p. 11). Students are required to keep logs or journals of their administrative activities by recording key events, steps taken, progress, setbacks or problems, and reflections on their practice for each week of the placement. These logs are central to field instruction discussions. They serve as a running account of specific activities on assignments, starting with brief statements of goals and objectives, student roles, level of responsibility, and initial and ongoing tasks engaged in each week. Logs should also include students' impressions and assessment of what they have accomplished in relation to assignments, logical next steps, impediments or problems, and progress or successes.

SAMPLE ORGANIZATIONAL/ADMINISTRATIVE ASSIGNMENTS

- Examining the agency's official mission statement, established goals and objectives, strategies for achieving goals and recommending policy changes if needed; developing alternative or contingency plans to achieve a particular agency objective.

- Defining the tasks and activities of various roles, positions, or programs in the agency, including the development of a job description for newly created agency positions or programs.

- Designing an orientation program for newly hired employees.

- Designing and implementing an in-service training program on a specific topic of concern to staff or the agency.

- Preparing an analysis of a meeting that the student chaired and evaluating how effective the student was in moving through the agenda and in facilitating communication.

- Supervising staff members or managing an agency unit, department, or program with several employees or volunteers.

- Identifying the criteria necessary for assessment of employee performance and conducting evaluations of staff.

- Evaluating the financial resource needs of an agency in the present or projecting the agency's resource needs and allocations over a 3- to 5-year period.

- Participating in the planning, development, and implementation of fundraising activities.

- Researching and writing proposals for additional agency funding.

- Presenting, interpreting, and justifying an agency or program budget to a board of directors or potential funding source.

- Writing descriptive materials, such as flyers, pamphlets, or brochures, about the agency's services or programs.

- Preparing press releases about agency activities for newspapers or newsletters.

Macro Practice With Communities

Interventions aimed at the community level of macro practice usually begin with identifying the target community's physical boundaries, its self-identification, and the community's structure, including demographic characteristics, values, power, economic structure, and the governmental service system (Landon & Feit, 1999). Pippard and Bjorklund (2003) propose that essential techniques/tools for community practice include understanding the use of influence in group decision making and facilitation of group process. They propose that community practitioners need to understand the techniques of force field analysis (FFA), nominal group technique (NGT), and Q-sort, Delphi, and managerial tools such as Performance Evaluation Review Technique (PERT) charts to be able to assess when to apply these tools differentially. Like agency administration, community organization and planning requires the development of skill in the areas of needs assessment and budgeting as well as an ability to develop "an expertise in group dynamics, conflict resolution, negotiation and political organizing" (Fauri, Wernet, & Netting, 2000, p. 104). These assignments provide unique opportunities for students to develop advocacy and empowerment skills (Richan, 1989). Community organization generally refers to practice in three distinct areas:

Organizational/group development for democratic collective action on social and community problems affecting health and well-being; and advocacy for change or creation of laws, policies, and programs to better meet human needs. Some assignments include providing technical assistance, preparing community needs assessment, constituency development through self-help/mutual support groups, coalition building, and social action campaigns.

Planning/program development for involvement of professionals and service constituents in the coordination of existing services as well as the development of new collaboratives or agency programs. Some assignments include resource development, fact-finding, interagency coordination, proposal writing, program evaluation, policy and legislative analysis, and lobbying.

Community education/leadership development for the acquisition of human and legal rights, self-actualization, self-determination, social cohesion, and community/client empowerment. Some assignments include developing information and referral services, educating and training staff, consumers, and volunteers through workshops or conferences, preparing newsletters, speakers bureaus, and community outreach.

As in other macro assignments, students are required to keep logs or journals of their organizing and planning activities, recording key events, steps taken, progress, setbacks or problems, and reflections on their practice for each week of the placement.

SAMPLE COMMUNITY ORGANIZATION ASSIGNMENTS

- Use various planning tools (e.g., census data and community directories).

- Distinguish between short- and long-range planning procedures and methods.

- Initiate a planning process that includes the participation of appropriate groups (e.g., citizen groups, boards, target groups).

- Forecast potential developments for a series of planning objectives.

- Prepare a time schedule for a comprehensive community-based planning process.

- Form a problem-solving task group from diverse agencies or consumer interest groups.

- Serve as participant on a task force.

- Identify potential areas of group conflict among committee members.

- Initiate contact with a group or organization for purposes of mutual cooperation.

- Develop and implement an agreement to coordinate services with another agency.

- Prepare documents and proposals for negotiating sessions with funding sources.

- Participate in lobbying efforts on local and state levels.

- Organize a speakers bureau.

Macro Practice Policy Analysis

Throughout its history, the social work profession has been in the forefront of social and political change. Intrinsic to these efforts has been the ability of social workers to understand and interpret social policies and, in turn, to influence the development of such policies. Social work education programs often remind students that social policies shape social work practice. Policy analysis requires a range of activities such as: recognizing how a social condition comes to be viewed as a social problem; collection and analysis of data measuring the extent and consequences of a social problem; identification and analysis of prior policy efforts aimed at solving a social problem; identification, analysis, and assessment of alternative policy options; and development and presentation of policy recommendations before legislative or community groups. These activities form the basis for possible student assignments in this arena.

SAMPLE POLICY ANALYSIS ASSIGNMENTS

- Conduct interviews with key stakeholders to gather and compare alternative perspectives on the extent and consequences of a social problem.

- Complete a stakeholder analysis that identifies key individuals and organizations, their interests in the problem and specific solutions, and their bases of legitimacy and power.

- Research the legislative history of an existing or proposed program.

- Complete a cost–benefit analysis comparing two or more policy alternatives.

- Critically review a policy or program proposal to identify potential implementation challenges and to generate possible solutions.

- Identify and contact groups and individuals to solicit support for a policy reform.

- Contact legislative or bureaucratic decision makers to explain/advocate for a policy.

- Organize and facilitate advocacy efforts.

- Present policy analysis and recommendations at a community meeting.

- Prepare and present public testimony in support of a policy or program reform for legislative or budgetary hearings or board meetings.

- Prepare and present testimony in support of a policy or program reform.

- Track and critically analyze the progress of a legislative or administrative reform.

Political Social Work and Policy Advocacy

Wolk, Pray, and Weismiller (1996) define political social work and policy advocacy in fieldwork in the following ways:

Governmental relations involves citizens and groups in activities to influence the formal decision-making process of governmental officials. Placements in this arena would be staffing the office of an elected official or staffing a constituency service or government commission, or being assigned to a lobbying office or group.

Electoral politics involves being assigned to work in the formal or informal systems that compete for power in government and might entail working for a ballot initiative or referendum, staffing a candidate's campaign or a political action committee.

Policy advocacy, development, and implementation might involve work in legislative or executive branch research offices, and work within professional organizations or advocacy groups. These placements offer exposure to policy-making and provide experience on which to develop necessary skills. The following questions are provided to guide the choice of assignments in this arena.

How does the assignment aid the student's ability to establish rapport and build relationships with colleagues and community leaders; develop use of initiative and leadership skills; demonstrate understanding of group processes, collaboration, coalition building, and conflict resolution; use organizational strategies and tactics; demonstrate professional communication and self-awareness; and function on a responsible and increasingly independent level?

How does this assignment aid the student's understanding of the agency's goals and objectives toward meeting client system needs; the nature of the problem; the administrative demands and operating policies?

How does this assignment aid the student's ability to understand the intent of the policy and its origin; assess the process used to develop the policy or changes to the policy; assess the political and administrative feasibility of policy alternatives; prepare written policy documents that are responsive to the population or issue; work with constituency and stakeholders to integrate policy into practice; and evaluate and monitor outcomes?

SAMPLE POLITICAL SOCIAL WORK ASSIGNMENTS

- Participate in voter-registration drives

- Research a legislative issue; write a legislative brief on the issue, and participate in or initiate meetings regarding this issue

- Prepare material for presentation to inform others on an issue

- Observe and partner with a legislative lobbyist

- Track local, state, or federal legislation regarding an issue pertinent to the problems of the community

Practice Research

Research assignments are appropriate within each practice method described, and designing such assignments emphasizes the significance of practice research in all aspects of social work practice.

Sample clinical research assignment. Using a single-system research design, students can be asked to identify client change or progress in achieving goals by gathering quantitative data. Include the following steps in evaluating the efficacy of a particular practice intervention: (1) provide data on client's behaviors or attitudes as the client/worker relationship begins; (2) describe the specific intervention model to be used with the client; (3) use an established research instrument to measure (pre- and post-test) interventions; (4) provide systematic data on client's behaviors or attitudes after the intervention model is employed; and (5) evaluate the effectiveness of the intervention model chosen.

Sample family practice research assignment. Formulate a research project that compares the advantages and disadvantages of strategic family therapy approaches (Minuchin, 1974) with diverse, single-parent families in which there is little family organization or delineated roles and responsibilities. After several sessions, how have strategic family therapy techniques helped to restructure and reorganize families? What techniques were most and least effective? How did the families participate in the process? What diversity factors were recognized in the process?

Sample group work practice research assignment. Design a research project to assess the effectiveness of a series of time-limited, educational groups with court-mandated youth in a community-based organization.

Sample community organization research assignments. Design and test a questionnaire that will help tap into the opinions of a select constituency or determine the feasibility for a particular agency program (day care center) or community project (reclaiming a park).

Sample policy analysis research assignment. Track the legislative response to a social problem at the city, state, and national levels. Locate and analyze survey data on the prevalence of a specific social or health problem, the populations affected, and the scope of the problem for a specific zone or area. Students could also conduct surveys of their own to evaluate staff or community support or opposition to program reform, elimination, or expansion.

Sample organizational research assignment. Organize a series of focus groups composed of a diverse staff to evaluate the level of cultural competence that exists in the agency and to ascertain what diversity training needs to be instituted.

Chapter 4

ADULT LEARNING, LEARNING STYLES, AND LEARNING STAGES

*W*hen teachers and mentors are attuned to the special learning styles of students, they are meeting the goals of diversity education in accord with the highest principles of democratic learning. (Goldstein, 2001, p. 85)

This chapter examines the application of adult learning theory, adult learning styles, and learning stages to field instruction. It is important for us to look at who we teach as much as what we teach. Students are diverse in age, experience, practice method and practice orientation, type of educational program, race, ethnicity, class, gender, sexual orientation, religion, and goals and aspirations. The following examples illustrate this diversity:

A. is a 22-year-old African American female with a BA in psychology and some work experience with emotionally disturbed children in a summer camp. She is extremely enthusiastic about her newfound profession and her desire to work with inner-city children, especially in an elementary school. She expected her 2 years of full-time graduate education to be similar to her undergraduate education, but soon finds that working in an agency several days a week and attending classes and coursework are surprisingly more difficult and exhausting than expected. She is being told that she lacks self-awareness and that her writing skills need improvement.

B. is a 30-year-old BSW Latina who comes into an advanced-standing program with 2 years of undergraduate class and field education in social work, plus 2 years of work on an in-patient psychiatric unit. Her graduate education will be over in 12 months of full-time study. She chose administration as her major method. A great deal is expected of her as a bilingual, bicultural, 2nd-year student in a community-based agency in a poor Latino neighborhood. She is also a lesbian and is having personal problems around her family's rejection of her sexual orientation and partner. She is already feeling burned out after just 3 months in the placement. She is beginning to doubt her decision to pursue an MSW at this point in her career.

C. is a 29-year-old male student of Orthodox Jewish background who has several years of experience in a child welfare agency, but has little formal education in social work. He brings his agency along with himself into a part-time, work/study program and is eager to learn more of the theory behind direct practice, especially as a group worker. He struggles to unlearn and relearn professional social work practice and finds himself defensive at times when his field instructor asks him to explain why he chose a certain intervention. He is not clear about why he needs to discuss race and ethnicity with his parent groups, or even why he needs to bring up the obvious fact that he is White Orthodox Jew. He feels like his experience, skills, and knowledge are constantly being called into question.

D. is a 40-year-old dual-degree student of Italian American background who is married with one child. She will need to negotiate two new professional identities as she pursues an MBA/MSW. She represents an elite group of students who are accepted into full-time, 3- or 4- year, dual-degree programs. She worked in the fashion industry for 15 years and is able to afford the money and time to complete the dual-degree course of study. She has very little prior knowledge of or experience with social work, but would like to open her own agency some day to serve special needs children.

It is a challenge to teach such a diverse group of students and to aid their transition to professional education. A theoretical framework provides direction to our task as field instructors and guides our responses to aid our students in the attainment of greater self-awareness and enhanced critical thinking skills. Adult learning theory has been used by a number of social work educators as a guide to this task (Cartney, 2000; Bogo & Vayda, 1993; Goldstein, 2001; Raschick, Maypole, & Day, 1998; Van Soest & Kruzich, 1994).

Adult learning theory, also referred to as andragogy, is the art and science of helping adults learn. "Andragogy is a set of assumptions about adults as learners and a series of recommendations for the planning, management, and evaluation of adult learners" (Kramer & Wren, 1999, p. 44). As espoused by Malcolm Knowles (1972, 1975, 1984; Knowles, Holton, & Swanson, 1998), adult learning theory proposes that "the learner's needs and interests are the appropriate starting points for organizing educational activities. . . . It follows that opportunities for self-directed participation, analysis, and application constitute the richest resources for learning" (Goldstein, 2001, p. 77).

Conducive Adult Learning Environments

Knowles based adult learning theory on 5 premises. These include: (1) the belief that a person's self-concept shifts from dependency to self-direction; (2) we accumulate an increasing pool of experiences as we mature that serves as a resource for learning; (3) our readiness to learn is increasingly related to the demands of our social roles; (4) our orientation to learning is increasingly problem-centered as we mature, and there is an inherent wish and need to apply our new knowledge; (5) and as we mature our motivation to learn is increasingly internal (Knowles, 1972; Smith, 2002).

Knowles emphasizes the importance of creating a conducive environment and connects this to the quality of learning achieved. According to Knowles, essential conditions include establishing a climate that promotes "informality, mutual respect, physical comfort, collaboration rather than competition, openness, authenticity, trust, non-defensiveness, and curiosity" (Knowles, 1972, p. 34). Not surprisingly, these qualities relate to characteristics associated with student satisfaction with field instruction, summarized by Bogo and Vayda (1987) as "availability, support, structure, promoting student autonomy, feedback and evaluation, and linking theory and practice" (pp. 39–40). The following section expands on conditions for a conducive environment identified by Knowles.

Informality. The differential power that exists between field instructors and students must be handled in a manner that creates comfort, promotes mutuality, and is responsive to student feelings and consistent with their cultural backgrounds. The way we define our role provides an avenue to lessen the power differential and to invite a more reciprocal relationship.

Mutual respect. This involves responding to students with both dignity and concern, which will promote the development of greater mutuality. We communicate our respect of our students by providing acknowledgment and integration of their experiences and by helping them bridge these past achievements with current learning. For example, students who have had considerable experience working with the elderly but are now placed in foster care agencies may benefit from assignments that involve working with groups of grandmothers who are acting as kinship foster parents. The familiarity from experience acts as a bridge to a new area of work and new roles and demonstrates respect for the student's achievements.

Physical comfort and physical environment. Physical comfort is achieved by providing rests, breaks, changes, and reminders that give students time to absorb new learning. The structure of the physical environment includes having a space for students to call their own that in turn increases their sense of belonging and the belief that their presence in the agency matters.

Collaboration rather than competition. This occurs when students are given increasing opportunities to share in planning their own learning experience. Collaboration builds on the mutual respect that exists in the relationship and involves mutual planning. In this way, the students are invited to own their learning, to make it their own, to build on their motivation, and to increase their self-direction.

Openness. This comes about when we provide opportunities for feedback. In addition to giving feedback to students, they should be encouraged to regularly give us feedback regarding learning environments, conditions, contexts, and assigned tasks. Eliciting student reactions to assignments allows them to disagree and encourages a dialogue about learning needs. This openness promotes mutuality in field instructor/student relationships.

Authenticity. This is achieved by honesty and meaningful connections to questions, by providing honest appraisals, and by tuning into student concerns. This means that we are straightforward in our approach to learning areas that require attention. Feedback contains a balance of pointing out achievements, strengths, and areas needing attention.

Trust and Non-defensiveness. These arise through the provision of opportunities to test abilities and to view learning as experimentation rather than as "doing the right or wrong thing" or "looking for success or failure." This involves creating a learning environment that encourages curiosity and experimentation with new ways of thinking. Providing the opportunity for ongoing feedback and evaluation aids the formation of mutuality and promotes risk taking toward the achievement of goals and objectives.

Curiosity. This involves demonstrating interest in our students as individuals and as learners. One way of achieving this is a detailed assessment of their learning needs. It means taking time to be clear and to adjust the pacing of our teaching accordingly. It means being curious about the effectiveness of our teaching and asking how our students are experiencing our efforts.

In addition, consideration of the following will assist field instructors in structuring the optimal field learning experience:

Time. Schedule consistent, private, uninterrupted field instruction conference time. This allows students to plan, and it provides a prism for viewing students' ability to use and organize time.

Space. Consider the physical setting for instructional conferences: Are chairs on different levels or different heights? Do students and field instructors face one another? Is the office or meeting place private? Do our offices include items that symbolize a variety of world views? Will students recognize their cultures as being valued through the artifacts represented?

Title/Status. How do we choose to be addressed? How do we choose to address students? How quickly is this issue settled?

Information sharing and access to resources. How available and accessible is information regarding some of the more routine aspects of placement settings? Are we the only persons from whom students can learn about the placement setting or obtain access to resources in the setting? How quickly can students obtain bathroom keys or find out where office supplies are located? How can we ensure that our students know that it is possible to make requests of us about placement settings?

Decision making. What is the process for decision making around assignments? How clear are these processes made to students? How are self-monitoring and self-evaluation encouraged? How frequently do we engage in reflective discussions? How achievable are the goals that are set? Are expectations discussed openly? Do we invite open discussion of what students expect?

Potential Blocks to Conducive
Learning Environments

Although these apparently straightforward suggestions can facilitate a conducive adult learning environment, they are often difficult to achieve. Bertrand Finch, Lurie, and Wrase (1997) identify the following pitfalls that may inhibit their achievement:

- Inadequate field instruction time because agency expectations and demands may conflict with the time needed for optimal student learning

- Difficulty in achieving a balance between our responsibilities to the profession, including the gatekeeping function, and the role of supportive educator

- Fear of loss of power and control over the progress and direction of the work

- Fear of liability and the pressures of accountability

- Conflict between stability and flexibility in accommodating the range of responsibilities students carry, including those related to work, family, and school

We may fear that accommodating to student needs may place professional standards in jeopardy. Working at a student's pace or taking the time to provide reflective supervision may be more labor-intensive and may create more pressure. It may seem easier to tell students exactly how to proceed in certain situations, both as a protection against something going wrong and as a time-saving device. Accelerating the pace of assignments or feeding students quick solutions to speed up the process to achieve a "correct" outcome are examples of this phenomenon. This apprentice model leads us to tell students, *"This is the way I would do it." "Do it this way." or "I am more experienced than you, so follow my instructions carefully."*

Helping students to reach their own answers and allowing for reasonable alternative approaches may take more time, but it is likely to yield greater results; for example, allowing a student to proceed with an intervention that is stylistically different from our own may be experienced by us as risky or as a more roundabout method.

It means being prepared to partialize and to break the learning down into manageable, digestible parts to assess the impact of this approach on our students. For example, when assigning new cases, beginning-level students may need instructions on how to contact clients and set up appointments before learning how to conduct initial sessions. Providing the context of what roles and responsibilities will be required also helps students meet performance expectations. Explaining the reasons why assignments are chosen and connecting them to learning objectives enables an approach to new learning that includes purpose and direction. For example, *"Our agency serves clients with a wide range of needs. One of the ways to get a sense of this is by working on telephone intakes, where you will have exposure to the broad range of requests we receive for services. So, I am assigning you to Wednesday morning intake sessions. Let's talk about what this task involves."* This open discussion aids understanding the reasons that lie behind our request to try something new or to put aside old ways of approaching situations. It promotes student curiosity about methods and approaches.

Another example is *"Our approach to working with families may differ considerably from the work you may have been introduced to previously. We begin by acknowledging the parents' efforts in caring for their children and our shared concern for their family's survival. We have found a focus on their past failures to be an unproductive way of starting. Let's talk about this approach as it relates to your role here and the way you are expected to engage families in this program."*

These variations require flexibility from us and our placement agencies. Confusion over whether we are lessening professional expectations may emerge. This is a particular challenge in today's practice climate. Being one step away from direct client contact is likely to create inherent tensions and fears. We are accountable for service delivery and carry responsibility for clients assigned to students. In response, we may seek safety by using an apprentice model rather than an educational stance. Balancing student learning needs and desires with learning objectives, timing, and needs of the agency create inherent tensions for us as we exercise the authority of our roles and power of our positions.

In summary,

- Education is a process. Learning and growth occur on a continuum.
  Learning is individualized and may proceed straightforwardly, but it is

also likely to occur in leaps and bounds with the occasional plateau and possible regression to earlier stages.

- Convey positive expectations, but expect "mistakes" as part of learning; have tolerance and patience for the process of learning. Adults may experience considerable embarrassment as they undertake new learning. As a result, students may attempt to disguise mistakes or avoid risk taking all together. Yet mistakes should be valued; they often carry the potential for significant learning. We have a responsibility to provide an atmosphere where mistakes can be tolerated and anticipated as part of the learning process.

- Provide a clear rationale for assignments that relate to identified goals and objectives. Adult motivation to learn is frequently connected to a perceived need to learn related to either work or personal growth. In addition, the ability to retain knowledge is often enhanced when the adult is able to apply the knowledge and to practice it.

- Create opportunities for a safe environment that provide adequate structure, promote risk taking, and allow students to test out their ideas in practice in order to develop their own practice style.

- Value what the student brings in terms of life experiences. These provide a rich resource for connecting new learning to previous successes. However, experience means that fixed ways of working and thinking may exist, and unlearning may be required to progress. Remember that new learning that contradicts what life experience has "proven" otherwise will be mistrusted or integrated more slowly.

- Allow for enjoyment and humor in the learning; however, remember that meaningful learning often has elements of fear, frustration, and anxiety-provoking risk taking. Discomfort does not always signal a bad learning experience and, in fact, it may often promote self-reflection and result in powerful learning. Promoting an atmosphere in which being able to laugh and enjoy the process of learning helps lessen discomfort and awkwardness.

- Student satisfaction is only one measure of success. Satisfaction may just as likely signal that the student has remained in a comfort zone or is joyful about surviving with minimal changes or challenges.

- Empower students to assume responsibility for their own learning. Simply because adults may plan, conduct, and evaluate their own learning does not mean that learning occurs independently. "Adults can be ordered into a classroom and prodded into seats, but they can't be forced to learn" (Zemke & Zemke, 1995, p. 32). Yet, motivation can be stimulated, and participation and responsibility can be increased.

- Provide feedback in an honest and clear manner. Adults may not always be certain what they do not know or what they need to learn. Many adults want and need input to decipher what additional knowledge they require or what they may need to relearn or unlearn. Communicate openly and consider how our own experiences, styles, expectations, and needs affect the learning process. Mutual feedback is an essential tool in this regard.

- Learning varies with tasks and with the person. Adults frequently use various styles and approaches that depend on what is to be learned, familiarity with the task, where it is to be learned, when it is to be learned, and the level of initiative involved. In addition, our approaches to new learning evolve over time.

- Discuss taboo and difficult subjects and establish an atmosphere in which it is possible to state: "This is something we talk about here. You don't have to leave it at the door." Expand creative thinking, encourage questioning and disagreement.

- Help students understand what is meant by integration of theory with practice.

- Exercise authority but seek to understand responses to powerlessness and compromise.

- Seek out supports from agencies, schools, field liaisons, other field instructors, and students.

Adult Learning Styles

In addition to promoting a conducive climate for learning, identifying learning styles is an essential field instruction component. Learning style refers to "a student's consistent ways of responding and using stimuli in the context of learning" (Claxton & Ralston as cited in Bogo & Vayda, 1993, p. 100). Adults have preferred ways of tackling new situations. These predominant and preferred ways of learning signify how adult students can best be taught to experiment with the application of new concepts. Identifying students' preferred learning styles enables adaptation of our teaching styles and assignment choices to facilitate learning. Once these are identified, it is then possible to help students expand and develop other ways of learning in new situations.

According to Hickcox (1995), adult student learning styles can be summarized into three major categories: (1) *physiological styles,* in which learning is influenced through the environment, sociological factors, and physical stimuli; (2) *cognitive styles,* in which learning is influenced primarily through the learner's mental activity or thoughts; and (3) *affective styles,* in which learning is influenced by the learner's emotions and feelings.

Environmental influences include such factors as individual responses to sound, light, temperature, and structural design of the learning environment. Sociological influences may include students' preferences to learn in groups versus learning alone, or learning in a structured situation versus a more self-directed approach. Even the time of day, the amount of activity and stimuli, or the ability to snack can affect each learner's capacity to assimilate new learning. Cognitive influences include the ways new situations are tackled, for example, through observation and reflection, doing and jumping in, theoretical approaches, or intuition. Affective influences include emotional associations to the task at hand. Gender, culture, and personal history can also play a crucial role in learning (Shen Ryan & Ortiz Hendricks, 1989; Granello, 1996).

No matter whose theoretical perspective is used or adopted, remember that adults learn in different ways, and that this is a critical component of how we teach. In order to improve our teaching techniques, we need to examine what is involved in learning, especially learning something new and difficult. Reflecting on our own assumptions about how to learn best expands our notions about the ways to facilitate our students' learning. This has powerful implications for teaching. It increases awareness of the complex needs of students, and it propels the search for ways of adapting teaching styles and structuring assignments. Remember that no one learning style alone describes an adult learner. All models of learning are used by adult learners in one pattern or another, but one style is ususally predominant. It should also be kept in mind that no style is considered better or more desirable than another for successful learning to take place.

Berengarten (1957) and, later, Papell (1980) studied learning styles of social work students. They identified three learning styles: Conceptual, Affective, and Operational. Papell's Self-Profile of Learning Styles is presented at the end of this chapter as an example of a learning style inventory for our use or for use with our students. More recently, field educators have applied Kolb's (1984) theory of experiential learning, which incorporates four learning styles—reflective, operational, conceptual, and intuitive learners. Kolb's interest is grounded in the processes related to experiential learning. He devised a learning cycle composed of four stages. Learners are presumed to enter the learning circle at any stage and progress around its circumference sequentially. The learner's preferred entry point signifies the learner's preferred learning style. Prior to an examination of Kolb's learning styles, an explanation of the learning process and cycle follows.

Kolb's Experiential Learning

Kolb's four stages in experiential learning involve a unidirectional circular process that moves from concrete experience to reflective observation to abstract conceptualization and, finally, to active experimentation. Kolb's model proposes that an individual learner may enter the learning cycle from any one of four distinct positions. These entry points are associated with a corresponding learning style. These are represented below.

STAGES OF LEARNING
THE LEARNING CIRCLE   **LEARNING STYLE**

1. "Reflective Observation"   Reflective learner (the Observer)
2. "Active Experimentation"   Operational learner (the Doer)
3. "Abstract Conceptualization"   Conceptual learner (the Thinker)
4. "Concrete Experience"   Intuitive learner (the Feeler)

Application of Kolb's model has resulted in attempts to adjust it to a more complex view of learning. For example, Jarvis (1995) assesses Kolb's learning circle as simplistic and sets forth a more dynamic model to reflect the complexity of learning. Likewise, Bogo and Vayda (1987) adapted Kolb's Learning

Cycle to provide a useful way of understanding the process of integration of theory and practice. Bogo and Vayda's "reflective loop" involves learning through retrieval, reflection, linkage, and professional response, which move back and forth in a manner that conveys more interaction and interrelation than is presented in Kolb's unidirectional circle. To be able to teach this process, Bogo and Vayda propose that we gain experience with the Integration of Theory and Practice (ITP) Loop Model. They suggest that "the process begins with the "*retrieval* [italics added] of the factual elements of a practice situation. The next step, *reflection*, focuses on the effectiveness of the retrieved interaction or intervention as well as the identification of personal values, attitudes and assumptions which modify the retrieved facts. These processes are then *linked* to professional knowledge that can explain or account for the findings of the preceding steps. This leads directly to the selection of a professional response to the initiating action that began the loop . . . A response or action is selected and its effect then becomes the focus of the same process" (pp. 3–4).

The ITP Loop Model provides a useful tool for working with our students as we attempt to explain and examine the processes involved in field learning. More recently, Miller, Kovacs, Wright, Corcoran, and Rosenblum (2004) report an exploratory study that builds on the work of Jarvis with groups of students and field instructors to examine the field learning process. Interesting modifications of Kolb's learning circle emerge that serve as a platform for further inquiry in this arena.

In spite of the recent works cited above that adapt Kolb's framework, his model and learning styles continue to provide important guides for our work with students. Urbanowski and Dwyer (1988) and Burack-Weiss and Coyle (1991) provide useful syntheses of learning styles and implications for our teaching. The following summary is based on both of these sources (see Table 1).

Kolb's Learning Styles

THE REFLECTIVE LEARNER (THE OBSERVER), "REFLECTIVE OBSERVATION"

These learners prefer to watch and observe in the context of new learning. They tend to be more comfortable reflecting on the work being done before taking action. They are able to recall accurately observations on multiple levels and they do a good job distinguishing between essential and trivial information. They also tend to keep an open mind, reserving judgment until all information has been gathered. A particular strength is their ability to look at many points of view and to organize this material into a meaningful order that enables them to generate ideas. Allowing these students to shadow or to sit in on sessions as a way of beginning is often helpful.

OPERATIONAL LEARNER (THE DOER), "ACTIVE EXPERIMENTATION"

These students learn best through direct action. They are anxious to get busy right from the start of their field placements and will be less comfortable reading case charts for a long period as a way to begin the placement. They are usually ready to take risks and to jump in. This enables them to test ideas and to learn from recurring activity. They are more able to discuss ideas and theories once they have experience on which to comment. Anticipating problems or possible outcomes does not come as easily for them. Linking assessments and interventions with theoretical underpinnings helps guide these students' practice. They may respond more easily to what needs to be done rather than to problems that involve less practical solutions. These students may need help to deal with the slow process of change and to experience the importance of assisting and supporting the client rather than acting and solving the problem for the client.

COGNITIVE LEARNER (THE THINKER), "ABSTRACT CONCEPTUALIZATION"

These students learn through literary and informational sources, thrive on learning theoretical approaches to problem solving, and often are helped by reading whatever information they can gather. They feel best prepared for action when they believe they have a grasp of the information they require, often through theoretical discussions about cases. Reading canned cases is helpful. It may take time before these students are prepared to discuss feelings, and we should not force this before they are ready. Seeing first what students think is a significant and useful way to begin rather than expecting them to report readily on the feelings evoked by the work. These students tend toward a question-and-answer probing format in sessions; they benefit from practice with more open-ended questions and interventions that promote exploration. Choosing a diverse caseload helps diffuse the conceptual learners' tendency to categorize and generalize.

AFFECTIVE LEARNER (THE FEELER), "CONCRETE EXPERIENCE"

These students learn best through the use of their senses, particularly their feelings and emotions. This personal experience is used to help formulate responses to problem solving. These students often need to move from personalized experience to reflection and conceptualization of the meaning of the experience. They demonstrate strength in their ability to connect with people, and they prefer to learn within the context of the "here-and-now." Process recording is particularly useful for these students, as it gives them an opportunity to reflect back on the process as separate from the feelings evoked. A review of several sessions often enables them to see patterns of behavior and to step back from the feelings involved. They are able to identify latent content, but may find themselves feeling along with their clients, and this may lead them into deeper water than anticipated. They will require help to identify their intuitive responses.

Table 1 is adapted from Urbanowski and Dwyer (1988) and Burack-Weiss and Coyle (1991) and presents a summary of learning styles and teaching responses.

Self-Assessment: Preferred Approaches to New Learning

Take a moment to reflect on your own preferred learning style and aspects of your learning patterns. You may possess elements of all types, but it is important to identify the strongest element operating in your approach to new learning. Your self-assessment can use Kolb's (1984) four models of learning styles or Papell's (1980) Self-Profile of Learning Styles (explained at the end of this chapter). Then ask yourself the following questions:

What learning style/s and patterns can you identify in your students' approaches to learning? On what evidence do you base this assessment?

How similar or dissimilar are your students' learning styles and your own? How might this affect field instruction?

What emerged for you in your attempts to identify your students' and your own leaning styles?

Table 1.

Learning Styles and Appropriate Teaching Responses (adapted from Urbanowski and Dwyer, 1988)

LEARNING STYLE	CHARACTERISTICS	TEACHING RESPONSES
Intellectual learners	Thrive on learning theoretical approaches, reading, and theoretical discussions Tend toward question-and-answer interviewing Analytical in approach to new learning	Select pertinent readings Reach for what students were thinking during an interaction rather than what they were feeling Canned cases or sample case files are helpful for these students to read A diverse caseload helps diffuse the tendency to categorize and generalize Practice open-ended questions and exploration Build on the analytical and advance planning skills
Observers	Watch and reflect before acting Provide accurate observations Open-minded and able to consider a variety of influences to broaden their assessments	Arrange an interview that students can observe Elicit their observations Build on their perceptions to increase comfort in discussion of theory
Doers	Action-oriented Take risks and jumps in Learn from recurring activity Anticipating problems or possible outcomes does not come easily May tend to take on more for the client than needed	Assignments that require immediate action Support links of theory to practice Discussion is easier after experience Explanations regarding the slow process of change
Feelers	Use senses and personal experience Connect easily with people Learn within the context of the "here-and-now" Lead with senses Have a good ear for latent content Often creative and able to respond to a range of clients and problems	Process recording is useful as it gives an opportunity to reflect back on the process as separate from the feelings evoked A review of several sessions enables seeing patterns of behavior and provides stepping back from the feelings involved Support and make conscious what comes intuitively

To summarize, knowledge of learning styles aids our teaching efforts in the following ways:

- *Makes learning more accessible.* For example, we can accommodate intellectual learners by selecting and offering readings that apply to the current placement setting and population, or by arranging for a joint interview for students who are more comfortable observing before performing tasks. Assignments may be chosen that require some immediate action for students who become anxious unless they are doing something active.

- *Stretches students' repertoire of learning styles.* By knowing students' preferred learning styles, it is possible to focus our support as they test out other means of learning. By assessing students' inner resources and providing learning opportunities that stretch their capabilities, it is possible for students to function in the many different roles and tasks required of them.

- *Recognizes the potential pitfalls and avoids "mismatches."* Identification of similarities and differences in preferred ways of learning and teaching provides a rich interchange that broadens approaches to new learning and problem solving, or it can explain tensions that cloud the educational task.

- *Matches teaching methods to shape assignments.* Understanding learning styles provides a framework for determining which teaching methods are needed and how assignments can be adapted to evaluate strengths and to help students reach their full potential. Asking intellectual learners to explain what was "felt" during particular client interactions may be met with blank stares. It may be more effective to ask what students "think" was going on at that point in the interaction.

Stages of Learning

Field instruction and student learning are influenced not only by learning styles but also by the stage of learning at which students find themselves when a particular task arises. Reynolds (1985) developed a five-stage model addressing the stages of learning a new social work task. These stages can be viewed as rites of passage that adult learners must pass through on the way to mastery. Reynolds proposes that these stages are experienced in all new learning situations. The identification of stages of learning facilitates the assessment of what our students require to adjust to new learning situations. Awareness of these stages provides guideposts to the potential stumbling blocks along the way. Reynolds recognizes that there is movement back and forth between stages. Learning does not occur in a linear fashion, and returning to earlier stages is normal and expected as the learner is faced with new facets of the tasks to be mastered. Reynolds emphasizes keeping the focus on what is happening to the learner and recommends beginning where the student is, using what the situation yields and building on the student's experience, and supporting the new learning to facilitate integration, assimilation, and application. Reynolds' five-stage theory includes the following:

1. *The stage of acute consciousness of self.* This is the stage where students feel that they do not have the capacity to succeed. During this stage students will respond by fight or flight, paralysis, feelings of inadequacy, stupidity, keeping silent, using humor, using aggression to mask anxiety, or becoming increasingly verbal. In this stage we need to help students to find the solid ground of personal adequacy they already possess. This stage is normal, expected, and usually short-lived. When students remain frozen in this stage beyond the 4th to 6th week of placement, it may indicate a cause for concern that should be brought to their attention and, if necessary, to the faculty liaison. It is not unusual, however, for students to return to this stage of learning over the course of the placement whenever they are faced with another new or difficult task or situation.

2. *The sink or swim stage.* Students are aware of expectations, but can barely keep up with the demands. Approval seeking and dependence characterize this stage. We can help by mobilizing students to trust their spontaneous or intuitive responses. We are responsible for providing support and conveying constructive criticism during this stage.

3. *The stage of understanding a situation without the power to control one's own actions or activity in it.* This stage involves freedom from preoccupation with the self and freedom to study the situation as it is. *"All at once it came to me. I thought I understood before what it was all about, but now I know I have been in a fog all this time."* Although students may be performing well and a sense of confidence is achieved

in this stage of learning, disillusionment quickly occurs when there are setbacks or when students find themselves regressing to previous stages of learning. This is a stage of progress and regression. Reynolds advises us to understand this stage so that we do not get disillusioned along with our students and lose confidence in our own teaching perform- ance. Many students achieve this stage of learning prior to graduation and may remain in this stage for several years after graduation.

4. *The stage of relative mastery.* In this stage, students can both under- stand what is involved and control the activity required. This stage is characterized by the integration of theory and practice. Confidence is gained, and students know they can deal with what is required of them. The activities become second nature to them, and they can autonomously analyze their own performance. In this way, students have achieved professionalism and can apply knowledge to solving practical problems, using themselves as instruments with their acquired skills. Not all students reach this stage of learning prior to graduation. It is common that the first 2 or 3 years after graduation are the years of consolidation and achievement of this stage of learning.

5. *The stage of learning to teach what one has mastered.* This stage acknowledges that once learners achieve mastery, they are often called on to offer consultation and to teach others. As new teachers enter this stage, they concomitantly return to the stage of acute self-con- sciousness and the expected anxieties faced by a new role. New field instructors often remark that they feel "acutely self-conscious" of themselves as field educators, which brings the process full circle back to Stage 1.

In Summary

The identification of similarities or differences in learning styles between our- selves and our students provides insight into how these styles might interact in field instruction. For example, if the field instructor and student are conceptual learners, they may enjoy reading all there is to know about a client population and delay assignment of cases. If both are operational learners, they may jump in and get the work done, leaving little time for reflection. Dissimilar styles pose other issues. An operational learner and conceptual teacher may clash over who wants to do and who wants to think and reflect first. Yet, in a similar fashion, these same differences in learning and teaching styles can enrich the interchange by broadening the approaches to learning and problem solving.

Learning/teaching styles interact in complex ways and are essential components in adapting teaching techniques to suit individual learning needs. Collaborative teaching requires an atmosphere in which honest and straightforward discussion of these issues can occur. In this way, adult learners are given the opportunity to accept personal responsibility for their own learning. Students can then begin to integrate their personal selves with their professional selves.

In addition, students have different relationships and patterns of approaching the persons who teach them and who are often in positions of authority. These patterns are similar to students' interpersonal styles; relate to their worldviews and cultural values, norms, and ways of being; and affect student/field instructor relationships. They often display themselves in the work and in student relationships to colleagues. Students' relationships to authority and to learning are critical in predicting how they will receive direction, take correction, and collaborate. All of these issues are integral to educational assessments of students, a topic discussed in greater detail in chapter 7.

In the same way that Kolb's learning cycle has been critiqued as failing to grasp the complexity of learning, concern has been raised about the limitations of adult learning theory and concepts of learning styles. Brookfield (1995) believes that chronological age or levels of maturity may carry less significance in explaining how learning occurs than other factors such as culture, personality, or political beliefs. He questions the advisability of attempting to espouse adult learning theory as discrete and unconnected to how we learn as children or as adolescents. Brookfield identifies areas for further research into adult learning, including appreciating the interaction of emotions and cognition; giving social context and culture their proper place in understanding how adults approach learning; understanding the role of gender in learning; and giving full weight to "whole person" learning rather than placing selected emphasis on experience and doing. These cautions point the way forward for new developments and research.

In spite of these expressed concerns, adult learning theory and understanding the different ways we learn is important to our consideration of teaching techniques and the methods we use.

Jarvis (1999) draws links between the necessary conditions for adult learning and the implied teaching approaches to these conditions. He proposes that andragogy provides a humanistic perspective to the approach of teaching adults. Jarvis (1999, p. 153) uses Knowles's 16 principles of teaching and summarizes the principles as:

The teacher:

- exposes learners to new possibilities for self-fulfillment

- helps learners clarify their own aspirations

- helps learners diagnose

- helps learners identify life problems resulting from their learning needs

- provides conditions conducive to adult learning

- accepts and treats learners as persons

- seeks to build relationships of trust and cooperation between learners

- becomes a co-learner in the spirit of mutual enquiry

- involves learners in a mutual process of formulating learning objectives

- shares with learners potential methods to achieve these objectives

- helps learners to organize themselves to undertake their tasks

- helps learners exploit their own experiences on learning resources

- gears presentation of his or her own resources to the levels of learners' experiences

- helps learners integrate new learning to their own experience

- involves learners in devising criteria and methods to measure progress

- helps learners develop and apply self-evaluation procedures

These principles can also be expressed as a creative endeavor. In the words of Robin Strauss, a social worker, field instructor, SIFI teacher, faculty liaison, and quilt maker: "The art of quilt making inspires the practice of field instruction. Both require a creative process that uses elements of design and an understanding of stages of development. Just as contrasting blocks give life to a quilt, recognizing contrast between field instructor and student offers vibrancy and meaning to the field experience."

Self-Profile of Learning Styles for Direct Social Work Practice (Papell, 1978)

Although this exercise was devised for use with social work students, it has multiple uses and is included in this text as a resource to field instructors. It may be given to students in placement or used directly by field instructors. This is not a study of how much you know, or how accurate your knowledge is, or how fast you learn, or how skillful you are, or where you learned what you know. It is a study of your particular style of learning. It has long been known that people have different styles of thought. Mental functioning seems to be a process of forming cognitive systems using combinations of body movements, sensory images, and language. Individuals seem to combine action, emotion, and word components of mental activity in unique patterns with different balances.

Learning is the development of new cognitive systems by experiencing, integrating, and transforming reality both from inside and from outside oneself in a problem-solving process. It is hypothesized that the process of learning in adults occurs by use of a combination of modes of cognitive activity—conceptual, affective, and operational. Social work learning for practice requires the use of all of these modes.

Step 1. Think about yourself and your process of learning for social work practice. In what kind of context—conceptual, affective, or operational—has learning been most comfortable or most productive for you? What is the pattern of your use of these three modes? Read the description on the following page of three hypothetical models to help you think introspectively about your own style or pattern. Remember that it is assumed that as a social work learner and as an adult you will identify in some way with each of the three models. Read the three hypothetical models of learners for social work practice.

Step 2. Study the descriptions of modes of learning activity, remembering that each is a hypothetical model. Which of these descriptions do you feel is most like you? Which is the least like you? What patterning of these models would best describe your learning style? Keep in mind that all modes are used by adult learners in some balance and pattern and that no pattern is considered to be more or less desirable for successful learning for social work practice. Remember also that classification systems are rarely, if ever, discrete or exact. Although there may be cultural values attached to one or another model, here we make the assumption that all learners share these processes in some integrated mix, and that social work learning in particular uses all three modes. Please try and be introspective about what you actually do as a learner and not what you think you should do.

   Step 3. Arrange these three models into a pattern of your own learning style, placing the three models in the order in which you identify yourself with each one. For example:

O	A
A	C
C	O

Three Hypothetical Models of Learners (Papell, 1978)

C

In this model, as a social work student, I learn with knowledge from the literature and theories. Theories are readily learned, even though it may be difficult to connect these to the client situation. Client situations have real meaning for me when there is a conceptual referent already available in my mind. I prepare myself for a new problem-solving situation by learning all that is available to me about the particular social and individual problem and feel best prepared to meet the client when I feel some mastery of the information. In my relations with my field instructor, a theoretical discussion of the problem is valued over actual suggestions for what to do. What I need is an adequate grasp of available knowledge. I can read "canned" cases and can use them to conceptualize. In writing papers about my own practice, I enjoy connecting my practice experience with concepts and theories, in fact, I feel uncomfortable if I have not done so. In process recordings, it is easy to record what has taken place within my current conceptual framework. It is sometimes difficult to get beyond what parameters to recognize and interpret what happened further. My practice analogue is a deductive, abstract one. I set deliberative, long-range goals.

A

In this model, as a social work student, I learn through my senses and by use of feeling. Important learning takes place when intense emotions are present in the client or in me. The emotional learning experience can be vicarious, that is, I can hear about it from someone else or read about it, but the significant learning occurs when I have caught the essential subjectivity of reality for myself. I trust my instincts and prepare myself for new problem-solving situations by self-reflection and getting my thoughts and feelings together. I prefer not to find out what previous workers have thought about practice situations, rather, I like to move in with my intuition functioning. I tend to resent practical suggestions by my field instructor. I prefer learning from live practice experience, my own or others', rather than from "canned" cases. My process recordings carry my subjectivity. It is easy to know the subjectivity but more difficult to identify what happened. I prefer to write papers about my own learning experience rather than about theories and concepts others have written in the literature. I am skeptical of theories because of their inherent abstractness. I prefer to create my language to describe my work. My practice analogue is expressive and unique. I have a reluctance to set specific goals, because they may get in the way of a process and feeling.

0

In this model, as a social work student, I learn by doing. Significant for learning is experience that occurs repetitively. I find myself or place myself in the act of confronting a client or evaluation with a client, but it is after the act that I find I learned what confronting or evaluating is. Concepts that have been read or discussed are real in my mind because they have been experienced in action. When faced with a new problem-solving situation, I prefer to get started. I feel most comfortable being busy with it, doing something about it. I appreciate specific suggestions from my field instructor, finding these helpful while I get moving into action. I find "canned" cases useful if the action is well described. In process recordings I sometimes find it difficult to describe what has happened in the practice situation. My recording is either too detailed or not explicit enough. It is easy to be specific but difficult to generalize. What others have written in the literature makes most sense when the concepts are discussed in terms of specific suggestions for practice. Concepts and theory are necessary but less instructive as a guide to action than my own personal momentum, judgment, and good sense. My practice analogue is practical and accomplishment-oriented. I set concrete, pragmatic goals.

Chapter 5

TEACHING METHODS

*F*ield educators are consummate teachers, but they use non-sanctioned teaching methods, ones not visible to the academic eye. The Ideal Type has educational vision and the ability to teach "standing up"—she uses every instance, positive or negative, and the process of field as a teaching tool for students...she is well versed in adult/learning/teaching styles, knows social work theories, and the continuum of practice...and knows the relationship between field and all parts of the curriculum. As a teacher of social work, she has, and models, a solid, integrated conceptual framework of social work as a profession. (Navari, 1993, p. 13)

We have all had the experience of being able to apply a professional maxim for the first time. Something "clicks" and we know that the insight is now a part of us. We have discovered the relevance of the knowledge. We need it. We can apply it. It works. The "teachable moment", then, is the time when what you teach can be immediately applied to what the student . . . needs to know. (Burack-Weiss & Coyle Brennan, 1999, p. 15)

The explosion of knowledge and information in the last several decades, due in great part to the development of the World Wide Web, has major implications for what social workers ought to know and how they acquire this vast knowledge. We are doing less and less direct teaching, but we are using more and more resources to help students learn. This shift has developed over time. "Current educational sources focus on the teacher's understanding of the student's learning style, the awareness of varied teaching methods, the use of innovative teaching technology, and the ability to integrate these into an efficient and effective learning environment" (Foeckler & Boynton, 1976, p. 38). Just as today's field instructors are called on to do more and more, so, too, are the demands on today's students. They have to hit the ground running, multitasking in complex agency systems, and dealing with the changes that learning produces while learning the craft of social work practice. Through a mutual and collaborative relationship, we help students to function in a specific agency environment. Simultaneously, we strive to help them become more autonomous critical thinkers and to achieve an awareness of themselves in their practice. These goals supersede specific agency contexts and fields of practice and refer to fundamental professional social work attributes required in any setting today.

In fact, we help students "live in three worlds: the immediate one that they face with their clients in their agencies; the broader world that they may practice in their various professional roles and functions; and the ideal world in which services are based on our professional values, historical commitments, theoretical knowledge, practice wisdom, and empirical research" (Goldstein, 1989, p. 9). Goldstein goes on to describe several teaching goals and objectives for field instructors:

- Teach professional values and principles.

- Affirm agency practice.

- Assess where students are.

- Bridge expectations and realities of agency-based practice.

- Explore possible constraints on performance.

- Convey positive expectations about growth.

- Know when to be active and structured versus nondirective and reflective.

- Expand capacities for empathy.

- Help to integrate theory and practice.

- Communicate openly.

- Become role models.

- Seek out educational supports.

Teaching Approaches

The most productive learning occurs within an environment that views the student and teacher as co-learners in the learning–teaching situation. Each participant in the learning situation at times exchanges the teacher–learner role, depending upon each one's unique knowledge or experience. Within this expectation, each member of the learning dyad or group may share the roles of expert, informational source, evaluator, or guide. (Foeckler & Boynton, 1976, p. 40)

The shift in social work education—from looking at teaching to looking at the whole nature of learning—continues to create challenges and to define best practices. The emphasis is on students as learners and our consumers. We, along with our agencies and social work education programs, produce their education. We can no longer think of teachers as all-knowing authorities who pass on knowledge to passive recipients. Active learning is preferable to passive listening (Roche et al., 1999).

However, some students will come to social work with a strong resistance to trusting or engaging in a "democratic educational processes" that is designed to lead to student-centered, direct, active, autonomous, effective, and in-depth experiential learning and teaching. Adult learning theory does not always take into account the experiences of oppressed groups within the educational system or of class and gender differences in opportunities for self-direction.

Co-learning and co-teaching occur in each step of the field instruction process, including the following collaborative activities:

- Defining what students want to learn

- Charting the learning course

- Preparing for field instruction conferences

- Sharing and exploring values, beliefs, and ethics

- Making informed statements, assessments, and judgments

- Expressing best ways to learn and teach

- Sharing the motivation to learn and to teach

- Being self-directed

- Meeting goals and objectives set for the learning situation

- Clarifying competency standards for field performance

- Meeting expectations set by the profession, social work program, and agency

- Providing open and honest feedback

- Discussing changing theories, client populations, and practice innovations

- Sharpening practice skills, knowledge, and values

- Improving performance when expectations fall below minimum standards

- Stimulating a spirit of inquiry

- Appreciating different teaching and learning styles

- Freeing ourselves to learn and teach in the most comfortable way

The possible opposite experience of co-learning may be described as the "games people play in field instruction" when students and teachers are caught up in power struggles for control of the learning/teaching situation (Kadushin, 1968; Hawthorne, 1975). If the student is not learning, then the teacher must be doing something wrong. If the teacher is not satisfied with the student's performance, then the student is failing in some way. Adult learners have developed various sets of behaviors to deal with the range of good and bad teachers they have encountered in their lives. Honest discussions about how students are experiencing the current field instruction experience may open up lines of communication and lead to new ways of teaching and learning.

There have been a number of studies that look at qualities and types of teaching that social work students want from their field instructors (Hartung, 1982; Knight, 1996; Lazar & Eisikovits, 1997; Navari, 1993; Rosenblatt & Mayer, 1975; Solas, 1990; Van Soest & Kruzick, 1994). In general, the most important component of overall teaching effectiveness appears to be the relationship between field instructors and students with the following components:

The supervisory skills that have been evaluated by students as particularly helpful are those that contribute directly to their learning and provide students with structure and direction in their work. Field instructors who are supportive, as well as those who actively involve their students in the learning process, provide instructive feedback to their students, and encourage their students to be autonomous, self-critical, and link the classroom to the field also have been evaluated as effective. (Knight, 2000, p. 174)

A summary list of significant student-ranked behaviors for effective teaching should support and encourage efforts to:

- Serve as role models for what a social work professional looks like

- Help incorporate professional values and ethics

- Challenge attitudes that are unethical or antithetical to social work values

- Regularly confer with students regarding progress or lack of progress

- Point to specific strengths or needs in practice skills and knowledge

- Introduce students to client populations and communities served

- Teach about diversity and model cultural competence

- Communicate with the social work education program regularly

- Help develop self-awareness and sensitivity with encouragement and empathy

- Evaluate progress formally and informally throughout the placement

- Introduce students to policies and procedures of the agency

- Define and clarify students' role in the agency

- Facilitate students' status as members of the agencies' professional staff

- Help students learn more than one method of practice

Teaching Methods

Teaching is a discipline in its own right, with its own vast knowledge base and skills. (Coulshed, 1993, p. 3)

Gitterman and Miller (1977) provide a useful definition of teaching: "The central task of teaching is defined as the selection and structuring of experiences that demand and induce creative problem solving" (p. 104). As field instructors, it is more important for us to orchestrate the learning experiences of students, and thus free them to learn, than to concentrate on what knowledge we will impart. "When education is oriented to the person who is to learn plus the situation to be mastered, there is something more to teaching than proving to the learner that one knows the subject" (Reynolds, 1985, p. 83). There are many ways of becoming this liberated learner/teacher. We can be selective in how much didactic content to offer students and how many experiential, concrete experiences to structure into the placement. We can select from a combination of teaching approaches that include auditory/visual technologies, Web sites, and distance learning; interactional/participatory face-to-face activities; use of role modeling and role playing; use of analogies or metaphors; and methods that employ all the senses in learning. It is useful to master several techniques to meet the various learning needs of students and to be ready to use a range of techniques given the particular learning issues being tackled.

HIERARCHICAL DIDACTIC TEACHING

In this approach, the field instructor is the expert who offers students information, guidance, practice wisdom, and suggestions primarily through a lecture format, and students are expected to pay attention, note down, understand, and recall the information transmitted. "The teaching and learning process in supervision, as in educational settings, has been profoundly affected by acceptance of the myth that teaching essentially involves transmitting existing ideas to learners who somehow absorb them and make the ideas as their own" (Shulman, 1984, p. 161). Power clearly rests with the teacher in this hierarchical approach to teaching. Many students are accustomed to "being fed" information and like it because they can gather a great deal of information quickly and then move on to the work. Didactic teaching may be preferred by students of particular cultural backgrounds where more self-directed or assertive learning/teaching approaches are not culturally syntonic or comfortable to them. For example, Asian students who are recent immigrants may view field instructors as authority figures imparting the wisdom of the profession and would not dare question or interrupt the field instructor's comments (Shen Ryan & Ortiz Hendricks, 1989; Shen Ryan, 1981).

It is important to recognize that the different ways of learning are discrete personal styles and it is essential that the field instructor be open to the fact that the student may perceive and process knowledge in different ways. There are students who must have hands-on experience in order to learn and others who operate in another way. (Van Soest & Kruzich, 1994, p. 61)

Didactic teaching may be essential in some contexts (e.g., large student units, fast-paced settings) where it can be enhanced by effectively using small-group discussions, problem-solving exercises, case studies, and projects that increase participation, reflection, and discussion among students. Yet, didactic teaching is not for everyone, and it has disadvantages such as overwhelming students with too much information all at once; expecting them to follow suggestions to the letter; preventing students from developing their own approach to assignments; and focusing on the field instructor as expert.

CONNECTED TEACHING

Paulo Freire (1993) challenged the didactic, prescriptive, "banking" form of education, calling it oppressive rather than enlightening. He believed that teacher domination robs the learner of self-respect, and he posed a theory of education as liberation in which teacher and student work toward mutual learning goals. Freire proposed the model of partner-teachers in which students are encouraged to speak in their own active voices and to think for themselves, as opposed to the traditional model of "banking" education or filling students up with the teacher's knowledge. The feminist approach to "connected teaching" welcomes diversity of opinion, recognizing "that each of us has a unique perspective that is in some sense irrefutably 'right' by virtue of its existence" (Belenky et al., 1986, p. 222). This approach constructs truth through consensus, feeling or sensing together, bridging private and shared experience. "The best teachers understand the issues and concerns of the person who is learning, see how each person learns best, find out what motivates a person to learn, appreciate what the person knows and what they still need to learn, and know when they are needed and when they are in the way" (Reynolds, 1985, p. 83). It is not so much the teachers' intelligence that is essential to learning, but that teachers are most effective when they understand different learning needs and are able to release the learners' intelligence.

Kolb's experiential model (1984), discussed in chapter 4, suggests that effective learning involves stages of learning—concrete experience, reflective observation, abstract conceptualization, and active experimentation. In this approach, experiences provide students with opportunities to build on their intuition and feeling and promote self-direction, autonomy, integration of theory with practice, and continued intellectual growth. Experiential learning assumes that all students are comfortable with operational (doing) and affective (feeling) learning versus more cognitive approaches to learning. Yet, not all students can "jump in" to the work of professional helping, and many students want help preparing themselves for this work. Sometimes the setting decides how we teach and how students learn. For example, in-patient units of a hospital may not allow students much time to acclimate to the work before they are expected to perform rapid assessments and hold their own as part of an interdisciplinary team.

It is most important that we be flexible in our approach to teaching, understand the constraints and opportunities of agency settings, and consider which teaching methods are best suited for which student's learning style. For example, a field instructor may assign a series of articles on support groups for cancer patients to a student. The student tries to read the articles, but they make no sense without direct experience to base the theory on. Realizing that the student prefers to learn from concrete experience, the field instructor suggests that the student get involved with a support group at the agency and read the articles later. "When learning blocks occur, an understanding of the learning styles of field instructor and student can help break down the barriers. Increased understanding of how differences and similarities in learning styles may influence the perceptions of both parties in the supervisory relationship can be a tool for improving communication and for successfully negotiating assignments and strategies for learning" (Van Soest & Kruzich, 1994, p. 67).

Range of Teaching Approaches

There are many ways to teach and many ways of learning. We should start by considering what teaching approaches are most comfortable for us—including lecturing on specific topics, discussing assigned articles, viewing videotapes together, using case material to stimulate discussions, requiring weekly journals, and teaching from recordings, which is the topic of chapter 6. Remember that we do not have to do all the teaching. It can be helpful to have other avenues for learning such as grand rounds, in-service training programs, conferences, field trips, films, etc.

In the beginning stages of field instruction, we may ask students to report on *observations* of staff meetings, client interactions, team meetings, and community or board meetings. These observations provide material on client/worker interactions as well as worker/supervisor interactions. In this way we model aspects of good practice and sound professional relationships. "Workers are particularly influenced by a supervisor who demonstrates skill in practice, maintains high standards, and shows excitement, curiosity, and openness to differing perspectives and possibilities. What effective supervisors 'say to do' needs to be congruent with what they actually 'do'" (Gitterman & Miller, 1977, p. 106). *Modeling* is an excellent way of teaching throughout the field placement, but especially in the first few weeks. Gradually, as the semester progresses, we shift to observing students in their interactions with co-workers, community leaders, administration, and clients. How students take on all these different aspects of their work is critical to their growth and development.

Role playing is a useful teaching method, especially when we reverse roles with our students so that we alternately play clients and workers. This technique can be effective in helping students develop empathy for client situations, in planning strategies for how to approach difficult situations, and in dealing with difficult and sensitive material. Role playing encourages students to pose their own responses and questions, rather than repeating what we might say. This exercise allows students to figure out and plan the best approaches to their work with individuals, families, groups, communities, or organizations. It enhances the development of their own critical thinking skills as they ponder next steps out loud.

Throughout our teaching efforts, we need to help students understand and operationalize *theoretical concepts* encountered in practice. This can best be done by linking concepts to examples or analogies that bring the concepts to life and enable students to gain a deeper understanding of theories. Some students respond very well to analogies that help make connections between their experiences and clients' experiences. For example, *"It seems like you are expecting yourself to act as a kind of superwoman! Let's consider your need to fix this* community's problems single-handedly" or "*You appear to be describing this part of the group process like a totally out-of-control freight train. Can you comment more on what was happening in the group at this point?*" Creating analogies that are relevant to the specific student/client experience, and are within the agency/community context, can be helpful when students are feeling overwhelmed and need to connect with the reality of the situation. It helps students to tune in and to understand how clients might be feeling.

Labeling or naming the skills used by students in particular interventions and identifying specific techniques used are helpful teaching techniques. Experienced students often do more than they know and need our assistance in identifying their intuitive or learned skills and techniques. It is also helpful to ask students to link learning from the classroom or readings to their work with clients. *Partializing* or breaking down a concept or task into manageable parts or steps helps students understand and appreciate complex ideas or interventions. For example, "*Assessment involves data gathering, evaluation of the data, and plans for intervention. Let's start with data gathering. What do you need to know in order to carry out this assignment, and how will you go about finding it out?*"

Throughout all of our teaching efforts, students need to get *feedback* on how they are doing. They need to hear that they are doing what they need to be doing and they need direction on how to improve their efforts. Frequent feedback or learning reviews help students to recognize achievements, to see where they are at in reaching learning goals, and to identify learning difficulties or gaps in their knowledge. Feedback also guides change in thinking, attitudes, and behaviors in desired directions. In a very real way, learning reviews are weekly evaluations of field performance. For example, we could say, "*You have achieved good rapport with this group of chronic mentally ill patients. Let's look at the specific ways you accomplished this*" or "*You were not afraid to deal with this client's anger or hostility. What was going through your mind as she raged at you?*" or "*You were extremely efficient getting the personnel manual done, but you are not so efficient getting this work group off the ground. Let's brainstorm together about the differences between these two assignments.*" Modeling, role playing, analogies, labeling, partializing, and feedback are just a few teaching techniques designed to enable students to offer ideas, suggestions, and hunches on how the work gets done.

Peer Group Supervision or Learning Teams

Group supervision, "a group learning climate conducive to the interactional processes of mutual problem solving and aid" (Gitterman & Miller, 1977), allows students to talk with other students and provides another atmosphere for learning. Learners become a resource to each other as they are "learning to learn by having to teach what has been learned" (Coulshed, 1993, p. 9). Students can either form themselves independently into peer groups for support or to research specific topics, or we can bring students together periodically for group supervision. One method of peer group supervision asks students to research the issues in a given assignment, analyzing, collating, presenting, and evaluating their findings. Sometimes the students present their findings to other staff members. The facilitators' role is to insure healthy group process and sound theoretical and research approaches. Other agency staff can be used to contribute to the peer group's learning by offering expertise on a special area of practice.

Peer groups can be empowering learning experiences that increase confidence and a sense of independence as students voice concerns about their learning or validate the field placement's strengths and limitations. Our perspectives as teachers are not the only "right" ones or the only perspective. Small-group discussions challenge assumptions, offer alternative perspectives, and broaden students' points of view as they learn to give constructive criticism to each other. Peers may more easily challenge each other to think outside of their usual frames of reference than we can. Equally, caution has been voiced regarding the lack of careful attention paid to the use of group supervision and the skills required to conduct group supervision of social work students. Walter and Young (1999) advocate for a combination of group and individual supervision, while Bogo, Globerman, and Sussman (2004) caution for greater examination of the skills required and increased training for this supervisory modality.

Developing Self-Awareness and Critical Thinking Skills

As a profession, we have tried to examine "how best to help students become self-aware, critical thinkers, capable of integrating theory with their practice"

(Caspi & Reid, 1998; Gitterman, 1988; Graybeal & Ruff, 1995; Neuman & Friedman, 1997). Adults who come to professional social work education programs are expected to have a certain degree of self-awareness. Education is meant to increase the capacity for greater self-awareness in relation to social work practice. Self-awareness involves our ability to assess how we react to people in the outside world and how the outside world reacts to us. Our role as field instructors is to help students figure out when the self is blocking learning in the course of the practice situation with clients, with us, or with other colleagues. We facilitate students' self-awareness in the context of an educational focus, because we *teach* and do not *treat* students.

Teaching students to increase self-awareness aids their ability to build on strengths, assume greater responsibility in sharing concerns, identify problem areas, and assess their own practice. The goals are to facilitate the progression toward autonomous functioning, recognition of their own limitations, and teach how to seek and obtain additional help when needed. We do this in various ways:

- We legitimatize students' right to have feelings about the work.

- We are sensitive to students' reluctance or readiness to examine feelings and reactions.

- We focus on feelings only as they affect specific aspects of students' practice/work.

- We avoid overgeneralizations that produce defensiveness.

- We move selectively, timing interventions when patterns emerge, giving specific examples of how the work is being affected.

Reflective field instructors model self-awareness and recognize how values and experiences affect our work with students and with clients. Self-aware students with solid critical thinking skills promise to develop into reflective practitioners (Paul, 1992). Reflective practice holds that "nothing is truly unusual and that preparation for the unexpected must be incorporated into the mental stance of the learner. . . . Providing this mental orientation may even reduce students' hunger for 'quick fixes' and easy-to-follow rules of practice" (Papell

& Skolnik, 1992, p. 22). However, this takes time and it is an ongoing process throughout one's career. We need to be patient and realize that we may not see our students progress to the extent we would like. However, once students recognize that we still grapple with these very same issues, they will be empowered to take risks in their own practice.

Engaging students to be reflective and to think critically is frequently a challenge. The aim is to engage students in an assessment of their values. This can best be achieved by involving students in clarifying their thinking processes. A learning atmosphere within which we encourage critical thinking is developed through the use of questions that probe assumptions, evidence, and implications. For example, questions that seek clarification may help students deepen their understanding of the issue at hand, such as, *"Could you put it another way?"* or *"Could you give me an example?"*

Questions that probe assumptions or look for reasons and evidence as distinguished from inferences may provide students with the opportunity to explain how they arrived at certain conclusions. *"How did you determine that the client did not want to go to the job interview?"* or *"What made you think the little girl was afraid of her mother?"* In a process parallel to client/student interactions, we seek answers to these questions for clarification of students' thought processes. This process is most productive if our questions are posed in a non-judgmental manner and phrased in such a way that causes students to gain insight into their own, and often unarticulated, thought patterns.

Similarly, questions that probe for implications and consequences, such as, *"What effect would that have?"* or *"If this and that are the case, what else must also be true?"* help students become more reflective as practitioners. By responding to students' questions with questions, we enhance their abilities to arrive at their own answers. *"To answer this question, what questions would we have to answer first?"* or *"Can we break this question down into smaller components?"* or *"Before I answer your question, can you help me understand what might be underlying your concern about this particular issue?"* Students' abilities to overcome obstacles in their work with clients will increase in direct correlation with their growing ability to think critically and to practice with growing self-awareness.

Field Instructor Self-Evaluation of Teaching Techniques

Responses to these questions can be included in the field instructor's reflective journal.

Following review of various teaching techniques in this chapter, field instructors should observe themselves for one week to self-assess the variety of techniques they actually employ in their teaching. For the second week, they should incorporate one new teaching technique into their repertoire.

- Which teaching techniques have you used?

- How does the new teaching technique fit with your teaching style?

- Have you noticed reliance on one teaching method over another?

- Have students' needs required you to extend yourself into a new arena of teaching or range of techniques?

- Which teaching methods are most useful in assisting your current students?

- Self-monitor field instruction conferences by asking yourself, "How well am I doing?" "How are my students doing?"

- How can you help students become more self-aware and confident in their practice?

- Are you going too fast or expecting too much?

- Are you guiding students to find their own professional style of working with clients?

Remember to also use this self-evaluation form at the end of a field placement experience to review whether your repertoire of teaching skills has expanded over the course of your work with students.

A Checklist for Skillful Teaching (Brookfield, 1990, pp. 192-211)

- Be clear about the purpose of your teaching.

- Reflect on your own learning.

- Be wary of standardized models and approaches.

- Expect ambiguity.

- Remember that perfection is impossible.

- Understand your students' backgrounds.

- Attend to how your students experience learning.

- Talk to your colleagues.

- Trust your instincts.

- Create diversity in your teaching methods.

- Take risks.

- Recognize the emotionality of learning.

- Acknowledge your personality.

- Don't evaluate only by student satisfaction.

- Balance support and challenge.

- Recognize the significance of your actions.

- View yourself as a helper of learning.

- Don't trust this list. Add your own truth!

Chapter 6

PROCESS RECORDINGS, LOGS, AND JOURNALS

*R*ecording and examining process using a variety of techniques provides students with a range of opportunities for reviewing their own reflection in action. . . . Recording and examining process stimulates inductive learning and generative theory building on the part of students. (Graybeal & Ruff, 1995, p. 171)

Some form of recording activities on assignments is required by all social work education programs for all students. Developing an effective written voice and being able to write in a variety of formats are important aspects of social work education and practice. "The use of student recordings has been a basic, accepted, long-standing fact of field instruction" (Hawthorne, 1987, p. 7). As early as 1917, Mary Richmond introduced written recording as a major tool in the development of social work professionals, and it quickly became the most efficient teaching method as practitioners write down everything that takes place in an interview (Wilson, 1980). Recordings for field instruction may be used on the full range of student activities in the agency, from telephone calls, collateral contacts, planning workshops, and agency meetings to client/worker interactions.

Traditionally in social work, process recordings refer to detailed records of student interventions with individuals, pairs, families, or groups. Logs and journals are more commonly associated with interventions with communities, organizations, or policy analyses. However, there are many kinds of recordings that students undertake in field placements associated with agency practice, including chart notes, uniform case records, psychosocial or community assessments, meeting analyses, critical incident recordings, group records of service, proposal writing, ecomaps, and genograms. Recordings for field instruction are different from any form of agency record keeping. Their function is educational and, as such, they are important teaching tools (Ames, 1999; Neuman & Friedman, 1997; Kagel, 1991). Whatever formats the recordings take, they are a method of communication between students and field instructors, providing us with a glimpse into students' work, from clinical interactions to progress on projects. They promote learning while also promoting accountability and the enhancement of social service delivery. Recordings are a principal way to monitor the student's work, and they provide the "raw material from which the instructor can understand what occurred, assess performance, develop and direct the teaching process" (Hawthorne, 1987, p. 7). These recordings are also a method of communication between students and themselves, since they stimulate an internal dialogue that allows rethinking of work with clients, including self-awareness, self-reflection, or "reflection in action" (Schon, 1983). Recordings promote autonomous practice and critical and organized thinking.

There have been many debates on the uses, formats, and purposes of recordings. Recordings, especially verbatim recordings, have been referred to as "questionable drudgery" (Nichols, Nichols, & Hardy, 1993) and "recordings are resisted and resented; misunderstood and misused; time consuming and anxiety provoking for both student and instructors" (Hawthorne, 1987, p. 7). But social work educators continue to promote the advantages of some form of detailed recording as a teaching tool (Graybeal & Ruff, 1995; Kagel, 1991; Kurland, 1989; Neuman & Friedman, 1997; Urbanowski & Dwyer, 1989).

Recordings provide us with a written account of the development of social work practice knowledge, skills, and values. These become the basis for teaching and educational assessment over time (Fox & Gutheil, 2000; Videka-Sherman & Reid, 1985). They serve as an educational tool to be used purposefully with specific learning objectives in mind that are based on an assessment of individual student learning needs. For example, they illustrate the use of listening skills and provide examples from which we can integrate theory into practice. They may be used to improve a student's self-reflection and to increase self-awareness (Graybeal & Ruff, 1995).

Recordings are valuable components to the learning experience, providing:

1. Written documentation that serves as a stimulus for reflective practice;

2. Information that furthers understanding of client needs and available resources;

3. Insights about the student as a practitioner and learner, which is the basis for the educational assessment and learning plans;

4. Information about collaboration with other practitioners;

5. Content for teaching about communication within the profession and with other disciplines;

6. Content for teaching about ethics, including privileged communication, informed consent, professional boundaries, and conflicts of interest;

7. Material for discussions about diversity and culturally competent practice;

8. Exercises to develop powers of recall and observation;

9. Ongoing documentation of student growth and development, achievements, and learning needs;

10. Practice in providing systematic accountability for practice;

11. Materials for classroom teaching; and

12. Data for practice research.

As field instructors, we teach students how to do recordings and what practical aspects are required, such as what content to include, what format to use, how often they should be done, and what procedures to follow. Going over examples of recordings with students gives them a concrete format from which to work and clarifies literacy and accuracy expectations. Clarification regarding why recordings are requested allays anxieties and feelings of risk. Giving time during field placement hours to do recordings provides a structure to the task and communicates the importance of recordings to the placement experience.

Confidentiality is essential in all recordings. Educational recordings are the student's property and belong to students, even if reviewed by field instructors and faculty liaisons. Recordings sometimes accompany classroom assignments as well. They are primarily communication from students to us and should be available only to those directly involved with teaching students. As such, they are not part of the agency's records. Methods to protect client privacy must be instituted by use of either code names or numbers. In this way, names and identifying information are disguised in recordings, especially as students take their recordings outside of the agency's premises. We may wish to keep copies of student recordings for our own records and for reviewing student progress, but recordings are most useful to students. Students should be encouraged to keep copies for their own review, for use in practice class, and for planning client interventions.

Recordings that contain wide margins on each page offer space for relevant comments, questions, and reactions to be made by students and field instructors. This provides a kind of running dialogue about the content presented. It also provides room for students to raise questions and concerns. We encourage meaningful student recordings by taking the time to review them and being prepared to discuss the students' questions and concerns. This exchange of ideas becomes the foundation for building student agendas for field instruction conferences. Ideally, our meetings with students are based on previously submitted recordings and on an agenda prepared by the student and shared with us in advance. This type of preparation enhances the teaching and learning.

A certain amount of risk taking is inherent in recording one's work. Students are asked to "go on record" about aspects of their work, activities that may seem vague or confusing at times and about which they may lack confidence. The inherent anxiety created in showing one's work to another should be acknowledged, and the courage that students display in trusting the process of learning should be validated. Still, it is inevitable that students consciously and unconsciously screen the content in recordings. Creating open and trusting communication holds this type of screening to a minimum. Effective recordings include information about behavior, thoughts, and feelings. The specific selections that students highlight, or obvious glaring omissions, indicate how students think about their work, their assumptions about expectations, and their assumptions about good professional practice.

Student resistance to handing in timely process recordings, logs, and journals may be a symptom of the need to slow the pace of work in field instruction. If this becomes an issue, it is critical to understand the nature of the student's difficulties. If not addressed, what begins as a possible sign of anxiety within the learning environment can turn into power struggles between us and our students. Understanding the factors involved and what may be preventing the student from producing recordings aids our efforts in avoiding the creation of undue student anxiety about recording and reviewing their work. If students are reluctant writers, we can let them start slowly by allowing for brief recordings and building from there. If students have difficulty recording what they were thinking or feeling during meetings, we can ask them to focus on providing one specific thought or feeling next time. Recordings then become manageable for students and easier for us to build from these beginning efforts.

Initially, we need to focus on major issues or questions in the recordings and avoid getting mired in details. We need to identify themes and patterns on which to comment. Gradually, we can do a line-by-line review, identifying emerging and significant patterns in practice. We can be specific when identifying what students do well in practice so that these behaviors or skills can be repeated, consolidated, and understood in terms of why they worked. As we work more closely with our students on a piece of recording, it often parallels the work in the actual assignment.

Another useful way of using process recordings is to read the passage aloud and to provide another vehicle for students to examine their interactions. Sometimes students take the role of clients while field instructors take the student role. This can be a powerful learning experience when students hear their own voice in a different manner. It brings the interaction alive and into the field instruction conference for greater scrutiny. In other words, as we work with process recordings, journals, and logs, we help students identify patterns in how they work with people as they emerge in the recording over time. We use what students are able to provide and build from there. If students continue to avoid writing the required recordings, we need to consult with the faculty liaison.

Variations in recording assignments individualize the help offered to students as they move through the learning process and reflect their progress in reaching learning objectives. Initially students may be asked to record all activities on assignments and all contacts with clients or other constituents. Once we have a sense of our students' skills and abilities, we may decide to ask for records of only first meetings, difficult meetings, or selective assignments. For ongoing practice experiences, students can use summary recordings or critical incident recordings. The decision regarding this progression of recording formats varies, but the general rule is that recordings should be used to help students move toward greater responsibility for self-learning and autonomous practice. Social work programs often have specific guidelines included in their Field Education Manuals regarding expectations for recordings, the nature of recordings used, and how many recordings are required.

Instructor Review of Process Recordings

There are some general guidelines to be considered in reviewing student recordings. They help students to:

- Look closely at the work; the data gathered in interviews, groups, or meetings; and the overall skills of helping.

- Look closely at efforts and interventions and examine how students use themselves in face-to-face professional encounters.

- Develop observational and active listening skills, the power of recall, and the ability to reflect on developing practice skills and knowledge.

- Focus on problem solving, critical thinking, and self-critiquing approaches.

- Record professional growth and development over time and record the content of teaching in field instruction.

- Gain feedback from field instructors and faculty liaisons. They also provide feedback to the social work education program regarding what is being taught and learned in the placement.

- Document assignments for evaluation of students or when raising issues or problems regarding student performance in the placement.

There are several points of view regarding written comments provided on student recordings (Urbanowski & Dwyer, 1988). When we write our comments on student recordings, it serves as a form of teaching while recognizing and respecting student efforts and work. Comments can be referred to during field instruction sessions and can be helpful in evaluating overall progress made by students in understanding their role and function. In addition, comments can help keep the focus on student learning objectives. Adequate attention to successful interventions should be given.

However, our comments tend to shape the discussion from our perspective before understanding students' assessment of interventions. Excessive comments on recordings may also be confusing for students and dilute the focus for learning. The comments may also increase student anxiety regarding "getting it wrong." Initially, the focus of comments should identify major issues or questions rather than getting "stuck" in the details of interventions made by students. This provides a positive learning environment and helps to build confidence. Too many comments can also affect students' capacities to critique their own practice or to raise questions in field instruction conferences. We may need to assume greater initiative in the beginning stages of learning and gradually increase our expectations that students direct their own learning. The struggle is to balance commentary based on students' learning needs with the need to increase students' professional autonomy (Dwyer & Urbanowski, 1965).

PRO: Comments serve as a form of teaching

Comments recognize and respect students' work

Comments focus the teaching content

Comments are helpful in evaluation

CON: Comments focus on field instructors' concerns rather than students' concerns

Comments can mobilize students' resistance

Comments may highlight mistakes or danger spots rather than strengths and progress made

Comments take away spontaneity in field instruction

Whether comments are used or not, the questions posed are geared to further student understanding of professional practice. For instance, take a piece of recording that a student prepares on a contact with an individual or group of clients and ask the student to consider identifying the knowledge, skills, and values he or she employed in the interaction as suggested below:

Social work knowledge: What knowledge of theoretical perspectives, interventive approaches, specific client populations, or needs assisted you in this interaction? Can you point to social work literature that supports your knowledge?

Social work skills: Can you identify specific skills you used in this interaction? Can you point to social work literature that supports your use of these skills? Could you have used different skills? How will you improve your interactions with this client in the future?

Social work values: What social work values were involved in this interaction? Why were values important in this interaction? Were you aware of any value conflicts in this interaction, and how will you resolve the conflicts? (Dettlaff, 2003).

These questions use recordings as a stepping-off point to plan next steps on assignments, specific tasks, interventions, overall direction with assignments, and the kinds of help students need. In this way, student questions become the basis for the field instruction conference agenda.

Agendas include questions or topics for discussion in field instruction conferences about recordings, interventions, assessments, resources, and general practice concerns or learning needs. Agendas are primarily student generated, but we can contribute additional topics for discussion. Agendas are valuable in that they:

- Help students comment on their own work

- Help students raise questions about their own practice

- Help students trust their own initiative

- Help students take responsibility for their own work and learning needs

- Help address students' specific questions and learning needs

- Model collaboration and mutual decision making

- Validate and support autonomous practice

- Facilitate the development of planning, organization, and prioritizing

Process Recordings

Process recording has traditionally meant just one thing: a student's attempt to create from memory a verbatim transcription of a social work interview. (Graybeal & Ruff, 1995, p. 169)

Process recordings are "a veritable gold mine of insight and teaching material." (Urdang, 1979, p. 1)

Through the details of the process recordings, the educational issues of the learner become clear so that the instructor can plan a focus for teaching and the student can analyze and become aware of his or her own process." (Hawthorne, 1987, p. 9)

Regardless of the value of recording, most social workers groan when the words, "process recording," are mentioned. We have all gone through this time-consuming, labor-intensive, and sometimes frustrating exercise, and we all tend to use recording formats that we were trained in or that are familiar to us. There are various formats for process recordings, and the most common form is basic observation and verbal reporting in which "students retell the story of their work (as they remember it) to the supervisor" (Graybeal & Ruff, 1995, p. 171). In other words, the student listens to the client's concerns and then organizes the verbal information into what is to them a familiar cognitive framework. Depending on the student's experience, values, and theoretical orientation, this representation may closely approximate the client's actual experience, but it will also reflect the student's subjective perspective about the client and the situation described.

As field instructors, we need to help students become aware of and sensitive to how they receive, sort, and store information, and help them identify the explicit ways in which they interpret and record this information. The process of reconstructing the interactions that take place in meetings with clients has many other benefits. The process forces students to remember forgotten material; to identify strengths and areas of difficulty; and it can also draw attention to details that may seem inconsequential but on second look may be important to the interactions taking place. This process orientation to recordings asks students to focus on their affective experiences and impressions of the interaction.

The process recording models that emphasize structure tend to be deficient in process orientation, and those formats that emphasize process are lacking in structure. Dwyer and Urbanowski (1965) advocate for structured recordings that blend in a process orientation and they offer the following format for process recordings: The student (a) writes down the purpose of the interview as determined before the session, (b) narrates in writing the observations, (c) describes the content of the session as closely as possible, (d) describes feelings experienced during the interview, and (e) records impressions and thoughts for ongoing plans for the client. "Process recording involves writing a verbatim transcript of the student client interaction using a format that consists of four columns: interview content (student client dialogue); the student's gut-level feelings; logical interpretations; and supervisory comments" (Neuman & Freidman, 1997, p. 237). Other popular structured models of recording include problem-oriented recordings (Martens & Holomstrup, 1974); problem-oriented logs (Burril, 1976); person-oriented records (Hartman & Wickey, 1978); and structured clinical records (Videka-Sherman & Reid, 1985). Some social work education programs have specific requirements for process recordings, while other programs allow more flexibility in choosing the type of recording format. Check the social work education program's Field Work Manual for specific suggestions. The following describes some of the variations in formats that can be used for process recordings.

Summary recordings. In this format, students summarize the major themes and content of sessions, but they can describe details about selective interactions between themselves and clients. These are chosen for explication and discussion because students have concerns about the interaction, or they want to identify underlying factors affecting the interaction. Although summary recordings take less time than verbatim recordings, the exercise requires students to select those parts of the session that they want to discuss in field instruction or that give them the most difficulty in their practice.

Verbatim recordings. Better known as "I said/ she said" or script recording, this style asks students to recall and record with as much detail as possible all aspects of the client/student encounter in a logical sequence. This type of process recording "involves writing a verbatim transcript of the student-client interaction using a format that consists of four columns: interview content (student-client dialogue); the student's gut-level feelings; logical interpretations; and supervisory comments" (Neuman & Freidman, 1997, p. 237).

This "accordion style" of verbatim recording, first developed by Wilson (1980), has several variations that recognize the different levels of information gathered by students. Wilson's work still stands as the most detailed discussion and explicit examples of techniques, outlines, and formats for recording. Column 1 includes verbatim recording or reconstruction of the dialogue between students and clients, recalling as much as possible what is actually said by both. Column 2 describes "gut-level reactions" or students' thoughts, feelings, observations, or commentary on what they say or what clients say. Column 3 is for instructors to provide feedback, observations, or commentary on students' work.

Narrative recordings. In this format, students recall as much as possible about the actual encounter with clients and retell the encounter in a running commentary that gives us the experience of actually being there with the student and client. Observations, thoughts, transitions, feelings, and comments are included as a part of the narrative, often in parentheses.

Whatever formats are used, the most important aspects of process recordings are that they communicate the dialogue and the content of client contacts accurately and precisely, and that the format facilitates discussions with students. "Indeed, process recording is an integral and viable tool for facilitating learning and integrating theory and practice in social work" (Tourse, 1994, p. 155). The following is an outline that covers the major areas usually included in recording face-to-face contacts with clients or constituents.

General Process Recording Format

1. *Identifying information.* Include student initials, client initials, date of interview, session number, and where contact takes place. It is helpful to state who is present during the contact (i.e., "4th contact with SJ; SJ and son were present" or "1st meeting; 6 community leaders were present"). On a first contact it may also be helpful to include other identifying data. Remember to instill the need to disguise clients' names to protect confidentiality.

2. *Objectives or goals.* Include the reason for the session or meeting, source of the referral, the initial or presenting problems, brief statement of any specific goals to be achieved during the contact, students' plans, and client system's agenda.

3. *Narrative.* Include a detailed description of what occurs in the session, including a narrative or word-for-word dialogue of the meeting from beginning to end to the extent the student can recall details. It should mention both client and student responses, and verbal and non-verbal communication. This is the longest and most important section of the recording.

4. *Students' feelings.* In parentheses or in a notation in a column or margin, students are required to reflect on unspoken thoughts, feelings, and reactions to the contact with the client or group as the session proceeds (i.e., "At this point I began to feel uneasy. I was uncertain about what to do next.").

5. *Critical thinking.* Students need to write down their thoughts about what is happening as the session progresses. For example, "I wonder what would have happened if I had reflected on the underlying mood of participants. I chose not to but I wonder whether I should have tried" or "SJ said she felt happy, but this seemed to contradict what she said earlier. I didn't think she looked very happy so I asked her to explain further."

6. Impressions. This is a summary of students' critical thinking and analysis of the entire session recorded. It includes attempts to self-critique interventions and responses. Students should reflect on their strengths in handling the session as well as areas needing improvement (i.e., *"The session answered most of my questions, but I think I should have allowed them to lead the group more."*).

7. Future plans and directions. In this section, students identify unfinished business, short- and long-term goals, possible service needs, and goals for the next session.

8. Questions. Questions lead to what students want to discuss in field instruction. These questions may come from the actual session, or they may arise from the actual experience of writing down the session as students reflect on the meeting and what occurred or did not occur. This section helps students to think more expansively about alternatives, provides for the integration of theory and practice, and leads to more autonomous practice.

Another possible inclusion in this outline is identified learning goals or themes at the beginning of the recording. Embedded in every interaction with clients are numerous learning opportunities, but students and field instructors select in advance which specific learning goals will be focused on in this particular recording. For example, initiating contact with clients and contracting for services is an important learning goal for a foundation-level student, while refining assessment skills is a more advanced learning goal. It is also important for us to note that recording is an acquired skill that needs to be done regularly and consistently, and students gradually develop the ability to recall and communicate essential elements of sessions with clients. It will take time for most students to produce useful recordings that effectively meet their needs and learning objectives.

Recording Group Process

Students need to record verbal and non-verbal behaviors engaged in by specific members of the group. The focus is more on the *process of the group as it emerges in the session* than on the content of what is said by each member (Garfield & Irizarr, 1971). Student recording of groups should be guided by the following questions:

1. *Description of the setting.* Describe the context, population, session number, and type of group.

2. *Structure.* How does the group organize itself to accomplish its tasks? What group rules emerge? What leader behaviors are displayed? How are decisions reached? How is information treated?

3. *Climate.* Describe the psychological/emotional atmosphere of the group. How are feelings, as opposed to points of view, dealt with? What non-verbal behaviors indicate changes in the climate? How do members' voices denote feeling tones?

4. *Facilitation* How do group members influence the development of the group? Does the group process run itself? What group-building behaviors (bringing in silent members, harmonizing conflict, reinforcing participation, etc.) are used and by whom?

5. *Barriers to the work.* What behaviors emerge that hinder the accomplishment of the group's task, e.g., what anti-group behaviors (blocking, recognition seeking, dominating, withdrawing, etc.) are seen? What communication patterns develop that block the group tasks?

6. *Group's demand for work.* How does the group move from independence to collective judgment? What behaviors promote agreement? What consensus-seeking behaviors are observed? What false consensus behaviors (such as "me too," "I'll go along with that") are displayed?

7. *Assessment of next steps.* What possible next steps would be recommended? What changes in plans might be feasible?

Student planning for the next steps in groups should be guided by the following outlined process (Glassman & Kates, 1988):

1. Context: Type of group, agency setting, group purpose, number of session, who was present/absent (remember confidentiality)

2. Pre-engagement preparation

3. Central themes discussed

4. Narrative of group meeting:

   a. Write the story of what happened in the group, particularly interactions between members and interactions between yourself and group members.

   b. Include verbatim dialogue and summaries, weaving your thoughts, feelings, and actions into the narrative.

   c. Include how the session started and ended.

   d. Using a wide right-hand margin, indicate a theme that the group is addressing, both latent and manifest, with each identified interaction.

5. Workers' impressions or interpretations of what took place in the group

6. Plans for next meeting

7. Questions regarding interventions and members' participation

Log or Journal Outline

The following log or journal format is offered as a helpful guide (Swenson, 1988):

1. *Brief description of assignment*—A few sentences that provide background, origin, and context of the assignment.

2. *Task plan*—A description of the purpose of the assignment and the need being addressed. The steps or primary activities required to complete the assignment should be listed in the order in which they will occur with projected completion dates, including any resources from within and outside the agency that are needed to complete the project.

3. Obstacles—Initial thoughts about problems anticipated.

4. Progress summary—Details of activities completed and progress achieved to date.

5. *Assessment of activity*—Questions raised in the process of attempting to complete tasks, and retrospective evaluation of practice about how activities might have been improved.

6. *Activity summary*—A description of primary project activities completed during the week and identification of problems or barriers encountered.

7. *Revised task plan*—Modifications in task plan and timetable as a result of problems encountered or experiences gained during conduct or work. If there is a major revision, a new plan should be described.

8. *Agenda*—Questions and issues for discussion in field instruction.

Teaching From Recordings

Recordings are for teaching and not just for monitoring accountability or reviewing evaluation. Hawthorne (1987, pp. 10–11) suggests some basic questions related to teaching from student recordings:

1. What teaching issues are identified in this recording?

2. Which ones should be selected for teaching at this time and why?

3. How should these be taught?

4. How should the student be involved in this process?

5. As a result of this teaching, what should the student continue doing? What should the student do differently?

Review the entire recording before adding comments or questions. This helps to focus on the more important aspects of the session, and it is an opportunity to identify learning themes and patterns. If written comments and feedback on student recordings are used, consider using additional sheets of paper to provide more space for comments and to prevent cryptic comments like "let's discuss." Try to identify and support good intentions, risk taking, and growth. Tune into student struggles and perceptions. What were students attempting to accomplish? Perhaps the delivery was off, but the students' intentions were on target. As mentioned earlier, help students manage the time it takes to complete process recordings, logs, or journals by incorporating time during placement hours for recording.

We can also help students to partialize interventions by breaking interventive choices into smaller steps and eliciting students' critique of their efforts and decision-making processes. Each activity contains a variety of possible interventions that may be equally applicable. Questions such as, *"What were you hoping to achieve?"* or *"What might have happened if you had done things differently?"* or *"What did the results mean to you?"* can help students dissect their thought processes and promote greater integration of intuitive responses with skills for future use. It is also important for students to remember that learning is a process, and that growth is identified from session to session and over time. We need to take the time to review student progress as it is made, and to encourage students to take notes on discussions of recordings so that they may review their progress over time. Hawthorne (1987, pp. 11–16) poses 10 principles for teaching from recordings.

Ten Principles for Teaching From Recordings

1. The student should learn something from every recording.

2. It should be case teaching and not case review that is an administrative function.

3. Teaching should be proactive and not merely reactive.

4. Teaching should deal with themes and patterns rather than specific points.

5. Teaching should be selective and focused.

6. Teaching should occur on both the empirical and conceptual levels.

7. Teaching should be progressive and sequential.

8. Teaching should be geared to strengths as well as problems.

9. The student should be an active participant in the educational process.

10. Teaching should employ a range of methodologies.

Other Forms of Recording

Although field education relies heavily on written recordings, especially process recordings, there are other forms of recording available. A survey of various graduate counseling programs found that verbal reports were most frequently used (64.7%); audio taping (15.6%), direct observation or sitting in on a session (14.4%), video taping (3.1%), and the use of one-way mirrors or closed circuit television (2.2%) were used relatively infrequently (Hart & Falvey, 1987). Perhaps it is time for us to be more creative in the uses of these alternative methods of recording that can enhance and expand the scope, depth, and utility of recordings. "Hearing or seeing oneself on tape is often a powerful learning experience, as is realizing how difficult it is to recall details from memory, or performing live before a field instructor" (Graybeal & Ruff, 1995, p. 170). These supplemental tools can be valuable in providing direct data about student interactions with clients and other professionals, including the pacing, tone, and attitudes of students.

Students must receive written permission from clients to use any audio or video taping of sessions, but there is one major advantage in that these forms of recording provide the most accurate account of interactions with clients. Then together, students and field instructors are able to see and hear how much or how little students talk and listen; the modulation, tenor, and emotion in student and client voices are evident; and attitudes and subtleties not available in written records can more easily be identified. Tapes are also easy to use, readily available, and relatively inexpensive, but reviewing them can be time-consuming. Often only segments of a session can be reviewed, but the audio or video tapes can be an enhancement to recordings. Students should still record their impressions or assessment of the session that is taped. As useful as these alternative training methods are, they do not replace the importance of requiring students to reflect, recall, record, and analyze interactions with clients and the choices made in practice.

Finally, live observations via a one-way mirror or with the field instructor sitting in on a session between students and clients is another form of observation of student practice. Students may feel under the spotlight with no place to hide mistakes or misdirection and, therefore, these training methods are usually introduced after the field instructor/student relationship is well developed, and the student is able to trust enough to risk being directly observed.

Table 2 offers an outlined summary of the different formats and training methods discussed in this chapter. Different combinations of these formats enhance field learning, especially when we find the method that best fits a particular student's learning needs.

Table 2.

A Continuum of Process Recording (Graybeal & Ruff, 1995, p. 172)

MODALITY	DESCRIPTION	PURPOSE
Cognitive-verbal	Verbal description of events	Immediate feedback
Cognitive-physical	Role playing, Sculpting, Drawing, Artwork	Reenactment
Written	Verbatim, Genogram, Eco-map, Progress notes	Recall of detail
Audio	Audio tape	Detailed reflection of verbal process
Video	Video tape	Detailed reflection of verbal and visual processes
Live observation	One-way mirror	Immediate feedback from supervisor or peers
Live observation	In session	Most immediate opportunity for *in vivo* teaching and learning

Purposes of Recordings for Students

- Serve as instruments to guide learning

- Help to clarify the purpose of the interview or activity

- Provide a basis for stimulating communication and self-awareness

- Develop observational and active listening skills and expand the power of recall

- Help focus on problem-solving, critical thinking, and self-critiquing approaches

Purpose of Recordings for Field Instructors

- Provide direction and structure for teaching

- Assist in the assessment of the student's ability to respond to the feeling or latent content of interviews or activities with various client systems

- Show the extent to which students are able to integrate knowledge and theory gained from previous field instruction sessions, client and group experiences, classroom courses, and outside readings

- Provide information about students as growing professionals

- Show a student's ability to collaborate with other professionals

- Provide an opportunity to look closely at a student's work, efforts, and interventions, and to examine a student's use of self

Teaching From Recordings, Logs, and Journals

The following questions focus teaching efforts around recordings. They promote the examination of the student's ability to accurately reflect content and feelings, to be client-centered, and to use purposeful interactions.

- Does the student produce recordings that convey the substance of client sessions or contacts?

- Does the student identify the purpose of sessions or contacts?

- Are the student's interventions or activities aimed toward achievement of goals?

- Do the student's verbal explanations reflect an understanding of role and function within this agency?

• Is the student following a personal agenda or the client system's agenda?

• Is the student helping clients to tell their story and focusing on their issues?

• Is the student able to start where the client is?

• Is the student able to hear what is being communicated?

• Is the student able to balance empathetic listening with appropriate responses?

• Is the student listening or attentive to non-verbal communications?

• Does the student maintain appropriate professional boundaries?

• Who does most of the work in the session?

• To what extent is the student receptive to the client's frame of reference?

• Does the student demonstrate awareness and sensitivity to diversity factors such as race and ethnicity, gender and sexual orientation, social class and status, religion and spirituality, age and physical or mental abilities?

• What level of self-assessment is evident in the recordings?

• Is the student able to identify when judgments or biases appear in his or her assessments?

• Does the student demonstrate the ability to self-correct behavior in a session or in comments about the session?

• To what extent is the student able to risk exposing mistakes, biases, *faux pas*, etc., in a manner that facilitates learning?

Sample Field Instruction Sessions Around Recordings

We have included two sample process recordings of field instruction sessions in which student recordings are discussed. The first sample is in a narrative summary style of recording and focuses on a 1st-year direct practice student's first contact with a client. The second sample is in a script verbatim style of recording and focuses on a mid-year 2nd-year student's recording of a clinical intervention with a client. After reading the recordings, consider the following questions:

- How would you characterize the field instructor's approach to the student?

- What are the teaching opportunities or "teaching moments" in the session?

- How does the field instructor teach the student?

- What teaching techniques do you see the field instructor using?

- What aspects of modeling do you see the field instructor using?

- Other comments?

PREPARING 1ST-YEAR GRADUATE STUDENT FOR INITIAL CLIENT CONTACT

Student. Female, 29-year-old married student with no prior social work-related experience. Majored in special education as an undergraduate.

Field placement. The agency offers services to survivors of domestic violence, including crisis intervention, advocacy, legal consultation, emergency safe housing, short-term group and individual counseling, and a hotline. Other services include community education and training and a residential shelter.

Student assignments. In a prior field instruction conference, student was informed of the general nature of her first assignments, and agency policies and procedures were reviewed. The student also read files on several clients. Student's initial assignment was to make follow-up calls to ascertain clients' present situations, need for further services, and outcomes of actions begun during previous agency contacts (referrals, court actions, housing, etc.). Field instructor and student role played making follow-up phone calls to previous agency clients. Student sat in on intakes and listened in on some hotline calls to become familiar with agency procedures and the agency population.

Client description. S is an 18-year-old, African American, mother of a 1-year-old child. She is living with her parents. S was referred to the agency last October by her OB/GYN clinic nurse because of reported physical abuse by her father. S described a history of abuse by her father and mother as well as abuse of her mother by her father. Client appeared depressed, hopeless, and helpless. She did not want to leave home, as it would leave her mother more vulnerable. S was reticent to talk about her family and was dirty and poorly dressed. She spoke more animatedly about training for a certificate as a nurse's aide, and the crisis counselor supported her interest. Although counseling was recommended, client only remained in contact with agency briefly. Several phone contacts were recorded. No follow-up was recorded.

Process of field instruction conference. The student and I read the S file aloud together. I asked her if she had any questions about the information. She responded that it seemed clear except for why the client was being encouraged to study nursing. "If she's in such need of therapy herself, how can she help others? You can't help people if you're a mess and don't even want to help yourself." My immediate reaction was shock to hear such a judgmental response from a student. However, I felt it would simply make the student defensive if I shared my reaction. I withheld my own judgment and asked the student what reasons the counselor might have had to encourage the client. She responded that it might be a way to encourage client to get involved in counseling. I asked student about her impressions of the client. She noted that S tended to start what she couldn't finish, seemed to want to help herself but got turned off. "She still lives at home even though it's dangerous." I asked student why a woman might stay in such a situation. She answered, "because of financial dependence, guilt, fears, hopes, and in this case because of S's age and her baby." I complimented the student on her insight. I was anxious not to let the concept of non-judgmental behavior go by and felt that now that the student had begun to think from the client's point of view it was time to refer back to her earlier comments about the client. I spoke about the importance of withholding judgments about our clients, especially those who have a low self-image. I introduced the professional value of maintaining a non-judgmental stance. We then discussed how the client might respond to a phone call from the agency. Student thought she might be wary and realized she needed to be prepared for that. I asked her how she could best approach the client. She suggested asking open-ended questions and indicating that the agency's concern for the client. I asked student what specific questions she might ask. Student asked, "Can I ask her how her baby is doing?" I answered that it might break the ice. The student thought that talking about someone the client loved would help her talk about herself. The student was concerned about client feeling that she was snooping if she asked her directly how she was doing. She expressed uncertainty about inquiring about any further abuse. I assured her that workers were often afraid to ask those questions, but that it was our job to help clients talk about difficult subjects by asking direct questions and not beating around the bush. I asked student to put herself in the client's shoes and how she might be feeling about herself. Student noted that S might be reticent to speak to a social worker because of her history of learning to be quiet in order to be safe. I complimented the student on her sensitive perception. We then role played the conversation they might have on the telephone, with me acting like the client. Student appreciated the opportunity to rehearse her first contact with a client. Student asked what resources we could offer the client, and we reviewed agency services once more. I acknowledged her hesitancy in making first contacts but encouraged her to make her calls as soon as possible, since waiting only increases anxiety.

Field instructor's educational assessment. It might have been more useful if we had reversed roles so that the student could have experienced the client more and observed me in the worker's role. The student's lack of confidence and judgmental attitudes will have to be addressed more directly after she has had more contact with clients. I can see how her initial self-doubts, personal behavior patterns, and insecurities will affect her work with clients in severe crisis. I may be expecting too much of her, but I will attempt to model client/worker interactions rather than lecture her on certain professional skills and values. Her responses indicate that she has the capacity to develop a more sensitive, open, professional stance in her work.

MID-YEAR FIELD INSTRUCTION CONFERENCE WITH 2ND-YEAR STUDENT

Introduction. The purpose of this supervisory session was to more clearly understand and focus in on student's difficulty in exploring or staying with feelings experienced by clients. With the M family, the problem was becoming worse rather than better. The student agreed that this was an area that needed work. The following is a section of a field instruction conference that focused on this learning need.

FI: I suggested that we track how B handles negative or intense affect in clients and discuss ways in which she can stay with the client rather than her own feelings. B agreed and we began on the first page of the process recording. I asked her how she thought Mr. M was feeling.

S: Clearly angry. I jumped in to defend myself, but I had a mixture of feelings here. First, I'm not sure that I agreed with the psychiatric team's decision, and I also felt like they were not being sensitive to the family's feelings.

FI: We talked about this dilemma for a while, and I stated that it is difficult to present a decision to a family that we do not personally support.

S: How do you handle that?

FI: I am often tempted to get defensive, too, but I try not to let that interfere. I focus on the family, stay with their feelings, and allow them to get angry with me.

S: I guess that is the other piece. I don't want them to be angry with me. I mean, I allowed them to express their feelings but with little encouragement on my part.

FI: I asked her how she could have stayed with Mr. M's angry feelings. We began to discuss anger, how uncomfortable it makes B feel, and how she tries to avoid these feelings. We then moved to the next page, and I asked B what she thought was happening here.

S: Mr. M was getting very angry, and I did not relate to his anger.

FI: I suggested that B was still trying to neutralize Mr. M's anger.

S: You're right! That's exactly what I did!

FI: We explored the risk of allowing Mr. M to become angry with B. She thought about this and began to realize that she had a considerable investment in being successful with the M family. It was the one family that she felt had the most capacity to change and the family that respected her authority and expertise the most. We went on to discuss B's need to feel successful, powerful, important, and worthwhile, particularly in this environment (a psychiatric institution, host environment, interdisciplinary team, etc.) that was intimidating to her. This was her "success" case.

S: I'm beginning to understand. It makes it harder for me to risk their anger. I'm probably afraid they won't come back. I remember how upset I was when Mr. M stated he did not need these sessions anymore.

FI: After establishing what was on the line with this particular family, we went on to track the process in the remaining two pages of the recording.

S: I can't believe it! Mr. M gets angry, and I jump in with a clarification or intellectual explanation for why he is getting angry. B laughed and said, "At least I'm consistent!"

FI: We continued to identify B's interventions away from the anger and went on to discuss the guilt that is stirred up in B as a result of Mr. M's anger. B had raised some personal issues in other cases related to her own family's way of dealing with angry feelings.

S: This has been very helpful. I'd like to watch for these digressions with my other families to see if it looks and feels the same.

FI: I suggested that since B was meeting with the M family this afternoon, she might not only be aware of her behavior during the session, but she might comment on her process whenever she felt that she was either staying with the anger or moving away from it. In this way she could begin to notice alternative ways of dealing with angry feelings and begin to define other feelings in clients that make her uncomfortable.

Chapter 7

EDUCATIONAL ASSESSMENTS AND LEARNING PLANS

*I*n field work, assessment is a dynamic, shared process leading to an educational plan which is negotiated, adopted, implemented, and refined.... Educational assessment involves the determination of a student's learning needs in relation to a common core of school and agency expectations. Educational needs are not considered problems in learning. If the student's performance is within an acceptable range, teaching addresses the gap between current knowledge and skills and objectives for learning. (Lemberger & Marshack, 1991, pp. 188–189)

When initial orientation programs are over, when student assignments have begun, when initial learning contracts have been established, and when field instructors, students, and agencies have begun to know what to expect of each other, it is time to begin the middle phase of field instruction. This phase of the learning experience includes ongoing refinement of educational assessments and learning plans. The refinement of the educational assessment occurs only after an environment conducive to adult learning has been established. It is within this atmosphere that students enter into an assessment of their own learning needs and abilities. Field instruction relationships that include trust, respect, and a spirit of mutual collaboration are essential for successful educational assessments.

The educational assessment is essential to identify learning needs and develop individualized learning goals. Educational assessment is an ongoing process that begins with the first meeting with students, continues throughout the entire placement, and culminates in the end of each term's final written evaluation.

Social work programs aid the task of educational assessments by providing "markers" throughout the academic year that act as guideposts to the process (see Table 3). Although formulating the educational assessment begins at the moment the placement begins, the first formal requirement is marked around the 6th or 8th week of the fall semester with what is often referred to as the "mid-semester oral evaluation" or the "6th-week learning plan." Each school recommends its own format for these required oral evaluations. First we need to define the terms involved in assessing student learning needs. The following list defines the terms, and Table 3 depicts the time frame involved.

Educational assessments—The ongoing process of assessment by which students and field instructors identify learning goals and needs that define the context of assignments and teaching approaches.

Educational Plans—The plans that outline the goals, objectives, and strategies for students' learning, usually formulated around the 6th–8th week of placement.

Learning contracts—An individualized educational plan that identifies barriers to progress and specific strategies and time frames for achieving educational objectives.

Informal and formal oral reviews—The ongoing dialogue within field instruction of learning goals and objectives. The formal oral review (described in more detail in chapter 8) usually occurs one month prior to the written evaluation due date.

Evaluations—The formal written end-of-term evaluation (described in chapter 8).

Table 3.

Time Frame for Educational Assessment

	6TH–8TH WEEK	1 MONTH PRIOR TO END OF TERM	END OF FALL TERM	1 MONTH PRIOR TO END OF TERM	END OF SPRING TERM	AS NEEDED
First Year	Educational plan	Oral review	Final evaluation	Oral review	Final evaluation	Learning contract
Second Year	Educational plan	Oral review	Final evaluation	Oral review	Final evaluation	Learnng contract

Purposes of Educational Assessments

Educational assessments provide the opportunity to:

- Identify foci for learning and the plans and measures to achieve learning goals

- Model how to engage in mutual collaboration and assessment of learning needs, professional growth, and field performance

- Delineate learning styles and consistent and repetitive learning patterns in approaches to learning that influence how students acquire practice knowledge and skills

- Identify learning stages and normalize the learning process

- Promote self-reflective practice through the involvement of students as active participants in the ongoing appraisal of their skill development and learning needs

- Place the learning goals and needs in the context of the learning opportunities available within the agency

- Provide the experience of a more formal feedback process that involves receiving constructive criticism from field instructors related to the social work education program's performance expectations, and prepare for the end-of-term evaluative process

- Highlight the uniqueness of each individual student's approach to learning, and guide the selection of learning opportunities, teaching techniques, and methods

The Process of Assessment

The seminal article on educational assessment in field education by Lemberger and Marshack (1991) reminds us that a "focus on learning tasks leads logically into consideration of the range and nature of opportunities for learning in the agency" (p. 193). The agency context for the learning is an integral part of the assessment. The educational assessment needs to include consideration of the types of problems, clients, and methodologies available in the agency. In addition, the assessment includes which types of problems, clients, and methodologies students' work with most effectively in contrast to those that present the greatest challenges. Identification of student responses to new learning is balanced against the types of challenges presented in the work. Repetitive patterns can only materialize over time, and therefore we must reserve our judgments until evidence emerges. It is in the identification of patterned responses that our educational assessments inform our choice of teaching interventions.

After the initial few weeks of placement, we begin to organize our impressions of our students into preliminary educational assessments with learning/teaching plans that emerge through mutual collaboration with students. This is relatively early in the relationship, but it is necessary to begin so that the process of ongoing educational assessments can be initiated and initial learning contracts can be established.

Ongoing assessment not only includes the opportunity for students to develop their capacity for self-reflection, self-assessment, and self-directed learning (Regehr, Regehr, Leeson, & Fusco, 2002), but it also incorporates evaluation of the conditions for learning by including mutual feedback. As we become accustomed to including mutuality as an integral part of the process, the assessment and evaluation of progress is increasingly individualized and made more meaningful.

Building the Educational Assessment

Throughout this discussion, refer to the Educational Assessment Outline at the end of this chapter and a sample educational assessment that is also provided. For the initial educational assessment, information is gathered to identify consistent patterns in how students learn and approach their work. We are examining what skills students possess, their progress over time in acquiring these skills, and what characteristic patterns of learning emerge as new skills and knowledge are integrated. This involves an appreciation of past experiences, intellectual capacities and personal strengths, distinctive ways of learning, capacity for interpersonal relationships, and learning opportunities available in the agency.

Although a written educational assessment is not always required by social work programs it is good practice to write one anyway. Experience in writing an educational assessment becomes particularly important when providing documentation on marginal or failing students. Whether formally written or just thought through orally, engaging in an educational assessment forms the basis of any learning plan and final evaluation, and includes consideration of the following elements (Bogo & Vayda, 1987; Fox & Zischka, 1989; Lemberger & Marshack, 1991).

POINTS TO CONSIDER IN STUDENT EVALUATIONS

1. *Past life experiences, skills, and professional attributes of students.* Describe the student's prior educational and employment history as well as other experiences relevant to learning in the field. This section highlights the student's strengths for professional development. It should include prior educational experiences and how this and previous field placements, employment, volunteer, and other life experiences relate to learning in the field of social work. Also include what skills and attributes have been identified that apply to the current agency context.

2. *Learning to the present and learning goals and objectives.* Describe the range and nature of learning opportunities in the agency, including available assignments and other resources for learning. In other words, what does the student need to learn in order to meet the criteria established by the social work education program for the student's particular practice method and level of professional education? What is the nature of the assignments made available to the student in the agency? How do these assignments relate to the student's current classes and attributes? What learning opportunities are likely to emerge from the context of these educational experiences? Begin to identify specific areas that need attention. It is useful to describe assignments and how these respond to the student's learning needs. Remember to refer to the social work education program's Field Instruction Manual for educational guidelines and competencies.

3. *Interpersonal style and characteristic learning patterns.* Evaluate the student pattern of response to the learning situation, including understanding of the learner role and understanding of professional performance expectations and criteria. Identify the type of learner the student

seems to be and the implications for teaching. The type of clients, problems, and social systems that the student works more easily with and those that are more difficult is an important factor for consideration. Observing how students use their intuition and how they give or withhold help in any given situation yields critical clues to this assessment. For example, what kinds of social work tasks does the student perform quickly, and what tasks does the student put off or hesitate to attend to? How flexible and effective is the student in organizing and scheduling tasks? What are the student's strengths, and how are these applied to work within this setting? Identify any obstacles to learning that impede performance at this time.

4. *Demographic characteristics of student, field instructor, staff, and clients.* Describe similarities and differences in culture, ethnicity, race, gender, class, age, sexual orientation, religion, and abilities between the student and field instructor. Consider these characteristic differences and similarities between you and the student, the student and agency staff, and between the student and populations served. Consider the implications of diversity on the work and the teaching and learning. What are the student's strengths and learning needs with regard to cultural competence? How is the student's self-awareness of his or her own culture demonstrated? How does the student express understanding of the role of culture in human development? Is the student able to demonstrate understanding of issues of diversity, power, privilege, and oppression in professional relationships?

This topic is discussed extensively in chapter 10, but for now it should suffice to say that diversity factors have implications for learning styles, characteristic patterns of learning, selective emphasis in field instruction, and how students respond to certain client populations or problems. From the beginning, it is our responsibility as field instructors to raise questions about cultural similarities and differences and their implications for teacher/learner relationships and client/worker relationships. We are generally aware of diversity factors, but are often uncertain about ways to incorporate diversity into teaching or learning plans (Marshack, Ortiz, Hendricks, & Gladstein, 1994). We need to be as straightforward as possible in naming the particular issue. For example, *"Isn't it interesting that we have been working together for a num-*

ber of weeks now and neither of us has yet raised the fact that I am a White female and you are a Hispanic man working with a culturally mixed female population? Let's take some time now to reflect together about how these dynamics might affect your work with clients and our work together."

5. *Learning plan.* Given the information obtained and performance observed, what learning goals have been established between you and the student? What unmet needs have been identified? What strategies are suggested to address identified learning needs? To what extent is there a shared vision of next steps to be taken? What additional assignments are needed to help with the achievement of learning goals? Are there any obstacles to the defined goals? If so, what action might be taken to aid the steps ahead?

Selective Emphasis in Field Instruction Conferences

Begin by noticing how students direct or respond to topics raised for discussion in field instruction conferences. For example, consider what questions are raised more frequently and what issues appear on students' agendas regularly. Consider whether students are primarily client-focused or self-preoccupied, concerned with themselves and with how their performance is viewed. Do students pose questions for immediate answers and immediate direction, or are questions focused on how social policies address social problems or on practice theories and how they are applied? Weekly field instruction conferences should touch on all of these areas at different stages in the learning process and for different reasons. When students are overly focused on any one area of learning, we need to consider why and introduce students to the advantages of expanding their views of field instruction as addressing many learning needs, not just one.

Assessment of students' organizational capacities involves identification of the kinds of tasks students perform quickly or those that are avoided, as well as their levels of productivity and efficiency. The manner in which students focus the discussion during field instruction conferences provides additional data for an educational assessment. Some students typically emphasize content about a task or problem situation, or the development of practice skills, or agency and administrative issues. Intermittent focus on self, or on us as field instructors, may facilitate learning, but a predominant focus on one or both of these areas may indicate impediments to learning and professional growth. Observe how students use what they have discussed in field instruction, and how they carry over learning from one assignment to another. This demonstrates their ability to integrate and apply learning and requires an appreciation of their distinctive style and pace of learning (Urbanowski & Dwyer, 1988).

In addition to the identification of the sources from which students learn best, we need to observe the tempo of learning, which might be relatively steady, occur in spurts with intervening plateaus, or be consistently accelerated or slow. As discussed in chapter 4, adult learners have preferred and characteristic ways of learning. Some prefer to develop broad conceptual frameworks about problem areas before actually meeting clients. Others want to get a "feel" for specific clients before giving thoughtful attention to facts about their situation. Still others prefer to rehearse their practice approaches through role playing or modeling their early interventions on observations of more seasoned practitioners. Understanding the student's preferred responses to learning as cognitive, affective, observational, or operational can help guide our choice of teaching interventions and extend a student's approach to learning.

Brookfield (1990) outlines factors that help us identify students' potential resistance to learning (see chapter 11, Teaching Challenges in Field Instruction, for more detail). Resistance may be misunderstood or labeled as a lack of motivation or lack of preparedness for work rather than as a natural and expected obstacle to change. For example, a student's hesitation to take on an assignment may be misunderstood as resistance, whereas the hesitation may simply be a request for further explanation, a reluctance to request a different activity, or a sign of a lack of confidence regarding the nature of the task. Brookfield's work facilitates our understanding of this delicate issue and is presented here for consideration of possible underlying reasons for resistance to learning and as a way of enhancing our educational assessments. The following summarizes these considerations.

- How intimidating is the placement setting? Are students given ample support if the setting involves performance that entails complex interactions with the public or difficult client populations?

- Has what is expected of them been discussed? How clear are the explanations about what is expected?

- What expectations of success or failure are brought into field instructor/student relationships? What is the level of investment in this endeavor, and how might this affect the learning contract?

- Are students supported to accept their right not to know and their need to ask questions? How do students approach the search for answers in the midst of uncertainty?

- How can students be made comfortable enough to take the risks involved in new learning?

- Are students prepared for the inevitable conflicts that will arise between their personal views of themselves or their culture and those of the profession or clients?

Some learners may have negative associations to learning. They may have been told they were "too dumb to learn" or "will never graduate." They come to field instruction with these perceptions of themselves. A fear of failure may inhibit their ability to tolerate moving ahead without clear and precise direction. Students may feel that asking questions is equated with being ignorant or foolish. Challenges to values and alternative world views may be confusing for some students. Experiences shape expectations around authority, disclosure, communication styles, and taboo areas that need to be discussed. Reframing resistance to learning as a response to facing the challenges to new learning provides a glimmer of new understanding and possible avenues for intervention (Brookfield, 1990).

Educational Plans

Once we have gathered enough information to assess students' approaches to learning situations presented by the placement, it is time to reflect on what has been learned from these beginning educational assessments and to craft educational plans that best meet learning needs. Bogo and Vayda (1987) provide helpful references to the task of developing collaborative educational plans. Hamilton and Else (1983) and Fox and Zischka (1989) advise that to be maximally useful, educational plans are developed mutually by students and field instructors. They individualize the experience for students in a particular agency, foster partnerships between students and field instructors, and specify what a student will be assigned within a given period of time. In this way, educational plans parallel contracting with clients for students.

Educational plans are based on the educational assessment. They form the basis of the final evaluation and provide an opportunity for ongoing feedback and frequent review of where students are in relation to mutually established goals and objectives. These plans link the professional knowledge to be acquired with performance objectives expected by particular social work education programs. Familiarity with the program's field practicum manuals and established evaluation criteria for student performance is therefore essential to this task.

Educational plans should be as specific as possible, including:

- Actual circumstances of the placement setting

- Learning goals and objectives

- Learning experiences and assignments used to achieve objectives

- Measurements or indicators of how to know when the goals are accomplished

- Time commitments

- Statement of roles and responsibilities

Several authors have defined the specifics of formulating goals, objectives, and learning strategies in field education (Bogo & Vayda, 1987; Collins, Thomlinson, & Grinnell 1992; Horejsi & Garthwaite 1999, 2002). Goals are generally described as broad concepts with long-range purposes such as helping students to become effective advocates, group workers, or program planners. Learning objectives are more specific and more often involve an outcome that can be measured. An example of a learning objective is helping a student obtain knowledge about motivational interviewing applied to mandated clients, or enabling a student's demonstration of community development skills. Learning activities are the tasks and situations undertaken to achieve the learning objectives. They are strategies such as assigning a student the task of developing a short-term parenting support group, having a student observe the agency's educational orientation series for new clients entering the drug and alcohol treatment center, or assigning students to conduct intakes with self-referred clients.

The teaching plan evolves from all the data provided above and in consultation with students. The plan identifies essential elements of students' learning needs, indicating both short- and long-term objectives, major teaching methods employed, and types of assignments planned to advance learning. Being as specific as possible when discussing future goals and how these translate into assignments aids the achievement of goals set. Specific behaviors and indicators provide evidence that skills are achieved. Remember to include goals and performance indicators for the development of culturally competent knowledge and skills.

Learning Contracts: When Problems Emerge

The discussion above describes educational plans as supportive to students in the development of focused self-directed learning. Whether formally written or not, defining goals for each student's experience gives focus and direction to the choice of assignments and improves the likelihood of success. However, when obstacles emerge in the learning situation, written learning contracts serve as guides and focus the teaching and learning efforts. "The learning contract is a means for making the learning objectives of the field experience clear and explicit for the learner and the field supervisor" (Fox & Zischka, 1989, p. 105). They provide useful boundaries and targets to identified priorities for learning that increase the possibility for change and success. A learning contract is derived from a shared experience, and we do them together with students so that they require mutual participation. Once a working alliance is established, both parties agree on a mutual purpose that is geared to promote learning and to push into new areas of learning. Ongoing review and evaluation are inherent parts of a learning contract that establishes reciprocal accountability, i.e., encourages students to take responsibility for learning so that field instructors, faculty liaisons, and students have individual, complementary, and shared (although not necessarily equal) responsibilities. The expectations of all parties concerned are made explicit. Learning contracts help identify what there is to learn as well as the best way to teach it. Specificity is essential so that field instructors and students can form a baseline from which progress can be assessed and gaps can be identified. Learning contracts help formulate priorities. Learning contracts are bound by time and reality, they are fluid and evolve over time, and not all there is to learn can be achieved in the time allotted. Therefore, goals and objectives are set based on the learning opportunities available and toward the possibility of success. Learning contracts require recurrent review and are meant to be dynamic in nature. They involve negotiation and redefinition of the tasks as "the work" of field placement proceeds, and they encourage self-evaluation and model a professional stance.

Learning contracts parallel the reciprocal, collaborative process of contracting for services with clients. In a similar vein, the field instruction contract "is an agreement between the consumer and the provider of service which specifies purpose and target issues" (Fox & Zischka, 1989, p. 104). We are providing an education service to student consumers. Learning contracts should include the following:

- Clearly stated goals and objectives;

- Outline of procedures;

- Anticipation of constraints;

- Details about roles and functions;

- Description of techniques to be employed;

- Determination of a specific time frame for completion of the contract; and

- An enhanced learner's involvement and responsibility in field education (Fox & Zischka, 1989, p. 105).

Examples of two learning contracts written to address difficulties arising in the placement are presented at the end of this chapter, along with two self-assessment field instruction forms. When students and field instructors regularly evaluate their own performance as teachers and learners, there is less need to develop learning contracts. Ongoing self-evaluation demonstrates a commitment to doing the best we can in our respective roles.

The collaborative nature of completing educational assessments presumes that we support students as they begin to answer some of the following questions for themselves:

- How do I see myself at this point in the learning process?

- What patterns do I notice in my learning?

- What patterns do I notice in my practice?

- Does field work reflect what I am learning in class work?

- How am I using field instruction conferences?

- What is most helpful in field instruction? What is least helpful?

- How do I learn best?

- What kinds of clients, problems, or systems do I work with best?

- What kinds of clients, problems, or systems do I find most challenging?

- How well do I work with cultural differences and similarities?

- How flexible and effective am I in scheduling and completing tasks?

- What kinds of tasks do I perform quickly and easily? What kinds of tasks do I avoid or find difficult?

- What areas of my practice can I identify as needing work?

- What new areas of practice do I want to learn?

The role of the faculty liaison is critical when issues arise in any of these areas, but as described below, the faculty liaison is a partner in each student's learning experience, providing support to both field instructors and students.

Faculty Liaisons

In most social work education programs, full-time and adjunct faculty are assigned to advise students in their academic and field performance. Each program's expectations of this role may differ, but there are some common responsibilities assigned to faculty liaisons. Liaisons act as a bridge or connection between the academic institution and the field instruction components of social work education, and they incorporate three primary responsibilities: advisory, instructional, and evaluative (Raphael & Rosenblum, 1987, 1983).

ADVISORY ROLE

Advice is given and suggestions are made to both students and field instructors. Faculty liaisons provide resources to the educational endeavor. They may offer suggestions on the modification of teaching methods and assignments, and they add their own time, effort, and expertise to increase the viability of the placement and learning experience for students and field instructors.

INSTRUCTIONAL ROLE

Clarification of a social work education program's expectations provides valuable information that helps students know what is expected of them in class and field instruction. It can also help develop a better match between a student's style of learning and a field instructor's style of teaching. In this way, faculty liaisons become advocates for and guardians of the student's educational experiences in the field.

EVALUATIVE ROLE

The final determination of the field instruction grade is submitted by faculty liaisons who independently gather information on student learning opportunities and field performance evaluations. Liaisons also evaluate field placements and provide information to the field education office on the learning opportunities within each setting.

Liaison Visits to Agencies

The tasks and nature of faculty liaison visits to agencies during the academic year also vary. Unless called on for a specific purpose, the timing of the visit often defines the focus and task. For example, a visit in the beginning of student placements will, by necessity, be focused on the educational task ahead and on an evaluation of the educational opportunities being made available to students. As the semester proceeds, it is then possible for faculty liaisons to begin an appraisal of student learning needs and competencies. Visits that take place during subsequent semesters incorporate the achievements of the previous semester and encourage anticipation of end-of-year goals. If the visit is close to the end of term, affirmation of student preparedness for entering the field and evaluation of the field instructor's contributions to the student's learning are addressed. Visits aim to promote communication between field instructors and students and to identify and clarify any learning issues needing attention. Liaisons are primarily concerned with promoting optimal learning situations and seek to strengthen the instructional relationships between field instructors and students.

Ideally, the agency meeting is usually held as a three-way session led by field liaisons. Students are meant to have an active role in defining their goals and in reflecting on their progress toward these goals. Liaisons and field instructors encourage students to take an active part in the discussions by eliciting their contributions. In this way, the meeting provides an opportunity for the integration of theory and practice, for evaluation of students' developing professional identity, and for their ownership of competencies and learning needs. It is an opportunity for field instructors to provide feedback to students and to restate issues needing emphasis.

Topics to cover during the field liaison's agency visit can include:

- The context and nature of actual and anticipated assignments that give liaisons a sense of the context and inherent challenges faced by students in the placement

- Identification of additional learning opportunities available to enhance the learning experience

- Issues related to field instruction itself, including how time is allotted, teaching methods used, and each student's use of the field instruction relationship and process

- Learning achievements and challenges

- Goals and objectives for the remaining academic term or next steps toward progress in the program or graduation or career choices

- Opportunities for integration between field instruction and the social work education program's curriculum

- Any other issues or concerns raised by students or field instructors

Students, field instructors, and faculty liaisons may request three-way meetings as the need arises. More often these meetings are initiated by faculty liaisons during their scheduled visits to agencies. Field instructors have the right to request an agency visit when none is offered. There are many more of us and students than any one school has faculty liaisons, and therefore, field instructors need not wait until liaisons make contact for a visit. Faculty liaisons offer support and guidance and provide a source of additional consultation, a third ear, around teaching and learning issues experienced in field instruction.

Outline for an Educational Assessment & Learning Plan

Present an educational assessment for your student using the outline provided. Be sure to include the student's demonstrated learning patterns and styles. Also discuss the specific learning/teaching goals developed, timing and sequencing of assignments, teaching methods chosen, and priorities set.

Field instructor:

Agency and placement site:

Student's status in the social work program (e.g., 1st year, 2nd year, advanced standing, etc.):

Student's major method or specialization:

I. Student's life experiences, skills, and professional attributes

Describe student's prior educational and employment history and other experiences relevant to learning in the field. Highlight student's strengths for further professional development.

II. Learning goals and objectives

What does the student need to learn in order to meet the criteria established by the social work program for his or her particular level of professional education? Identify specific areas that need attention. Refer to the Field Instruction Manual for guidelines and competencies. Give examples to support your statement.

III. Demographic characteristics of student, field Instructor, staff, and clients

Describe similarities and differences in culture, ethnicity, race, gender, class, age, sexual orientation, religion, and disabilities and their implications for the teacher/learner relationship. Include how you teach students to work with diverse clients and staff.

IV. Student's characteristic learning patterns and problems

Evaluate the student's pattern of responses to the learning situation, including understanding of the learner role. Identify the type of learner and implications for teaching. Note student's strengths as well as any obstacles to learning that impede the student's professional performance.

V. Learning opportunities

Describe the range and nature of learning opportunities in the agency, including available assignments and other resources for learning.

VI. Educational plan

The teaching plan evolves from all the data provided above and in consultation with the student. The plan should identify essential elements of the student's learning needs, indicating both short- and long-term objectives, major teaching methods employed, and types of assignments planned to advance learning.

Sample Educational Assessment and Learning Plan

Field Instructor: D. J.
Agency & Unit: Family Support Program
Student: R. L., 1st Year

AGENCY AND PLACEMENT CONTEXT

R is placed in a youth and family outreach program within a large social services department that serves a predominately culturally mixed, working-class, metropolitan community. Families are served only if there is a youth between the ages of 10–18. Services provided are free. Other younger children in the family may also be included in service, as long as the youth ages 10–18 has been identified as needing services. Contact is time-limited and referral is negotiated if the initial contract of 6 months proves to be inadequate for resolution of the presenting difficulties. A waiting list is maintained; at present the waiting list for services is approximately 1 month. Family work is mandated as part of the contract for services. Issues addressed represent the full range of problems faced by youth in today's society. Individual and group student supervision is provided. Two other students are placed within the agency at this time. The agency has had a long-standing relationship with provision of graduate student placements.

STUDENT'S LIFE EXPERIENCES, SKILLS, AND PROFESSIONAL ATTRIBUTES

R is a young, enthusiastic woman who comes to graduate school with some volunteer experience with the elderly in a senior center and as a candy striper in hospitals. Her volunteer work has aided her quick assimilation into the rather hierarchical structure of this agency. R was an English major in her undergraduate education and has done considerable reading in this field and in self-help psychology; additionally, she has done reading on social change movements and on social work practice. R demonstrates the ability to relate easily and comfortably with most clients and is open about her discomfort with child abuse, spouse abuse, and any form of family violence—all new areas for her. Her volunteer work provides her with a beginning sense of the need to understand the total picture and not just the presenting problem. She is eager to learn social work clinical skills and to explore issues or problems of concern with her clients. She demonstrates a caring attitude with her first few clients, and like many 1st-year students has a tendency to rush in to relieve the client's pain or unhappiness. She has a developing sense of self-awareness and this facilitates open discussion of her interventive choices.

LEARNING GOALS AND OBJECTIVES

The specific learning tasks for R this semester will be to develop beginning helping skills. In particular, interviewing skills, engaging clients in helping relationships, formulating beginning contracts and interventive plans, and gathering information for biopsychosocial assessments are identified for focus. Exploration, support, sustainment, and engagement are the primary skills to be worked on in the weeks ahead. Familiarity with agency policies will be provided. The ways these policies affect service delivery will be addressed. Her social work education program's foundation 1st-year curriculum requires that she be assigned some individual clients within this first semester and, ideally, that other modalities be assigned as available.

DEMOGRAPHIC CHARACTERISTICS OF STUDENT, FIELD INSTRUCTOR, AND CLIENTS

Student is 22 years old, born in Puerto Rico and raised in a suburb of a large metropolitan city. She has had 16 years of Catholic schooling and a middle-class upbringing. She is partially bilingual and is working to improve her Spanish. Many clients in this agency speak Spanish, and she is being given as diverse a workload as possible in terms of age, race, ethnicity, religion, social class, problems, etc. The field instructor is a 43-year-old, Orthodox Jewish woman who has supervised many students in almost 20 years as a social worker. Student and field instructor have discussed these apparent cultural differences. Field instructor is fluent in Spanish, and both she and the student love to cook, read mystery novels, and collect antiques.

STUDENT'S CHARACTERISTIC LEARNING PATTERNS AND PROBLEMS

R is an intellectual learner as shown by her efforts to relate her clients' problems to what she has read in books or journal articles. In supervision, she is quick to formulate theories to fit her cases. R is able to verbalize the concerns and interests of adult clients, and she is developing her ability to demonstrate the same ease with children. She is less comfortable in her work with children. She has more difficulty listening to or understanding their problems and more often reverts to advice giving or lecturing than in her work with older, verbal adolescents and adults. R thinks this may be related to her being an only child, not having siblings while growing up, and having more experience in relating with adults in formal situations. She has demonstrated ease in establishing rapport with clients and understandably needs help in how to continue with the helping process. R's empathic response to clients her age or older is well formed. A focus of supervision will be to explore extending this capability to her work with latency-age children or younger children or less verbal adolescents. R's self-assessment of her work has sometimes been critical. We have agreed to make this a continued teaching/learning agenda by maintaining a balance of work with clients from a range of ages. R's strengths and self-awareness indicate good potential for learning, growth, and change.

LEARNING OPPORTUNITIES

This agency serves a wide-ranging client population, located as it is in a diverse community. R will have cases involving children and adults of all ages, mostly African American and Latinos, who present problems that are concrete, emotional, and socially based. Most clients will be assigned following the family assessment. She will begin with individual youth, and as she demonstrates the potential, R will be able to work with family groups and will have the opportunity to form a parenting group. R is planning to provide information sessions about agency services to the local schools and youth centers, and in time she might develop an information and referral service.

LEARNING PLAN

R will be given additional assignments, youth, children, and families with varying problems to build up her caseload. Additional readings will be used, especially those related to work with children, youth, and play therapy, to strengthen her intellectual capacity for the work. Role playing will be used to prepare her for more difficult cases. R will observe families in sessions through a one-way mirror in order to prepare for family meetings.

Reflecting on Educational Assessment and Planning

Referring to the sample educational assessment and plan provided above, consider the following:

1. What information about the student's educational background and prior work experiences is particularly important for the field instructor to note?

2. What learning opportunities are being provided in the placement?

3. What personal attributes and abilities does the student possess that are resources for further professional growth and development?

4. What are the specific learning tasks that the student needs to accomplish in order to meet the school's criteria for field performance?

5. What are the student's characteristic patterns and techniques of learning?

6. What potential obstacles to learning can be identified? In other words, are there any defensive or self-protective behaviors that inhibit professional growth? Do you see the student exhibiting healthy resistance to control the tempo and amount of learning in order to promote integration?

7. Does the educational plan distinguish between short- and long-term objectives, the teaching methodology to be used, and types of additional assignments that will advance the student's learning?

8. In what ways might this educational assessment be more finely tuned to meet the identified learning needs of this student?

Components to Learning Contracts

A learning contract is comprised of the following components:

- It is derived from a shared experience. It is done together and requires mutual participation.

- It sets up a working alliance and establishes permission to push into new areas of learning.

- Parties agree on a mutual purpose that is geared to promote learning; therefore, questioning, review, and evaluation are inherent.

- It establishes reciprocal accountability, i.e., encourages students to take responsibility for learning so that field instructors, field liaisons, and students have individual, complementary, and shared (although not necessarily equal) responsibilities.

Expectations of both parties are made explicit:

- Helps identify what there is to learn as well as the best way to teach it

- Specificity is required to help form a baseline from which progress can be assessed and gaps can be identified (i.e., gaps in the learning and in the teaching)

- Helps formulate priorities

- Defines what is and is not possible (a matching of hopes, expectations, and opportunities)

It is bound by time and reality:

- It is fluid and evolves through time.

- Not all there is to learn may be achieved in the time allotted.

- Goals and objectives set are based on the learning opportunities available and are formulated toward the possibility of success.

Involves recurrent review and is dynamic in nature:

- Involves negotiation and redefinition of the tasks as "the work" of field placement gets underway

- Encourages self-evaluation

- Models a professional stance

Sample Learning Contracts

The following are learning contracts in which concerns about a student's performance were identified. Evaluate the examples on their clarity, provision of mutual roles and responsibilities, and specificity in relation to strategies to meet objectives and goals. Finally, consider how you would improve each contract to better serve the teaching and learning efforts.

LEARNING CONTRACT—1ST-YEAR, 1ST-SEMESTER MSW STUDENT

A meeting was held to address concerns held by the field instructor and task supervisor. Present were student (S), field instructor (FI), and faculty liaison (FL). Although the student is enthusiastic and eager to learn, she is having difficulty understanding what is required in completing paperwork requirements and in understanding the difference between process recordings and progress notes required by the agency. In addition, there are concerns about her use of time and organizational skills. The quality of the written work submitted to date has been disorganized and often late, and the student has also been late for essential meetings. As a result, the field instructor has felt unable to assess this student's work and is questioning the student's commitment to the placement and to learning. The following learning contract specifies goals related to administrative tasks, use of time, and process recording.

Administrative goal. S will complete administrative assignments in a timely manner and will maintain appropriate agency records and produce weekly process recordings.

1. FI and S will clarify what paperwork needs to be completed on each assignment. S will review with the task supervisor how to complete each form and what is entailed in the progress notes. FI will provide S with examples of such recordings. FI will provide S with additional guidance in the completion of these requirements within supervision.

2. S will ask questions within supervision for needed clarity. Additional guidance from the task supervisor will also be sought as needed.

3. Progress notes will be completed on each of S's clients on a weekly basis. They will be submitted in draft form to be reviewed in supervision and then entered into the client's chart by the end of each week S is in placement.

Use of time/organization goal. S will organize and use time productively, including attending meetings on time.

1. S will purchase a daily planner and write the daily/weekly schedule of meetings and appointments in that book, including where meetings and groups are being held.

2. FI will coordinate assignments and review the use of S's time in placement at the start of each supervisory session.

3. One hour per week will be booked into S's week for completion of written work.

4. S will inform FI if there are any blocks of time that are free and not occupied.

5. S will attend meetings on time.

Process Recordings

1. FL will review S's process recording during the next 3 weeks as additional support to S while S is becoming familiar with the requirements of process recording.

2. S will submit one process recording per week 1 day prior to supervision for the next 3 weeks. Following the period of 3 weeks, this requirement will return to the prescribed 2 process recordings per week for the remainder of the term.

3. FI will review process recordings and make comments on them for S's review. Process recordings will also be reviewed during supervision.

FL will be available to FI and S and will return for a follow-up visit in 4 weeks to review progress and next steps. S will contact FL with any concerns during this 4-week period. The next meeting will review what aspects of this plan have been achieved and what further work in these areas is still required.

LEARNING CONTRACT—2ND-YEAR, 3RD-SEMESTER MSW STUDENT

A meeting was held to discuss learning objectives and goals for a 2nd-year student placed within a large metropolitan hospital. Present at this meeting were the student (S), field instructor (FI), agency student coordinator (SC), and the faculty liaison (FL). Concern was expressed regarding the student's sense of being overwhelmed by the pace and demands of this setting. Specific concerns related to timeliness, appropriate self-reflection, and ability to prioritize work expected of a 2nd-year student. Another area of concern was difficulty of moving from beginning engagement to a clearer focus of work with long-term rehabilitation clients.

To aid the student's success within this setting, the following agreement was reached:

Student will:

1. Contact FI at the start of each placement day to review the work plan for the day.

2. Daily progress notes will be kept on each of S's clients, and these will be emailed to FI at the end of each placement day.

3. An agenda will be created by S for weekly supervision.

4. Two process recordings will be submitted weekly one day prior to field instruction conference. The end of each recording will focus on S's reflection on the work and possible next steps to be taken. The specific areas to be addressed are S's thoughts and reactions to the client inter-action, identification of any unfinished business, unaddressed emotion-al content during the session, and thoughts on possible next steps.

Field instructor will:

1. Provide an uninterrupted supervisory hour for S to review process recordings submitted and to address S's supervisory agenda.

2. Provide feedback on both what S is doing effectively as well as on what may need attention or improvement.

Faculty liaison will:

1. Maintain contact with S to support efforts made and to be an additional resource.

2. Maintain contact with FI.

3. Coordinate a follow-up meeting with S and FI within the next month.

4. Review one process recording prior to the next visit.

Field Instructor's Self-Assessment of Field Instruction

This form is meant to be used intermittently during the academic year.

	YES	NO	TO SOME EXTENT
Was I prepared for what the student discussed today?			
Did I convey interest in my student's agenda?			
Was I preoccupied?			
Did I prevent interruptions to our session?			
Did I give the student enough time to talk?			
Did I encourage elaboration?			
Did I invite questions?			
Did I listen?			
Were my questions inquiring rather than leading?			
Did my questions encourage critical thinking skills?			
Did I encourage student self-reflection?			
Did I provide feedback?			
Did I provide the opportunity to link theory with practice?			
Was I in touch with my own feelings?			
What "unfinished business" is left for our next session?			
What issues/patterns emerged in my teaching?			
What issues/patterns emerged within the student's practice?			
Identify an area in which I have noticed improvement in my teaching.			
Identify an area in which I would like to see more improvement in my teaching.			

Student's Self-Assessment of Field Instruction

This form is meant to be used intermittently during the academic year.

	YES	NO	TO SOME EXTENT
Was I prepared for field instruction today?			
Did I prepare an agenda of my concerns?			
Was I preoccupied?			
Did I prevent interruptions to our session?			
Did I share my views freely?			
Am I pleased with how I communicated?			
Did I voice my questions and concerns?			
Did I listen?			
Was I able to link theory with practice?			
Was I able to ask for explanations when I was unclear?			
Did I engage in self-reflection?			
Did I provide feedback?			
Could I engage in a critical analysis of my work?			
Was I in touch with my own feelings?			
What "unfinished business" is left for our next session?			
What issues/patterns emerged in my learning or my practice?			
Identify an area in which I have noticed improvement in my practice or understanding.			
Identify an area in which I would like to see more improvement in my practice or understanding.			

Chapter 8

EVALUATION OF FIELD PERFORMANCE

*G*iving evaluations is one of the most difficult, demanding and complex tasks teachers have to face; yet, done well, it is also one of the most significant spurs to learning. Because teachers' evaluations are invested with enormous significance by students...a critical comment from a teacher can be psychologically devastating. So giving evaluations is, quite rightly, the feature of practice that gives rise to the most continuous soul-searching. . . . And this is as it should be. (Brookfield, 1990, p. 132)

The process of evaluation provides students with the opportunity to self-critique their own practice, an essential component to professional practice, particularly in learning to become autonomous and self-reflective social workers. The written evaluation and the process leading up to it provide us with the platform from which to tackle this fundamental task. The written evaluation is the culmination of the ongoing evaluative process that involves a partnership and collaborative feedback throughout the entire academic year. Students take increased responsibility for self-evaluation as they advance through their placements, but the emphasis in field instruction is always on mutual responsibility and collaboration. This aims to support students in their professional development, to aid in their ownership of learning achievements and needs, and to recognize the instructor's responsibility for the use of power and authority associated with the evaluative role. "For the experience to be of maximum benefit, the student must actively engage in the evaluation process rather than passively accept or reject imposed judgments" (Gitterman & Gitterman, 1979, p. 105).

Writing individualized, balanced, and clear statements about how students can improve their performance and incorporating ongoing evaluations as part of the placement experience are critical components of the learning process. The evaluation is *individualized* and addresses a specific student's learning needs and demonstrated competencies as opposed to generalized statements that would fit any student. Evaluations need to be *balanced* between what the student is able to do well and what learning goals are identified. It is rare to have a student who has not demonstrated any strengths or positives. Providing *clear* guidance as to how performance can be improved gives focus to the work ahead and promotes the possibility that additional growth can be realized.

Evaluations aid our efforts to contribute to the professional development of our students by providing the opportunity to emphasize a teaching point or to restate a learning goal. They also provide an occasion for discussion and negotiation regarding how an attribute or learning goal can be described or conceptualized. Giving students the chance to read and absorb their evaluations before signing them is built in to ensure due process. It also provides another occasion to model mutuality and collaborative feedback. The review of the written evaluation is an opportunity to modify our description of the student's skill level, to take into account additional evidence, and to clarify our educational assessment. As adult learners develop self-observation about their learning progress, this awareness can be articulated and used to fine-tune our teaching interventions. For example, if a student continues to resist speaking up in staff meetings, we may need to help the student to retrospectively consider what might have been said and to imagine how these comments might have been received. We could also point out that dealing with colleagues and other disciplines in staff meetings is an important component to our professional role. If professional development in this area continues to be uneven, that is, sometimes the student speaks but most of the time the student is quiet, this progress is acknowledged while also looking at what is getting in the way of more consistent performance.

Although the specific requirements, terminology, and formats for evaluations may differ, the process of evaluation is generic. Some social work programs require 6-week learning contracts, and others require written educational assessments and learning plans during the first half of the first semester. These tools enhance and contribute to the eventual formal evaluation process. All social work education programs view evaluations as ongoing educational processes, regardless of their structures and formats. The major components of all evaluations are similar to those presented in chapter 7, Educational Assessments and Learning Plans.

The end-of-term evaluation usually focuses on:

- Identification of the specific context of the field placement and of assignments and learning opportunities available in the placement setting;

- Confirmation of student achievements of stated performance expectations;

- Examples or evidence of student achievement of goals or needs; and

- Identified areas of strength and issues identified for focus of future learning.

Preparing for the Written Evaluation

PERFORMANCE CRITERIA

Preparing students for what to expect from field performance appraisals enables them to be more fully equipped and able to participate as equal partners in the process. We need to take the time to explain the context of evaluations, that every social work education program is required by the Council on Social Work Education's (CSWE) educational policy and accreditation standards to have field performance criteria and outcome measures, and that these are contained in field instruction manuals. These criteria form the basis of the formal evaluation and provide a guide to the aims and objectives for student performance.

Charlotte Towle's classic text, *The Learner in Education for the Profession as Seen in Education for Social Work* (1954, pp. 395–411) includes a summary of indicators of movement in learning that are useful criteria for evaluation. Some of these indicators are that students' attitudes toward clients change; they demonstrate a readiness to identify with clients; they can individualize people and situations and are less prone to stereotyping; they develop the ability to analyze a situation, break it down, and examine its parts; they demonstrate lower anxiety and increased emotional growth; they are able to accept criticism and participate in self-evaluation; they can proceed more slowly toward goal attainment in the helping process; they can establish and maintain constructive working relationships; they can accept not knowing everything; and they demonstrate increased independence, creative thinking, and appropriate autonomous actions.

Dore, Epstein, and Herrerias (1992, p. 353) offer eight universally recognized learning objectives for the evaluation of student performance in the field, based on an analysis of 98 social work education programs:

Objective 1. Development of specific skills for micro practice, including skills in engagement, problem exploration, exploration of feelings, goal setting, contracting, and termination, as well as knowledge of how and ability to apply various treatment modalities.

Objective 2. Development of critical thinking, including conceptual understanding, application of values in practice, and ability to use theory in action.

Objective 3. Development of the capability for self-directed learning, including the ability to manage one's own dependency and to seek out and accept new knowledge.

Objective 4. Enhancement of personal characteristics thought to be associated with professional competency, including flexibility, initiative, and risk taking.

Objective 5. Enhancement of leadership qualities, including communication skills, advocacy, and commitment to social change.

Objective 6. Facility in caseload management, including knowledge of community resources, time management, and management of workload.

Objective 7. Development of interpersonal skills, including the use of self in relationships, relational capacities, and the ability to form collaborative relationships.

Objective 8. Development of administrative skills, including preparation of case materials and the ability to be self-evaluative in relation to practice.

"Field instructors identified four core areas when asked to characterize a passing student: (1) the ability to work with clients in terms of capacity to build and sustain appropriate relationships and to understand how the clients viewed their situation; (2) personal characteristics in terms of maturity, honesty, tolerance, warmth. A knowledge of self and an ability to cope with stress, conflict and crisis were also important here; (3) the amount of growth or movement during the placement; and (4) an ability to understand and work within the social work agency" (Wilson & Moore, 1989, p. 22).

Field performance criteria are often abstract or global and can benefit from concrete examples to give a clearer picture of what is meant. For example, stating a performance expectation as, "the student demonstrates the ability to engage clients in professional relationships" is not specific enough to describe a student's performance in this aspect of the helping process. It is better to make statements like, "Student has established a good working relationship with a 7-year-old client and her family and has explained her role and function clearly to teachers and guidance counselors in the child's school."

It is good practice to examine performance criteria and evaluation formats together with students. This review provides us with ample opportunities to discuss the definitions and meaning of terms used so that we both have the same interpretation and understanding of the criteria. Field performance criteria spelled out by each social work education program form the basis of student evaluations. The following questions (Horejsi & Gathwaite, 1999) can be used alongside the review of the program's established criteria.

• How clear are the social work education program's performance criteria in describing student learning growth and patterns?

• What terms require clarification?

• What questions arise when thinking of a particular student's performance in relation to the stated criteria?

• Are there aspects of the student's performance that are not covered in the criteria?

Although the aim is to be objective and to form value-free judgments based on evidence, this is not always easy to achieve. Students require support to be able to describe and evaluate their skills and to specify what they believe they have learned in relation to expected practice competencies. This can best be achieved by giving examples and highlighting illustrations of key performance criteria. In summary, we need to identify to what extent students have demonstrated their performance criteria and then expand on these criteria by providing specific examples.

Preparing for the Written Evaluation

THE FORMAL ORAL REVIEW

Field performance evaluations include ongoing discussions, but the-end-of semester written evaluation is often preceded by a formal evaluation conference to discuss progress. If a social work education program does not require a written 6th-week plan or contract, verbal evaluations usually occur during the mid-semester time frame. This verbal review generally involves a structured discussion that gives students an opportunity to evaluate how much they have achieved and how much they still need to accomplish toward learning goals and objectives. A summary of these verbal evaluations should also be shared with faculty liaisons.

Each field instruction conference is viewed as an opportunity to evaluate achievements toward learning goals. Then the more formal verbal review conference can be seen as an opportunity to take stock of how much students have grown in their skills development and what they still need to accomplish to successfully meet field performance criteria. Through this process, students who start as passive learners are encouraged to exercise initiative in defining the direction of their learning and in taking responsibility for their learning. Likewise, students who are active learners are encouraged to become active evaluators of their own work.

We should have a date in mind for the mid-semester oral evaluation throughout the entire semester. As the date approaches, we can review the baseline data established in the initial learning plan discussed at the beginning of the field placement. The baseline includes what knowledge, skills, and values students brought to the learning situation, and what overall abilities and competencies they possess. Once the baseline is specified through the process of the educational assessment, it is then possible to evaluate how far students have come in achieving learning goals:

- What new skills have students acquired?

- What new knowledge have they incorporated?

- What professional values and ethics have they demonstrated?

- Where have students met expectations?

- Where is further progress needed?

These questions help students focus on areas to be discussed in more detail. In preparation for the verbal evaluation conference, we can review the student's written process recordings, logs and journals, case records, field conference notes, and agendas. If field instructor journals are kept, these also provide additional information useful to the task. These ongoing oral evaluations are important steps in our gatekeeping function, and any serious concerns about field performance need to be discussed with faculty liaisons as soon as possible. If difficulties persist in being able to talk to students about issues of concern, or if students have difficulty hearing issues of concern, the faculty liaison can serve as a useful resource or third party to facilitate this discussion and review.

The oral evaluation concludes by establishing new or expanded learning goals and objectives with students. This paves the way for the formal written evaluations due at the end of each semester in placement. Oral evaluations also lead to new or more challenging assignments, depending on student progress. These evaluations may also indicate changes needed in teaching approaches based on student learning needs. If oral evaluations are done well, students will have increased comfort with and confidence in the field evaluation process. They will understand the benefits of mutual feedback and will be prepared to give input on their final evaluations as active participants in the learning process.

Writing the Evaluation

Despite mutuality and collaboration in the evaluation process, we have overall responsibility for writing evaluations of our students. Students need ample time to read, digest, discuss, and give feedback on evaluations. Mutual feedback includes allowing students to voice their disagreement with the substance of a statement, or wording, or a given rating. Disagreements may also reflect miscommunication or deeper differences of opinions regarding field performance.

A formal evaluation conference set aside to review the final evaluation provides time to consider and make any suggested changes.

Formats of evaluations take on many different configurations. Gitterman and Gitterman (1979) suggest six principal areas for evaluations: (1) an introduction that describes the agency and student's assignments; (2) professional practice skills; (3) use of learning opportunities; (4) work management; (5) professional influence; and (6) a summary that characterizes the student's uniqueness, progress, and specific learning and practice directions. Evaluations may be unstructured, as when a social work program poses a series of open-ended questions, or they can be highly structured using specific criteria and rating scales, or they can consist of a combination of both. More and more social work education programs are using rating scales in their field evaluations.

For example, a 1st-year criterion for field performance that would be rated on a 5-point scale ranging from 0–5 may look like this:

	0	1	2	3	4	5
By the end of the 1st semester, student demonstrates an understanding of the NASW Code of Ethics and identification with the ethics of the profession.						

0 = no significant opportunity; 1 = unacceptable; 2 = needs improvement; 3= satisfactory; 4 = very good; 5 = outstanding

An example of a 2nd-year criterion for field performance that is rated on a 5-point scale is:

	0	1	2	3	4	5
By the end of the 4th semester, student demonstrates commitment to and application of the values and ethics of the profession in practice.						

See 1st-semester criterion above for point values.

Evaluations using rating scales usually provide space for commentary so that we can give examples of situations that have occurred in the placement and that point to specific responses made by students in meeting a criterion. It is these examples that make the criterion specific, real, and balanced, more than the actual number that is circled on the evaluation. Again, giving examples of how the student recognized ethical conflicts and struggled to arrive at solutions demonstrates the achievement of the above criterion.

Written end-of-semester evaluations normally consist of a series of responses to questions about established field performance criteria; are signed by both the field instructor and student; are submitted to field education programs; become an integral part of student records; and are the basis for field performance grades. They are generally viewed as summaries or recapitulations of what is already known about each student's field performance to date. All written field evaluations should be mailed to students' respective social work education program in a timely fashion. Timely submission of evaluations is important for several reasons. First, students benefit from the written feedback to tackle the next steps in the achievement of their learning goals. Next, field instruction grades cannot be submitted without the proper documentation. And finally, for graduating students, the timely submission of grades can determine their eligibility for licensure exams and employment.

Because the written word sometimes delivers a more powerful impact than either field instructors or students anticipate, students should not be presented with surprises in written evaluations, even if new learning needs are identified. This means that prior dialogue has occurred, and the written evaluations simply reflect prior discussions. The major difference between written and oral evaluations is that students see in writing what has been verbally discussed over time.

Written evaluations require the signatures of both field instructors and students, although a signature does not mean that both agree with everything stated in the evaluation. Some social work education programs generally ask students to write addenda to evaluations, and it is expected that field instructors see student comments before they are forwarded to field education departments. The ongoing process of evaluation and feedback should provide students with the opportunity to seek clarification regarding field instructors' evaluative comments. However, it can happen that in the final writing of the evaluation a field instructor sees the total picture differently, and decides that this must be reflected in the written evaluation. In these situations, the expectation that no surprises should be presented to the student in the final written evaluation still holds true. Field instructors need to patiently explain their thinking, and still give time for students to consider the comments and make any suggested modifications. In other situations, despite prior verbal discussions, students may react as if it is the first time they have heard the concern or critique. In these circumstances faculty liaisons are available for consultation or feedback. In most social work education programs, it is the liaison who actually grants the grade for the field performance, and he or she can offer consultation on the wording or handling of potentially complex or delicate situations.

In general, evaluations of field performance tend toward a "leniency bias," which refers to the fact that field instructors often rate students higher than students would rate themselves or than is demonstrated in their performance. Field instructors usually have no problems with identifying a student's strengths, describing "stars" or "neophytes" to the profession, or praising student accomplishments. Field instructors have more difficulty in critiquing students' work, especially when they seem unaware of their limitations. Approaching discussions of sensitive issues with students, such as student limitations and weaknesses, biases and value conflicts, rushes to judgment, resistance to learning, or personality conflicts, needs to be tackled in a straightforward manner. If there are extenuating circumstances that have affected students' experiences in the placement (illness, inadequate assignments, strikes, field instructor's leaving an agency, replacement of students, agency policy changes, etc.), these should also be discussed in the evaluation.

Another evaluation pitfall relates to field instructors' avoidance of putting in writing the full extent of the concerns about a student's performance. A discomfort with confronting students with a negative critique of their performance is often expressed as, "*I did not want to write this down. I am afraid of the student's reaction. It will only make my work with her more difficult*" or "*I didn't think I spent enough time addressing his grant-writing skills in field instruction, so I didn't feel it was fair to comment on his lack of skill in this area.*" Both comments reflect problems in seeing the written evaluation as an important tool in teaching. Both comments signal difficulties. One way to tackle these problems is to create a regular and recurrent time within field instruction conferences to review progress made or not made.

Summary of Suggestions for Reviewing and Constructing End-of-Semester Evaluations

- Three components of an evaluation include the "what," which describes and evaluates the skills; the "when," which describes and evaluates progress over time; and the "how," which describes student learning patterns and learning styles.

- In addition to being ongoing, evaluations are dynamic. We invite students to participate and take ownership of assessing their performance throughout the placement experience.

- Evaluations should be personal and individualized, identifying what is unique to students in the ways they approach practice and learning.

- They should be comprehensive but should also focus on specific areas of learning. Students' practice skills and patterns should be described, incorporating examples of assignments and other illustrations.

- Evaluations should be based on appropriate expectations that relate to the level of training and are within the context of placement opportunities and constraints.

- Oral evaluation notes, educational assessments, student recordings, or learning contracts should be used for background and support.

- Agency descriptions and assignments should be brief and should focus on the specific context of practice that shapes learning assignments (i.e., short-term crisis intervention with runaway youth that requires collaboration with a variety of service organizations and outreach services to families).

- Evaluations should always include goals for future learning for either student's next placement or job as a graduating social work practitioner.

- The final written evaluation builds on prior reviews and marks the end of each academic term in field instruction. It underscores a student's transition from one stage to another. It culminates each respective term's learning and, therefore, does not present new information or critiques that have not already been discussed with students.

- Even if a final evaluation form is predominantly objectified through the use of rating scales of performance, a written section of comments or summaries provides evidence and valuable feedback that furthers the work ahead.

Chapter 9

PROFESSIONAL ETHICS AND VALUES

*I*n addition to didactic learning about ethics either through a separate course or integrated approach, students learn ethical behavior through observing their teachers. (Congress, 2002, p. 153)

Teaching about professional ethics and values is central to field instruction, since ethics and values guide our everyday practice (Congress, 1999; Linzer, 1999; Lowenberg, Dolgoff, & Harrington, 2000; Matthews, Weinger, & Wijnberg, 1997), and it is a given that ethical dilemmas will arise in practice. Students are often introduced to professional ethics in orientation programs and through classroom discussions, and thus, ethics surfaces as a topic for discussion from the very beginning and throughout their education. The Council on Social Work Education (CSWE) has included Values and Ethics as the first foundation content area in its *Educational Policy and Accreditation Standards*. "The educational experience provides students with the opportunity to be aware of personal values; develop, demonstrate, and promote the values of the profession; and analyze ethical dilemmas and the ways in which these affect practice, services, and clients" (CSWE, 2001, p. 10).

As field instructors, we are in the best position to teach students about these core ethical concepts by framing ethical dilemmas as issues or conflicts that arise between:

personal and professional values;

professional social work colleagues;

students and clients;

students and particular agency philosophies or policies; and even

field instructors and students.

We model how to handle ethical content and conflicts in practice. As teachers, we provide non-judgmental, reflective forums for discussions of ethics and values in field instruction conferences, and we help students frame how to deal with ethical dilemmas honestly and directly. "As part of social work education students learn the importance of using supervision when faced with serious ethical dilemmas" (Congress, 2002, p. 154). We cannot expect students to learn professional ethics and values automatically. If a student exhibits inappropriate behaviors such as judgmental remarks or violations of confidentiality, we might move too quickly to our gatekeeping function and rush to remove a student from the placement before considering whether we taught the expected behaviors in a clear, deliberate, and precise manner. It is a question of whether the student's behavior is a reflection of lack of knowledge and experience or whether it is a reflection of a serious inability to function as a professional social worker (Berger, Thornton, & Cochrane, 1993). Discussions of ethics are also important in reinforcing the common base of values and ethics in the profession that permeate different practice methods. This is particularly important in light of the ethical dilemmas posed by the challenges to social work practice today, such as the expectations of managed care providers that might conflict with our commitment to clients (Brooks & Riley, 1996; Strom-Gottfried & Corcoran, 1998). Attention to professional ethics is core-curriculum content in the foundation year, and the expectation is that more advanced attention to ethics is included in the 2nd-year curriculum or year of specialization. Professional ethics are included as specific goals and objectives in field performance evaluations of students, and an appreciation of ethics and values is seen as essential to professional development.

The National Association of Social Workers Code of Ethics

Field instructors are encouraged to use the National Association of Social Workers (NASW, 1999) Code of Ethics in all discussions about professional ethics. Most social work education programs include the Code of Ethics in student handbooks as well as in field instruction manuals, or the Code can be accessed directly by going to www.naswdc.org. Students are generally informed that they will be held to the standards of professional behavior outlined in the Code. We should read the Code of Ethics with students and have some initial discussions of any questions or issues that are brought up by the profession's values, principles, and standards that may apply specifically to the setting and population of the field placement. Students are generally willing and able to identify with and uphold fundamental professional values like respect for the individual, right to confidentiality, and right to self-determination. It is the ethical dilemmas that arise from conflicting values that are much more difficult to deal with. The Code of Ethics contains standards for social workers in six principal categories that outline the social worker's responsibilities: (1) to clients; (2) to colleagues; (3) in practice settings; (4) as professionals; (5) to the social work profession; and (6) to society. For the first time, the Code of Ethics adopted in 1996 made specific mention of supervision and consultation, education and training, and performance evaluation (see Standard 3 in the Code).

There are a number of ways that ethical issues emerge in field instruction. One of the first things students ask us is, "What do I call myself?" Section 3.02c of the Code states we "should take reasonable steps to ensure that clients are routinely informed when services are being provided by students." This ethical standard is an opportunity for us to discuss how students should introduce themselves, and to raise the ethical responsibility of students, field instructors, and agencies to accurately inform clients exactly who is providing services. "Secrecy regarding student status and its lack of congruence with social work values creates dissonance within the social work curriculum and in the formation of professional identity for the student" (Miller & Rodwell, 1997, p. 73).

Section 3.01a of the Code states supervisors and consultants "should have the necessary knowledge and skill to supervise or consult appropriately and should do so only within their areas of knowledge and competence." We need to interpret the meaning of this standard for ourselves and our students. New field instructors may read too much into this standard fearing that they do not know enough to teach to a student's practice method or to meet a student's learning needs. We need to remember that we do have expertise and knowledge gained from education and years of practice. Yet, we should also avail ourselves of opportunities to expand our knowledge and skills as professionals. Social work education programs are additional sources of support, and faculty liaisons are equipped to help us in our role as teachers of social work students.

The Code mentions the evaluative role of field instructors and supervisors and exhorts us to "fulfill such responsibilities in a fair and considerate manner and on the basis of clearly stated criteria" (Code 3.03). We can use this standard to introduce the topic of field evaluations, preparing students for what to expect from the evaluation process, what the social work education program's criteria are for their field performance, and what their role is in field performance evaluations.

Over and above these supervisory standards, ethical content should be integrated and infused throughout the course of field instruction. After we have read the Code, we can begin to consider the most common ethical issues that arise in practice within our particular settings. Pre-planned situations or scenarios between students and clients may be used initially to stimulate discussion (a few examples of these are included at the end of this chapter). But gradually, teaching points about professional ethics emerge from students' practice experiences in the agency and with clients.

Social workers operate from a common base of social work practice, and there are core values that inform service delivery, helping relationships, and all practice methods. The preamble to the Code outlines these core values as service, social justice, dignity and worth of the person, importance of human relationships, integrity, and competence. Discussions about the meaning of these values and what kinds of ethical dilemmas students can expect to see in their work with clients aids integration of these ethical values and principles. Some common ethical themes that emerge in the course of field instruction include conflicts of interest, confidentiality, and dual relationships and boundary issues. Process recordings often bring to light such issues.

Conflicts of Interest

A 45-year-old African American student is working with a 30-year-old Hispanic mother of a 10-year-old boy and 8-year-old girl who have been in foster care for almost 6 months because of their mother's substance abuse problems and neglect of the children. The mother wants her children returned to her care and plans for her mother to come here from the Dominican Republic to help her care for the children. However, she has not been able to follow through with this plan nor has she followed through with any drug treatment, and she has failed to keep several visitation appointments. The agency is demanding that a permanent plan be made for the children. Because they cannot be returned to their mother, they should be placed for adoption.

This is an example of "the diversity of value systems which enter into work with clients and the impact of these competing values on ethical-decision making" (Congress, 1993, p. 27). In discussing this example, we need to support development of the student's awareness of personal values about single mothers of color, substance abuse, and child neglect. This can be contrasted with professional social work values that emphasize self-determination of clients, and agency values that focus on administering social policies and procedures. The safety of the children is a paramount consideration. Furthermore, the student and client are both women of color, and they have similar and different cultural values and ethnic/racial life experiences. We can also use this example to demonstrate how conflicting values inevitably occur among personal, societal, cultural, and professional values, and how these converge in the real world of social work practice.

When teaching about professional ethics and values, we often focus on the relationship between personal and professional values and their impact on practice (Black, Hartley, Whelley, & Kirk-Sharp, 1989). Adult learners come to social work education with a range of ethnic, racial, class, and regional backgrounds as well as varying sexual orientations, ages, and religious beliefs that may be challenged by the professional code of behavior. Social work students may come from other careers or have degrees in other fields such as nursing or business where they have inculcated different perspectives on professional values and behaviors. Conflicts can easily arise as a result of enthusiasm and idealism, biases, and differing world views, or when personal values clash head-on with stated professional values such as in the case of "pro-choice" versus "pro-life" points of view.

The diversity among fields of practice and social work roles and functions in hospitals, schools, mental health clinics, or for-profit settings complicates students' perceptions of professional ethics. Multiple role strains related to employment, family, and school can put students under enormous stress to perform efficiently and effectively in all spheres of life and erode their capacity or time for reflection on value conflicts. We begin discussions on ethics by giving students permission to raise concerns about conflicting values and beliefs, and letting students know that together we will try to figure out the most appropriate stance in a given situation.

One such example involves a 2nd-year student—a former police officer who was placed in an agency that provides advocacy and support services regarding employment discrimination and rights of immigrants and migrant workers.

Following September 11, 2001, this student experienced a conflict in allegiances—commitment to civil protection and loyalty to ex-colleagues who had lost their lives in the World Trade Center versus loyalty to his current placement, which was attempting to advocate for more lenient policies for immigrants in an immediate post-9/11 atmosphere of fear. His assignment involved facilitation of a committee discussion regarding protection of immigrants against discrimination and possible community responses to a burgeoning problem of intolerance. In supervision the anticipated obstacles identified were how to manage the range of opinions and attitudes so that a balanced discussion and basis for decision making might ensue. The student did not believe he could hold a balance. He expressed the strength of his feelings regarding the need for a tightening of protocols dealing with immigrants following the recent terrorist attacks. His field instructor did not attempt to eradicate the student's conflict, nor did he question whether this student might be better placed elsewhere. The student was praised for his honesty, and the situation was seen as an opportunity to work with the realities of this issue. Given that the student's values were also a reflection of societal values that would be represented within the committee discussion, the issue was translated as a practice dilemma that the student and field instructor examined together in terms of the skills and tools that this situation might require. The student was supported in this exploration, and next steps were devised to enable the student to feel able to take on this task.

We can help students anticipate potential value conflicts or conflicts of interest (Code 1.06). These may occur between agency-based professionals around such things as case planning or disagreements between agency policies and the needs of clients. They may occur between students and the agency around disclosure of a student's status, or between students and clients involving judgmental behaviors or issues of self-determination (Code 1.02) and informed consent (Code 1.03). Value conflicts may even occur between students and ourselves if there are blurred boundaries from either socializing outside the placement situation or when we fall into a counseling role with students. It is helpful if we discuss value conflicts with students before they occur and support students in confronting them when they do occur. However, some conflicts seem to arise out of nowhere. It is precisely the nature of "being taken off guard" that makes ethical dilemmas difficult issues to deal with. An example is a field instructor who is committed to providing home visits to the population being served but is shocked when a student takes a stand against doing home visits. A teaching point in terms of service delivery and ways of reaching out to clients quickly becomes a conflict rooted in the values of service, social justice, and dignity and worth of the person. If it is not recognized as a professional issue for discussion, the conflict may be translated into "this student cannot remain in this placement because of refusal to participate in home visits." Only through the discussion of this potential conflict of personal values and the values of the profession can any resolution, plan, or compromise be reached.

Confidentiality

Students need to learn about the relationship between the law of privilege (the client's right to confidentiality) and the ethics of confidentiality (our ethical commitment to confidentiality). This helps them answer the question, "What do I tell clients about confidentiality?" (Kagle, 1991). Privacy and confidentiality are given extensive attention in the Code of Ethics under Standard 1.07. Confidentiality is usually introduced at the beginning of field instruction when students are informed about the importance of maintaining confidential records of all case materials. Classroom and field educators generally emphasize the need to disguise case materials when writing papers or process recordings or when making case presentations that involve real clients and their life situations. Confidentiality between field instructors and students or among students placed in the same agency should also be stressed. For example, we need to be clear about what information we will share with faculty liaisons or our own supervisors regarding what takes place in field instruction. Students, in turn, need to consider what field instruction material or client information they will share with others for professional purposes versus casual discussion. As future licensed practitioners, students need to be made aware of their rights and responsibilities under the laws of the state in which they practice. The laws are generally very specific about the limitations on confidentiality.

Students quickly learn that confidentiality cannot always be promised or maintained. "It may be discouraging for students to discover that answers are not always clear and ethical dilemmas frequently arise in deciding when confidentiality should be breached" (Congress, 2002, p. 154). We need to stress that protecting clients is the major goal underlying confidentiality. However, there is no such a thing as absolute confidentiality, and in this modern technological age, there are many real limitations on confidentiality that make this a difficult value to uphold in practice.

Upholding confidentiality may conflict with state and agency policies that require disclosure of client information for a variety of reasons. The NASW Model Licensing Act of 1973 indicates four exceptions to confidentiality: (1) the client or someone acting on the client's behalf, waives privilege, giving written consent for disclosure; (2) the client brings charges against the social worker; (3) the client reveals in confidence the contemplation of a crime or harmful act; and (4) the client is a minor who may have been the victim of a crime (Kagle, 1991, p. 56). Social workers are obligated to prevent harm to clients or others such as in cases of child abuse, suicide, or homicide. Students frequently feel inept in assessing suicidal risk or conflicted when reporting child abuse incidents. This is understandable. Agency and professional guidelines are not always well defined or clear regarding the protocols for such situations. It is incumbent upon us to explain agency policies in such cases, to prepare students for what may or may not occur in the field placement agency, what should or should not be kept confidential in case situations, and what to do when confronted with such situations. A typical example arises when a student learns of a potentially harmful situation reported by a parent, but does not recognize it as a reportable incident to child protective services. Upon disclosing the information to us, the student's failure to see the seriousness of the situation and its implications may be viewed as a deficit or lack of professional behavior or as an indication of overidentification with the parent. Of course, it may indicate these possibilities, but it also indicates a need to educate the student on the importance of value judgments beyond the facts and protocols of reporting regulations.

The current climate of brief therapies and third-party accountability policies has confronted practitioners with many dilemmas in relation to service delivery. The Code of Ethics advises social workers to inform clients of the requirements of third-party payers (Congress, 2002) such as:

- Discussing with clients the extent of the knowledge that will be conveyed to managed care companies;

- Making clients aware that they will need to waive their privilege of confidentiality;

- Sharing with clients the reports that will be forwarded to insurance companies; and

- Asking clients to sign releases for reports to be shared with third-party payers.

It is not uncommon for social workers to find themselves in a conflict-of-interest situation when they wish to advocate for client needs, but are confronted with funding policies and programs that seem to deny clients a continuum of care. We should not shield students from these realities of practice, but rather, we should help them think about ways to provide care under existing agency policies while simultaneously becoming advocates for change on behalf of clients. The Code includes a statement of the social worker's role in social and political action under Standard 6.04, which is the last standard in the Code. As agency-based practitioners, students need to learn how to provide quality services within professional guidelines while maintaining their commitments to the agency (Code 3.09) without jeopardizing the financial base of service delivery. Students also need to identify gaps in agency services that fail to meet client needs. These are tough issues for us to teach and for students to learn.

HIPAA Privacy Rules

An important and timely example of new measures to protect client confidentiality can be found in the Health Insurance Portability and Accountability Act (HIPAA). HIPAA privacy rules, enacted on April 14, 2003, affect all social workers and aspects of field instruction. Field instructors and students need clarification on whether there are any agency policies regarding HIPAA that affect student learning practices, such as policies around review of agency records, or field instruction recordings, or removing records and recordings from agencies.

These federal privacy regulations refer to the use and disclosure of individually identifiable health information ("Protected Health Information" or

"PHI") by "Covered Entities," which are health plans, health care clearing-houses, and health care providers that transmit health information in electronic form in connection with HIPAA standard transactions (e.g., billing or claims eligibility determinations). HIPAA prohibits Covered Entities from using or disclosing PHI, and thus may even include information collected by a social service agency or counseling program if the agency or program is a Covered Entity, except as authorized by the patient/client, or as permitted or required by the regulations. The privacy regulations provide a de-identification "safe harbor" that requires agencies to remove a list of 18 specific identifiers, namely birth dates, treatment dates, and addresses.

Student Research Projects

HIPAA regulations also affect students conducting research in agencies. Students are required to sign a limited-data use agreement in which the researcher pledges, among other things, not to try to re-identify the data and to use the data only for the designated research purposes. The Code includes a rather explicit statement on evaluation and research under Standard 5.02. Social workers who engage in research involving clients as human subjects must follow strict guidelines and protocols that are designed to protect clients. This entails gaining approval for such research from institutional regulatory bodies associated with the social work program or agency, but it also requires some discussion of the ethics behind such protocols and guidelines.

Dual Relationships and Boundaries

Professional social work has been remiss in directly addressing issues of "dual relationship" abuse within student-supervisory relationships. But such relationships, especially of a sexual nature, may lead to violations of confidentiality and objectivity, exploitation, psychological damage, and educational distortions. (Bonosky, 1995, p. 70)

Cautions against dual or multiple relationships are extensive throughout the Code of Ethics (see Standards 1.09, 1.10, 1.11). In the last few years, dual relationships and boundary issues have received serious attention in social work literature (Bonosky, 1995; Congress, 1996, 2000; Kagle & Giebelhausen, 1994).

The Code clearly states that "social workers who provide supervision or consultation are responsible for setting clear, appropriate, and culturally sensitive boundaries" (3.01b). The boundaries issue is an important one for us to uphold and model for students. A case in point is taken from an article on violations of the supervisory relationship (Jacobs, 1991):

> Sally's supervisor liked to tell Sally about her own cases during supervision. At first Sally enjoyed hearing about her supervisor's work, but gradually she began to get frustrated at not having enough time to review cases she had questions about during her supervision. When the supervisor began using the time to tell Sally about some problems she was having with her children, Sally became alarmed. She recognized that the supervisor was acting inappropriately but she wasn't sure how to address the issue. To complicate matters, the supervisor had also disclosed to Sally that she was a personal friend of Sally's faculty advisor for the placement. Sally was concerned that if she raised the matter with either instructor, the two of them would join forces against her and undermine her credibility. (p. 130)

This example demonstrates how students can feel vulnerable to the power of the field instructor, faculty liaison, and even classroom instructors. Although we are very clear about how to maintain professional boundaries with clients, we may not always be so clear about our field instruction roles and functions. Boundary violations within the field instructor/student relationship involve more subtle differences than boundary issues in clinical situations with clients. In chapter 1, we differentiated between teaching and treating students, however, field instructors becoming therapists of their students occurs more often than we wish to admit. We must guard our role as educators and avoid any pretense of inappropriateness such as becoming a friend, therapist, romantic or sexual partner, or employer of our students. Some of us, highly sensitive to power differentials, may overcompensate by abdicating our power and authority and establishing relationships with students based on rules of friendship or collegiality, or we may try to help students with personal problems rather than maintaining an educator stance. The worst case scenario are field instructors who engage in personal or sexual relationships with students.

> It may be argued that no student is able to enter into this relationship in a truly voluntary way because of the power faculty members [and field instructors] have over the students especially in the form of grades which affect students' academic progress and future career options. (Congress, 1996, p. 333)

First and foremost, field instructors "should not engage in any dual or multiple relationships with supervisee [students] in which there is a risk of exploitation of or potential harm to supervisee [students]" (Code 3.01c). Dual relationships with students, particularly as they pertain to educational policies on sexual harassment, are generally included in field instruction manuals. Refer to chapter 11, where teaching challenges are discussed in more detail and issues of sexual harassment are examined.

Field instructors are key figures in modeling for students the importance of avoiding dual relationships and maintaining professional boundaries at all times. "Discussing types of dual relationships and helping students discuss relevant dilemmas may strengthen their skills in deciding when dual relationships are appropriate and when they should be avoided" (Congress, 2002, p. 160). This also involves demonstrating how not to abuse power and authority by maintaining appropriate working relationships. We need to be aware of our own tendencies to use covert or overt power to control students or their behavior. Students are sensitive to their vulnerability in instructor/student relationships. The reality of being evaluated by field instructors places students at a felt disadvantage, or they feel dependent on our good wishes or integrity. Congress (1996, p. 336) poses six key questions to evaluate the possibility of dual relationships with students:

1. Does the dual relationship with the student involve assuming a role of sexual partner, friend, therapist, or employer?

2. Does the dual relationship exploit or have the potential of harming the student?

3. Does the dual relationship take undue advantage of the educator's greater power in the relationship?

4. Does the dual relationship have an impact on other students?

5. Is the dual relationship with a current or with a former student?

6. How do other colleagues view the dual relationship?

The following guidelines (Congress, 1994) are suggested for dealing with possible dual-relationship conflicts in field instruction.

• Clearly define the nature of dual relationships to students.

- Carefully examine with students the risk of exploitation or harm to vulnerable persons.

- Help students anticipate the possible consequences, positive and negative, of proceeding with a dual relationship.

- Address with colleagues and supervisors the prohibition against maintaining dual relationships.

- Teach that the responsibility of professional social workers is to avoid even the possibility of exploitation or harm of vulnerable persons, whether they are clients, supervisees, or students.

In Summary

As our society has developed and grown, the complexity of choices for professional social workers has increased. Although there are certain consistent ethical rules that are unquestionable, like not exploiting clients or not having sexual relationships with students, there remain vague areas and new situations that will arise in the course of a social worker's career. Many of these should be discussed in field instruction in order for students to become ethically competent practitioners. We should remind ourselves that, unless students "learn to examine themselves and what they really value, their command of ethical theories and their ability to think about ethics from diverse perspectives are not likely to bring them any closer to being willing and able to do the right thing" (Marino, 2004, p. B5).

Ethical Dilemmas Scenarios

The following ethical dilemmas in field instruction are presented as scenarios that may be used to stimulate reflection on these issues.

- You are having a party for your son's graduation and are inviting many of your colleagues from the agency. Do you invite your 2nd-year student? If yes, why? If no, why not?

- Your student presents you with an expensive gift at the end of the field placement. Do you accept the gift? If not, how do you handle this situation?

- A few weeks into the placement, your student discloses that he is gay and wonders if you are gay also. How do you respond?

- Your student is going through a painful divorce and custody battle and mentions it to you during a field instruction conference. How can you be helpful and supportive to the student? Would you encourage the discussion of your student's mental and emotional state around this situation? How do you maintain objective, professional boundaries and distance without appearing uncaring or indifferent?

- You and your student are both women of the same age, have the same number of children, are single parents, and are both African Americans. You sense that the student is eagerly trying to be your equal and looking for ways to make you a friend rather than deal with you as her field instructor. Your student is also avoiding responsibilities in the field placement and jokes when you request recordings or question work-management skills. How do you maintain a professional working relationship without appearing aloof or bossy?

The following ethical dilemmas in social work practice are presented as scenarios that field instructors might use with students.

- An adolescent client is having a graduation party and enthusiastically invites the social work student to attend. How do you help the student discuss the pros and cons of accepting or rejecting the invitation?

• A client presents the student with a rather expensive gift at the end of the field placement. How do you help the student handle this situation?

• A few weeks into the placement, your student asks you whether he can tell this one client that he is gay because he thinks it would help the client feel more comfortable in coming out to him? How do you respond?

• Your student is running a group for women dealing with domestic violence. She discloses to you that she, too, is a survivor of domestic violence. How can you be helpful and supportive to the student in dealing with the painful memories that the group evokes in her? Do you discourage the student from connecting her experiences with those of the women in her group? Or do you encourage the student to discuss her mental and emotional state at the time of the domestic violence as a way of helping her gain self-awareness?

• The student is female and her client is male. Both are of similar age, from similar middle-class backgrounds, and both are Italian Catholics. In process recordings, you sense that the student is trying to be overly objective and distant from her client and has established very rigid boundary lines. This behavior is strikingly different from how she works with other clients. Do you ask the student if she feels a physical attraction to the client or if she senses that the client is physically attracted to her? How do you help the student maintain a professional working relationship while allowing her to connect with the similar life experiences of the client?

Chapter 10

CULTURAL COMPETENCE AND DIVERSITY

*C*ultural competence does not come naturally to any social worker and requires a high level of professionalism and sophistication, yet how culturally competent practitioners are trained is not clear in professional education or practice. (Ortiz Hendricks, 2003, p. 75)

The development of culturally competent knowledge, skills, and values is critical for social workers, particularly given certain social, political, economic, and professional realities operating today. Among these realities are the changing population demographics, data on the underutilization of mental health services by clients of color, and the profession's most recent accreditation and ethical standards on diversity (CSWE, 2001; National Association of Social Workers [NASW], 2000; Yutrzenka, 1995). Over the last few decades, social science practitioners and researchers have generated guidelines on what is required for the development of cultural self-awareness and competence (NASW, 2000; Sue & Sue, 2003).

Cultural Competence Standards

In 2000 NASW established *Standards for Cultural Competence in Social Work Practice*, which were endorsed by the Council on Social Work Education in 2003. These 10 standards can be used to create goals and objectives for what needs to be taught and learned about cultural competence in field education.

Field instructors and students should review the standards and discuss how they can strive for cultural competence in their work.

Standard 1—Ethics and Values starts with our ethical obligation to be culturally competent practitioners as stated in the NASW Code of Ethics (1.05).

Standard 2—Self-Awareness refers to the widely held belief that self-awareness is the hallmark of cultural competence in social work practice (Harry, 1992). This standard suggests that in order to facilitate self-awareness in students, we need to develop and continue to nurture self-awareness of our own cultural backgrounds and identities.

Standard 3—Cross-Cultural Knowledge speaks to the specialized knowledge that we need to acquire and continue to develop in order to understand the history, traditions, values, family systems, and artistic expressions of the client groups we serve.

Standard 4—Cross-Cultural Skills addresses the need to use appropriate methodological approaches, skills, and techniques with clients that reflect an understanding of the role of culture in the helping process.

Standard 5—Service Delivery encourages us to be knowledgeable about and skillful in the use of services available in the community and broader society in order to make appropriate referrals for diverse client populations.

Standard 6—Empowerment and Advocacy charges us with the responsibility to advocate for and empower clients, and to be knowledgeable about the effects of social policies and programs on different client populations.

Standard 7—Diverse Workplace requires us to recruit and hire diverse workers in programs and agencies to ensure diversity within the profession.

Standard 8—Professional Education holds social work programs responsible for the education and training of culturally competent practitioners.

Standard 9—Language Diversity emphasizes the importance of speaking the language of our clients and that this is a special skill that should be recognized and compensated by employers.

Standard 10—Cross-Cultural Leadership promotes our role as cultural competence leaders both within and outside the profession.

Cultural Self-Awareness

A broad definition of cultural self-awareness includes an appreciation of the following factors:

- Our own values, beliefs, attitudes, behaviors, biases, prejudices, knowledge paradigms, and how these may differ across worldview and value orientations

- Differences within broad categories of diversity and differences among and within groups. For example, Hispanic/Latino or Asian American encompasses a variety of different nationalities, social classes, histories, immigration experiences, and geographic locations

- The many dimensions of diversity including race, skin color, ethnicity, gender, sexual orientation, religious or spiritual beliefs, social class and status, age, different physical or mental abilities, language, national origin, and geographic locations

- Issues of power and privilege and the complexity and interchangeability of these statuses

- The impact of historical trauma, oppression, dominance, and exploitation on human development and mental health

- Identity development issues, including stages of racial identity formation, sexual orientation identity, and gender expression

- Multiple status integration and intersectional identity issues (i.e., biracial young adults struggling to solidify their gay identity), or growing into or maturing as a way of coming to understand one's racial identity and gender identity. The challenge for each of us is to be cognizant of individual features of diversity while understanding the multifaceted and intersectional nature of these factors.

- Cultural awareness in social work practice across methods including clinical work, administration, program development, policy analysis and advocacy, and community organizing

- Culture as part of personality development and mental health and not just an economic, social, or political variable

- The impact of the "isms" like racism, sexism, and heterosexism (Latting, 1990) on the beneficiaries as well as the victims or survivors of these unequal power systems

Achieving Cultural Competence

Achieving cultural competence is an ongoing, lifelong process for all social workers, and field education serves as the perfect laboratory for the development and enhancement of culturally competent professionals. Although cultural competence in field instruction is presented as a separate chapter, it is assumed that discussions of diversity are infused throughout field instruction and are integral to all teaching and practice efforts. "Instructors need to demonstrate the belief that differences are normal, healthy and useful in the educational process; instructors should reach for them and encourage their expression" (Raphael & Rosenblum, 1989, p. 116). The goal for us as field instructors is to model the integration of cultural competence content throughout the field placement.

When talking about cultural self-awareness, sensitivity, and competence, we need to include a number of significant factors such as the capacity to develop authentic relationships with persons who are culturally very similar or different from ourselves; the ability to understand the daily experience of people whose realities are different from our own; an appreciation of the social, political, organizational, and economic arrangements that maintain racism, oppression, internalized oppression, dominance, and privilege in our society; and the emotional, psychological, and mental health cost of internalized dominance and privilege. Cultural competence also requires us to understand how all these experiences are rooted in a historical context, and how each moment in social work practice is shaped by that history. These considerations are experienced differently by people based on their life experiences and their capacity to understand the content. Therefore, developing cultural competence is more about the capacity to listen, hear, and understand than about specific information that is being taught or delivered. Understanding the experiences of the "other" has a crucial impact on our interactions with client systems and communities. A commitment to continuing education in this area is strongly recommended for the ongoing development of cultural competence in social work practice, field education, and supervision.

Identity theory, including racial and sexual orientation identity (Helms, 1990; Sue & Sue, 2003), is key in developing an understanding of these complex levels of worldviews. Racial identity theory aids our ability to recognize what is involved in being authentic in cross-racial relationships. For example, early stages of White racial identity correlate with feelings of anxiety and discomfort or anger and fear in interactions with people of color, or feelings of guilt and shame manifest in behaviors and attitudes of "wanting to help those poor victims," which translates into "helping them be more like us." Early stages of identity in people of color imply an overidealization and identification with the dominant culture and may cause conflicts with other people of color who are at more advanced stages in their development.

In summary, cultural competence is more than just the development of cultural self-awareness and sensitivity to biases and stereotypes. It implies more than just being aware of our values, attitudes, and worldview perspectives. Cultural competence requires an understanding of within- and between-group differences, identity development, power and privilege statuses, and the experience of multiple statuses. It presupposes an understanding of how these factors influence all stages of micro- and macro-level practice (Franks, Hess, Sheiman, Walters, & Wheeler, 1999). Awareness also extends to an understanding of specific cultural dimensions as part of personality and human development (Carter, 1995), and an understanding of the consequences of racism (Jones, 1997) and other forms of oppression and dominance on the beneficiaries as well as on the victims of these systems (Bowser & Hunt, 1996).

Basic Assumptions on Teaching Culturally Competent Practice

- People need to feel predominantly positive about their cultural identity and group connectedness, although some ambivalence is natural.

- Clarity about values, including value conflicts, enhances one's functioning.

- Distortion and bias take on greater significance when they are used to justify power arrangements that oppress and exploit others.

- Power touches all levels of functioning for both the oppressed and the privileged. Because of their student status, students may experience oppression and feel powerless, but they also find it more difficult to discuss their power and privilege.

- Social workers must transcend distortions and biases, because they are destructive to effective work with clients and they undermine the values and goals of service delivery and the profession.

• Transcending distortions and biases involves a search for solutions on a societal and interpersonal basis.

• We should understand the distortions and preconceptions that are internalized, their etiology, and the purposes they serve. We also have a responsibility to change these and the societal structures they justify.

• A relationship in which there is trust and support enables the self-examination necessary to clarify one's values, to confront racial and other cultural biases, and to appreciate the costs to benefactors and victims of bias.

• Emotional growth occurs via self-confrontation. Conflict, if managed with sensitivity and respect, will enhance growth.

• Understanding one's power (feelings and experiences as persons of power and non-power) deepens the understanding of the self in the social context and offers an opportunity to avoid embracing power for destructive or selfish purposes.

• Students need us to support their reflection on generalities and specifics, sameness, and difference to encourage their critical analysis of these issues. This forces us to think in terms of relativity and variability and protects against tendencies to use concrete thinking to generalize or to oversimplify complex diversity issues.

• This experience helps students see others, especially clients, in multiple ways and free from personal biases and assumptions (Pinderhughes, 1989).

Teaching Cultural Competence in Field Education

Diversity in social work practice requires infusion of this content throughout the placement experience for students, and creating opportunities for discussions of differences and similarities arising between students and clients, students and agency staff, and students and field instructors. There are many teaching moments around diversity. For example, process recordings are full of illustrations of potential value conflicts arising from differences or similarities in gender and sexual orientation, race and ethnicity, social class and status, age and abilities, or religious and spiritual beliefs. Highlighting the range of client systems or communities that characterize the field placement is a straightforward way to orient students to diversity and to make it clear from the beginning of the placement that this is an appropriate issue for discussion.

Inquiring about how the social work education program acquaints students to this material facilitates integration of diversity content and brings these experiences into the realm of field instruction. For example, some programs provide students with sensitivity training at orientation; others have ongoing diversity-training programs, or the content is deliberately interwoven throughout the curriculum. Knowing how a student is exposed to and is assimilating this material supports our role in teaching about diversity. We can build on these curriculum efforts by using some of the same exercises, readings, and content in field instruction to ensure continuity in student learning.

An initial consideration toward culturally competent field education is creating a climate where cultural differences and similarities are discussed openly and freely and viewed as a normal and regular part of the field instruction agenda. The development of trust will be hampered if students feel that they need to leave these issues or parts of themselves "at the door." Bringing such issues as cultural experiences, racism, sexual orientation, or social class into the room helps to build a relationship on which openness and trust can emerge, and the ability to think through diversity dilemmas can occur more naturally.

Additionally, it is important to encourage that diversity issues be included regularly on students' agendas, in their process recordings and reflective journals and in both oral and written evaluations. The educational assessment and learning plan discussed in chapter 7 specifically asks questions that force us to describe and assess differences and similarities that exist between students and us, or with clients and agency staff. We are asked how these factors influence the teacher/learner relationship and how we teach students to understand diversity in the field placement. A study of field instructors' responses to this question (Marshack, Ortiz Hendricks, & Gladstein, 1994) noted that field instructors were adept at describing diversity factors, but hesitant to discuss how they would teach about diversity. Emphasizing the importance of diversity as integral to practice is essential to the field performance evaluation process. It provides a path to monitoring and assessing students' abilities to integrate this material into their practice.

Finally, we help students handle the difficult and often uncomfortable feelings stirred up by diversity discussions by acknowledging that these feelings are normal given the history of social oppression and dominance in this country and the taboo against talking about such issues as race and sexual orientation. We need to develop the ability to help students manage the feelings, anxieties, fears, and projections that emerge in such discussions and not to hide or resist these discussions as a way of avoiding the feelings of discomfort. In this way, we model how to create a climate for such discussions with clients. Differences are merely differences and should not connote "better than" or "less than," but simply "different from."

Power Dynamics and Diversity in Field Education

> Attention only to similarities without attention to differences reinforces the orientation that all people are the same and invites ignoring or denial of difference. Attention only to difference without attention to similarities reinforces distancing, separation, and barriers between people. (Pinderhughes, 1989, p. 27)

The reluctance of students to admit to the power they have, the defenses they erect to avoid this knowledge, the pain that is embodied in unequal power relationships, the compulsion to defend against it, and the problematic behaviors that are used to maintain defenses are all issues that make it difficult to understand and manage the power dynamics in cross-cultural encounters. We need to help students to become more aware of the resistance, withholding behavior, tension, and dissatisfaction generated by diversity by identifying and naming the resistance in a non-judgmental manner. We achieve this by sensitively confronting students with their resistance and natural defenses. We can create safety and trust by sharing our own experiences and giving examples of how we have dealt with issues of power and differences and similarities encountered in practice.

If students retreat to intellectualization or to tangential material, we can best handle this in a respectful but firm manner that steers the discussion back to the emotional plane. Persons who are unclear, ambivalent, in conflict, or predominantly negative about their cultural background may attempt to protect themselves from the discomfort mobilized by the effort to answer the questions placed before them. Recognition of one's bias can stir up feelings of disappointment, embarrassment, guilt, and helplessness. People fear rejection and loss of status as a result of showing vulnerability or making statements that may be considered offensive. Commenting on the strength that is demonstrated in honestly confronting oneself and risking vulnerability can result in increased freedom and comfort in discussing these issues. Expressions of anger are a necessary step for some students before they can begin to listen to others and look at themselves. Anger and projection might indicate movement among the continuum of racial identity development. We should not lose sight of the fact that it is only in an atmosphere of safety that people attempt to examine, understand, and master biases.

Power, or lack of power, exists for everyone in varying degrees and on varying levels. Understanding the degrees of power, its nuances, and how it differs or is the same for individuals, including oneself, can help practitioners become aware of their own power. The power they possess as a product of their roles as group worker, caseworker, community organizer, and administrator must be used effectively and not abused (McRoy, Freeman, Logan, & Blackmon, 1986).

Ortiz Hendricks (2003) developed a five-stage model for the development of culturally competent social work practice.

Table 4.

The Five Stages of Learning and Teaching Cultural Competence in the Practice of Social Work

Stage I	I am so embarrassed. I am afraid of saying the wrong thing.	Cultural self-awareness
Stage II	I jump in for better or worse and hope for the best.	Cultural sensitivity
Stage III	Somehow, what I do works. I handle diversity encounters quite well, but I cannot explain why.	Beginning cultural competence
Stage IV	I understand what I am doing and use a range of culturally competent knowledge, skills, and values.	Relative mastery of cultural competence
Stage V	I can teach others to be culturally competent practitioners or supervisors.	Teacher/learner of cultural competence

The five stages are based on Reynolds's (1985) framework for learning and teaching social work practice described in chapter 4. They demonstrate the progression from cultural self-awareness to the ability to teach someone how to be culturally competent. They are fluid stages, visited frequently, in a fluid life-long search for culturally competent social work practice.

This model has many strengths: (1) it recognizes the need for conscious attention to new or diverse experiences encountered in everyday practice; (2) it helps social workers evaluate how far they have come and how much they still need to accomplish to become more culturally competent; (3) it provides a safe perspective from which workers and supervisors can question and assess their individual cultural competence; and (4) it acknowledges that cultural competence requires stage-specific developmental steps for any success or relative mastery. Supervisors can utilize the framework to challenge workers at various levels of cultural competence, noting the stumbling blocks along the way, and being supportive of each worker's natural right of passage through these stages on the way to mastery of culturally competent knowledge and skills. (Ortiz Hendricks, 2003, p. 76)

Introducing Cultural Competence Discussions With Students

- Initiate dialogue regarding the meaning of diversity, attitudes about others, and the psychological benefits of maintaining cultural biases

- Neutralize the anxiety that is mobilized in interactions with culturally different or similar others

- Aid our understanding of our students' cultural backgrounds and support the development of their awareness of their culture

- Foster change toward more effective cross-cultural interactions

- Provide an experience for unraveling the multifaceted complexities involved in culturally competent practice

- Teach students how cultural identity and issues of power and powerlessness influence the various levels of human functioning, including the worker/client relationship

- Clarify how students' behaviors affect service delivery

Ways to Achieve
Cultural Competence Objectives

• Facilitate exploration of feelings, perceptions, and experiences of diversity factors presented by the client populations students are working with, such as issues of race or religion.

• Support identification of predispositions and biases and explore the origin of these feelings and perceptions that influence students' behavior with culturally different or similar others.

• Assign work that provides direct experience with, not just intellectual understanding of, the differences and similarities between students and others to increase appreciation of the importance of cultural identity, respect for differences in people, and to increase comfort in cross-cultural interactions.

• Foster new ways of thinking and behaving through the development of critical analysis of these situations.

• Support students in their assumption of responsibility for their values and biases on both an interpersonal and societal basis.

In the final section of this chapter, the authors offer some specific tools to help us with discussions of diversity. First there is the "Cultural Self-identity Interview," which can be used by field instructors with students or in small-group discussions. Next, there is a discussion followed by a series of questions to help us evaluate the experiences of gay, lesbian, bisexual, or transgender students. And finally, we offer a series of five "diversity scenarios" designed to trigger and stimulate field instruction discussions of diversity.

A Cultural Self-Identity Interview

The Cultural Self-identity Interview can guide the cultural self-examination process that we all must go through. For individual reflection or small-group discussion, review the following questions and reflect on how you would answer them.

1. What is your cultural heritage? Include as many dimensions of your

cultural heritage as possible, i.e., multiple generations, races, ethnicities, social classes, religions, sexual orientations, languages spoken, disabilities, national or regional affiliations, etc. Organize this information on a genogram or family tree.

2. What were the values, norms, beliefs, and behaviors that you grew up with? What were your family of origin's structure and norms of behavior? What was the approach to child rearing, and how were you disciplined? Were there other relatives around during your childhood? What role did your grandparents play in your family of origin?

3. What is your primary cultural group identity at this stage of your life? How do you identify? Include as many dimensions as possible in your identity, e.g., generation, gender, races, ethnicities, social class, religions, sexual orientations, languages spoken, disabilities, etc.

4. When did you first become aware of yourself as different and unique from "others"?

5. Which dimensions of your cultural identity are the most affirming and empowering aspects of your identity and why? What do you like most about your cultural heritage?

6. Which dimensions of your cultural identity are the most troublesome and difficult to manage and why? Are there any painful experiences associated with your cultural heritage that continue to affect your cultural identity today?

7. Have you ever tried to deny or reject any dimension of your cultural identity and why? Which dimensions of your cultural identity do you think "need work" and why?

8. What generalizations do people make about you that reflect their misinformation about some aspect of your cultural group identity? What would you like to teach people not of your cultural group about your cultural heritage and identity?

9. Which dimensions of your cultural identity are most helpful and least helpful to you as a social worker?

Gay, Lesbian, Bisexual, Transgender (GLBT) Students

Significant questions and issues arise in field instruction around how best to work with GLBT students in a social agency. These often come from discomfort or lack of experience in knowing how to manage the unique concerns faced by GLBT students in placement settings. The following are some recommendations for working effectively and sensitively with students who are "coming out" or being "outed" in an agency.

As with all issues of prejudice, discrimination, and bias, it is appropriate and necessary for us to take a proactive role with our students in reducing racism, sexism, heterosexism, or other "isms" in the placement setting. With a GLBT student, we need to identify and position ourselves as student allies and create a safe space for them to express their concerns. This means taking an active role in intervening around homophobic statements or behaviors exhibited by staff members. Homophobia can be effectively reduced or eliminated when heterosexual people challenge and correct misinformation about homosexuality. An example of this may relate to staff reactions to a student's chosen gender expression in the form of dress or mannerisms. Although a delicate issue, even this can be handled in a straightforward and affirming manner by advocating on the student's behalf when behaviors or dress are within acceptable professional boundaries. Furthermore, GLBT students should not be put in the position of being spokespersons for all gay people, particularly if they feel unsupported and alone in the agency. This is similar to Latino, Asian, or African American students who are expected to speak for all ethnic communities encompassed by these broad ethnic categories.

Being "out" or freely identifying as gay or lesbian on the job is professionally acceptable, even though societal pressures continue to prohibit open discussions of bisexuality or transgender issues. It is also professional not to disclose one's sexual orientation. Students can be helped to discuss their sexual identity and experiences with homophobia as these pertain to effective service delivery and functioning within an agency. It is particularly helpful to students to experience a supportive environment and to receive accurate information about the agency in order to make informed choices about the nature and extent of disclosure/nondisclosure they may wish to make about their sexual orientation. For example, if students choose to disclose their sexual orientation, it is appropriate for us to discuss the issue with a focus on the "work" and how disclosure of one's sexual orientation may affect clients. Sexual orientation is like any other issue of difference or similarity that may affect a social worker's role and function with clients.

If we initiate the discussion of sexual orientation, it is important to accept that students may not feel safe to discuss the issue and may first need time to build trust in the field instruction relationship. Open communication and support are vital when dealing with differences and similarities, especially because GLBT persons often face silence. Openness and a willingness to learn—as well as to teach—are basic to good practice and good field instruction.

Discussion Questions for Field Instructors on GLBT Issues in Field Education

Have you ever worked with a student/worker who self-disclosed his or her sexual orientation at the agency? Yes ___ No ___
If yes, to whom did he or she self-disclose? Check all that apply:
___You
___Another field instructor or supervisor
___The educational coordinator of your agency
___Another social worker or professional in the agency
___The faculty advisor
___A nonprofessional staff member of the agency
___Other student(s)
___Client(s)
___Other(explain):_____
Was a student/worker ever "outed" in your agency? Yes ___ No ___
If yes, by whom was he or she "outed"?
___You
___Another field instructor or supervisor
___The educational coordinator of your agency
___Another social worker or professional in the agency

___The faculty advisor

___A nonprofessional staff member of the agency

___Other student(s)

___Client(s)

___Others (explain):_____

If a student/worker self-disclosed to you, when did he or she do it?

___At the beginning of your supervisory relationship

___Middle of your relationship

___End of your relationship

Have you ever had a student/worker that you thought was gay, lesbian, bisexual, or transgender but who did not self-disclose? Yes ___ No ___

Would you describe your agency as a "safe" place for

GLBT persons? Yes ___ No ___

Is there anyone at your agency who is openly gay? Yes ___ No ___

If a student/worker self-disclosed or was outed at your agency, do you believe it affected the student/worker's? (check all that apply):

___Work with clients

___Relationship with you

___Relationship with other staff

___Work with other agencies

___Other (explain): _____

Diversity Scenarios for Field Education

CULTURAL COMPETENCE AND RELIGION

How do you support a student in managing differences with respect to the religious beliefs of clients?

A White student is running a "Parents Group." An African American male group member has been talking more and more about his religious views and beliefs. In a recent session, this client talks about ways to use prayer to ease pain and anxiety and begins to pray in the group. Two group members join him in prayer while other group members just look uncomfortable. The student interrupts the client saying, "We understand that your faith is very important to you, but we are here to talk about ways to raise our children and not to pray." The client says that one cannot raise healthy children without a belief in God. He asks group members if they agree with him.

The student is very uncomfortable and distressed by this confrontation. First, because the student's leadership in the group is being challenged. Second, the student has never faced this situation before and it is confusing. The student is not sure how to proceed. And last, the student was raised in a rather religious family, but she is now nonreligious and a little conflicted about it as an adult. The student says to the group that sharing religious beliefs is important, but that they have come together to get help with being parents. The student asks the group if they should not get back to their common purpose for being together. Everyone agrees, including the "religious" client.

In a subsequent session, an issue arises with an adolescent son who has just found out that his girlfriend is pregnant. The religious client tells the parent that abortion is a sin and urges her to put her faith in God. The group erupts into a heated discussion about the pros and cons of abortion. The client dramatically claims that he cannot go against his religious beliefs and will have to quit this "sinful" group.

1. *What are the diversity dynamics present in this scenario? The power dynamics? The group-work dynamics? What are the professional values raised by this scenario?*

2. *What identity development issues of the religious group member, student, and field instructor are to be considered in field instruction with the student?*

3. *How can the field instructor support the student to integrate the competing demands of culturally competent practice?*

4. *How can the student be helpful to the group's development?*

5. *What are some of your own issues around religious or spiritual identity that might appear in your working with the student and the organization?*

CULTURAL COMPETENCE AND SEXUAL ORIENTATION

"Coming out" in the agency: Issues for field instructors and students!

A 24-year-old student in a well-known child guidance agency informs her field instructor that she is a lesbian and wants everyone in the agency, including clients, to know about her sexual orientation. The field instructor, who identifies as straight, is totally surprised by this student's "coming out" request, since she never questioned the student's sexual orientation. She is also somewhat concerned about how others in the agency will take this new information. The field instructor responds by saying that the agency and staff are rather traditional and conservative, and she feels that such an announcement would be counterproductive for the student and would interfere with the student's professional relationships. The student seems to accept the field instructor's advice in the matter.

During a supervisory conference, the student tells her field instructor that she wants to start a discussion group for adolescent clients who are having identity confusion around their sexual orientation. She wants to provide them with an opportunity to discuss their concerns and with a safe place to arrive at some resolution of their sexual identities. The student is asking for support to raise the idea of the group at the next staff meeting.

The field instructor finds herself discouraging the student from such a course of action, stating that the staff would not be receptive to the idea. However, the student is convinced that her clients need this service and she urges the field instructor to let her bring up this group idea with other staff. The field instructor is upset and angry that the student is so adamant in her position and is suspicious that the student may have an ulterior motive in wanting to bring this issue to the staff's attention.

1. *What are some of the sexual orientation identity issues for the field instructor and for the student? What are some of the field instructor's and*

*student's attitudes, behaviors, and values around sexual orientation that
can help you understand their respective stages of identity development?*

2. *What are the field instructor's responsibilities in dealing with the
agency's homophobia and heterosexism?*

3. *What practice and organizational issues are operating in this situation?*

4. *How would the field instructor support the student to integrate the competing demands of culturally competent practice?*

5. *As a field instructor, how would you assist this student in "coming out"?
What are some of your own issues operating that might appear in your
working with the student and the organization around sexual orientation?*

CULTURAL COMPETENCE AND ETHNICITY

*How does a field instructor address a Latina student's culturally incompetent
practice?*

A 54-year-old student with 10 years of baccalaureate-level social work
experience has recently been placed at a shelter. She was raised in Ecuador,
educated in Europe, and has been living in the United States for 12 years.
She is fully bilingual in English and Spanish. The agency is thrilled to finally
attract a Latina student to intern in a homeless-family shelter serving mostly
Puerto Rican and Dominican families. The shelter director and field instructor
is a 27-year-old White male with 3 years' post-master's experience. He participated in the interviewing of this Latina student and had initially expressed
concern over their age and background differences.

After a few months of placement, the field instructor finds himself deferring to
the new student's opinions, thinking that she is the expert on the Hispanic community. He fails to confront the student when she does not follow through on certain
assigned tasks and notices value-laden and judgmental statements coming
through in the student's records, with such statements as "weak, unfit mother,"
"dirty, ill-mannered child," and "low-class parents." When clients begin to miss
appointments with the student, the director brings his concerns to her attention.

She complains vehemently about the futility of engaging such difficult clients in therapeutic relationships. She is being expected to work miracles with low-functioning clients and to meet unrealistic demands from the field instructor. She also tells him that her interviews are actually better in Spanish, and that the English notations make her sound more judgmental than she really is with clients.

The field instructor is beginning to suspect that the student is not so culturally sensitive or competent. He still feels inadequate in supervising such an experienced Hispanic student, but he is concerned with how she is responding to client needs.

1. *What are the practice and diversity issues and dilemmas confronting the student? What are the within-group issues that are shaping the student's work with clients? The between-group issues that are shaping the field instructor's work with the student?*

2. *What assumptions are being made about Latino/a social workers working with Latino/a clients? As a field instructor how can you work with this student in a culturally competent manner?*

3. *What are the issues of power, privilege, and oppression present in the student/field instructor relationship? What are the identity issues for both student and field instructor that can help to inform the student/field instructor relationship?*

4. *What are some of your own issues operating that might appear in your working with the student and the organization in terms of ethnic identity?*

CULTURAL COMPETENCE AND RACE

How do you support a student in talking with his or her clients about race and racism?

The student is a highly experienced White intern who is culturally sensitive and aware of the importance of creating a climate in which race and ethnicity can be openly discussed in the helping relationship. The client, an African Caribbean woman, is having career-transition, financial, and relationship difficulties. The student and client have been meeting together weekly for 6 months in an employee assistance program in which most of the professional staff is White and most of the clients are people of color, mainly African Americans and Latinos.

In their individual sessions, the student has discussed the importance of cultural issues in the client's life, and has raised the issue of racial/ethnic differences between the student/client and how this might affect their work together. The student feels that she has modeled for the client openness in discussing these sensitive issues. However, despite the student's encouragement, the client refrains from joining her in these discussions and stops short of expressing how race or racism affects her problems at work or in relationships. Rather than force the issue, the student decides to wait until the client is more comfortable to voluntarily raise these issues.

One day on her way to the waiting room to meet this client, the student overhears her client and another client of color talking animatedly about a racial incident covered in the media that day, and about how Whites still think they rule this country. The client goes on to say that her White boss was so condescending she made her feel totally incompetent. "She even had the nerve to comment on my accent. That's why I left that job. I was so stressed out trying to act White." The student is confused, hurt, and angry that the client is not able to trust her sufficiently to discuss these race matters with her.

1. *How are race and racism clinical issues in this scenario? How are they shaping the dynamics of this student/client relationship?*

2. *What are the racial identity issues affecting the student/client relationship? What are the issues of power and trust that need to be considered?*

3. *What are the organizational and agency-based issues that are affecting the relationship? What can the agency do differently?*

4. *Knowing all of this, how can the field instructor work with the student to understand how these dynamics shape what is going on in the student's relationship with the client and ways she can intervene toward a more authentic relationship?*

5. *What are some of your own issues around race, racism, and racial identity that might appear in your working with the student and the organization?*

CULTURAL COMPETENCE AND DIFFERENT ABILITIES

What does it mean to "accommodate" the special needs of a student?

The student is a 36-year-old White male student who has suffered from cerebral palsy since childhood. The field instructor is a White woman without physical disabilities, 5 years his junior, and has never supervised a student with special needs. The student is confined to a wheelchair, has good control of his upper body motor activity, communicates well verbally without any assistance, and is adept at using a word processor. He is currently interning as a direct practice student in the agency. He presents as a capable, intelligent, personable, and easygoing person who makes jokes about his disabilities. He lives at home with his mother, an aunt, and a younger sister.

The field instructor is having trouble engaging this student in a supervisory relationship because he is always joking around with her and acting like her friend rather than her student. The field instructor is getting conflicting messages from the student, who at times is seductive or flirtatious, while at other times behaving in a way that seems to mask enormous rage and dependency needs.

The student states that he is getting a great deal from his supervisory sessions with the field instructor, but he is often late arriving for supervisory appointments claiming transportation difficulties. He cancelled three successive appointments with the field instructor claiming fatigue and transportation problems. The field instructor is reluctant to confront him about his behaviors because, "He has an excuse ready or just talks circles around me." The field instructor feels she is "getting nowhere fast," and frustration has increased to the point where she is asking to have this student reassigned to another field instructor.

1. *What are the identity development issues that are affecting the student/field instructor relationship, including disability/ability, gender, and within-group issues of race?*

2: What is reasonable accommodation for a person with such severe disabilities?

3. What resources are necessary to support this student in serving the agency's clientele and in becoming a competent social worker?

4. How can the field instructor engage this student in a field instruction relationship? How can the field instructor work with this student in a culturally competent manner?

5. What are some of your own issues around disability/ability identity that might appear in your working with the student and the organization?

Chapter 11

TEACHING CHALLENGES IN FIELD INSTRUCTION

*W*hen problems arise...they are usually considered in isolation without notice of how they interconnect. They include: due process, liability, how to articulate and institute normative standards of practice regarding students in general, and the gate keeping role of the practicum. . . . Other matters include idiosyncratic issues of how to best match the student with an appropriate practicum and how the individual roles of instructor, liaison, and field director are coordinated. . . . The decision to fail a student is thus based upon a conglomeration of interrelated factors that cannot be addressed in isolation. (Coleman, Collins, & Aikins, 1995, p. 256)

There are many special challenges we face as we collaborate in the professional development of students. "Constant change and multiple pressures within the social environment, agency structures, and higher education further challenge the fulfillment of this mission" (Lager & Robbins, 2004, p. 3). Even the very nature of agency-based field instruction is under scrutiny. "Evidence indicates that the turnover of field instructors is high, thus threatening the quality and costs of social work education...[and] the voluntary and somewhat precarious nature of university-agency partnerships for social work education needs to be reconsidered" (Bogo & Power, 1992, p. 178). On the other hand, sometimes field instructors may feel like they are fighting for the privilege of being field instructors in their agencies (Rhodes, Ward, Ligon, & Priddy, 1999).

Other challenges emerge from students themselves, like providing reasonable accommodations for students with disabilities or special needs, some arise related to allegations of sexual harassment in the placement, and some challenges arise due to our own difficulties with our role. This chapter looks at some of the challenges that emerge from the changing context of social work practice and the stressful conditions of service delivery such as the impact of managed care on clients and practitioners. It also emphasizes our role as gatekeepers because we as social work educators "are responsible for graduating professionals who are academically, behaviorally, and ethically suitable to practice as social workers" (Cole & Lewis, 1993, p. 150).

The Changing Context of Social Work Practice

We need to be mindful of the challenges facing social work today, and how they affect student placements and field instruction, mainly: (1) the climate of modern social work; (2) preparing students for self-directed learning; (3) the implications of managed care on field placements and social work practice; (4) the increasing complexity of presenting problems and the limited resources to redress them; (5) the changing context of diversity and the demand for cultural competence; and (6) accommodating for the special needs of students (Globerman & Bogo, 2003; Jarman-Rohde, McFall, Kolar, & Strom, 1997; Raskin & Blome, 1998; Reisch & Jarman-Rhode, 2000). And because we live in a violent society, social workers may serve potentially violent populations, and it is possible for social workers to experience violence at the workplace. We need to think about how to teach students to assess the environment for potential violence, how to deal with violence, and how to deal with the aftermath of violence (Tully, Kroff, & Prick, 1993).

These conditions place special strains on preparing students for self-directed learning and autonomous practice and, by implication, on the ability of students to meet these demands. Donner (1996) points to three major limitations that are radically altering the world of practice and the ability of social work education programs to train social work students today: (1) the shift from long- to short-term services; (2) payment restrictions mandated by Medicaid or other managed care decision makers that limit student caseloads; and (3) cutbacks in agency support for student supervision (p. 317). There are several constraints in the social context of practice (privatization, managed care, the public image of social work); in the agency context (fiscal problems, pressure for students to produce labor-intensive work, and liability concerns); and the educational context (funding cuts, financial aid limitations, and the increased demands for field placements in the face of decreasing resources). In light of these constraints, Jarman-Rohde et al. (1997) recommend strengthening the viability and visibility of the profession; strengthening our gatekeeping functions; and expanding social work curricula to include content on the changing human service environment and its impact on clients (pp. 34–40). These realities set today's context of social work education and remind us of the dynamic interplay between education for practice and the context of practice.

The Idealized Student and Field Instructor

Both students and field instructors have strong opinions about how each should respond to the other. Research has shown that students' perceptions of "good" field instructors are largely dependent on their availability, use of process recordings, amount of supervision they give, the skill of the field instructor, and the quality of the learning experience provided (Knight, 1996, p. 16). Sometimes idealized pictures alter our perceptions and affect what we consider acceptable. Navari (1993) reports on student perceptions of ideal field instructors:

> In summary, the Ideal Type Field Educator is the consummate provider of service, has a 6th sense, a mega-memory, is assertive, tactful, idealistic, pragmatic, has a strong sense of self, but is caring, sensitive, and empathetic. The Ideal Field Educator has a strong sense of justice, is organized in her brain . . . , is comfortable working in two very different organizational environments—the academic and human service—and recognizes the strengths and weaknesses of both, genuinely enjoys students, teaching, and doing social work. In sum, the Ideal Type Field Educator can "leap tall buildings in a single bound."

In a similar vein, Goldstein (1989, pp. 12–13) offers a profile of the ideal student:

An ideal student:

1. Lightens the field instructor's workload and can function autonomously with a minimum of supervision;

2. Looks up to the field instructor and validates his or her competence;

3. Is a source of pride to and reflects well on the field instructor;

4. Appreciates the field instructor's time pressures and is mature enough to sometimes listen to the field instructor's concerns;

5. Learns easily, is organized and efficient, particularly in written documentation, and integrates theory and practice spontaneously;

6. Is open, self-aware, and self-reflective but not inappropriately revealing, self-indulgent, or self-centered;

7. Is empathic with, sensitive to, and caring about clients without being overly identified and showing poor boundaries with them;

8. Is confident in approaching clients but cautious in raising challenging or embarrassing questions in staff meetings;

9. Confides in the supervisor but does not expect the supervisor to lessen workload expectations and demands because of the student's personal problems;

10. Is committed to social work values and realizes that agency practice is valuable;

11. Helps clients and is good enough to be hired by the agency; and

12. Feels that the field instructor has been a wonderful role model.

Challenges from Students

Even students making satisfactory progress can plateau or become "stuck" during the middle phase of field instruction. The plateau may be experienced as a stalemate, and we feel challenged by the task of helping students overcome these impasses. Ongoing heightened anxiety, personality conflicts, or lack of growth and development as practitioners should concern us and are issues to be tackled in field instruction when they impede progress. In a thoughtful and planned manner, students need to be confronted about their learning needs and problems. We seem to have greatest difficulty confronting students who have questionable values or exhibit inappropriate or unethical behaviors (Cobb & Jordan, 1989). The field placement agency and the program need to consider the legal basis for student dismissal from the program and the agency, including poor academic or field performance, inappropriate or questionable behaviors, psychiatric problems, or outright violations of the Code of Ethics. Most social work education programs have clear and precise procedures for dismissing students that recognize the rights of all parties concerned.

Older, experienced students may feel tested by their transition to the student role, or students whose employment becomes their field placement may struggle to separate their student/employee roles. Problems may arise when students express reluctance to work with certain populations or certain issues, and this reluctance is exhibited as difficulties to engage with the clients or client issues. Sometimes students struggle with other staff members or the agency context (Tropman, 1977) such as when resources are limited, or there is a clash with the agency's mission.

GIFTED OR EXPERIENCED STUDENTS

Gifted or experienced students can present specific sets of challenges in field instruction. We may feel like we have nothing to teach these students, and they may feel like they are understimulated and underchallenged. Gifted or experienced learners may pose challenges, but it is equally rewarding when we are able to look beyond the norm of satisfactory field performance and find new and unique learning/teaching opportunities that take these students into new realms of learning. In these situations we may be challenged to find ways to enhance teaching/learning expectations by going beyond the status quo of agency service delivery. We may need to devise additional learning opportunities or find unique ways to build on students' experiences. For example, it may be possible to extend the agency's repertoire of services to include family, community, or research assignments in order to provide learning experiences for students who are otherwise unchallenged by the usual range of service delivery in the agency. Maintaining the demand for work may involve expanding our own repertoire of knowledge and skills, or finding task supervisors with specialized knowledge and skills to stimulate student learning. The temptation is to allow the learning to slide and to accept the level of competence gained rather than to push for new levels of competence.

MARGINALLY PASSING STUDENTS

> Supervisors must be empathic about the strains faced by students who are experiencing personal problems, and be sensitive to the effects these can have on their work. . . . However, it is not helpful to stop making expectations of students or to try to cover for a student who is having a hard time. It is better for the supervisor to maintain expectations about the work and thus help troubled students to function effectively in the agency, which, in turn, can help them deal with their personal problems—and ultimately those of the client. (Shulman, 1994, pp. 35–36)

Difficulties arise when students' anxiety levels remain heightened over an extended period of time, or if the anxiety prohibits appropriate progression in achieving learning goals and objectives. Students who are excessively anxious regarding their field performance are often inhibited from taking the necessary risks for new learning. This often creates a level of frustration for us as teachers. Behaviors that most frequently signal teaching challenges are open resistance, avoidance of learning, and failure to take responsibility for learning. These behaviors hamper our ability to offer the kind of critique required and also impede the development of self-reflective practice. Some students are self-preoccupied due to personality traits that demand continuous reassurance and expressions of positive regard from us. Any attempt to provide constructive criticism is interpreted negatively or as an attack on the person. In these situations, it is often very helpful to have three-way conferences with faculty liaisons that can reinforce the educational program's expectations and clarify the field educator's role and expectations. This also serves to remove us from the role of task master and shifts the focus to a shared responsibility between the social work program and the agency, freeing us to reestablish a teaching focus over and above the struggles encountered. A number of steps can be taken when students experience learning difficulties, including revision of field performance expectations; clarification of learning objectives; assignment of remedial work; setting time limits on requirements; changing assignments, placement, or field instructor; and extending the time in the placement (Kilpatrick, Turner, & Holland, 1994). These are usually stated in clear and specific learning contracts that are valuable tools in these situations. Learning contracts measure students' growth and development toward achieving field expectations and delineate reciprocal responsibilities of each stakeholder—field instructor, liaison, and student. Refer to chapter 7 on Education Assessment and Learning Plans.

EXCESSIVE ABSENCES OR LATENESS

Excessive absences or lateness inhibit the flow of the educational experience and signal more serious conflicts or performance issues. Sometimes absences or lateness indicate health or family problems that interfere with the rigorous period of study required by social work education programs. They can also indicate a lack of commitment to the profession or strong resistance to the demands of field instruction. Either way, excessive absences or lateness may prevent students from remaining client-focused. Before any issues arise in this area, we need to review with our students their understanding of the requirements regarding time and attendance. Timeliness is an organizational skill that needs to be learned, and not all students understand how this behavior demonstrates commitment to service and accountability in their new professional roles. Being explicit about the time and commitment required to meet field placement expectations and its relationship to achieving a satisfactory grade in field performance is essential. However, if problems persist, the faculty liaison should be called on to reinforce these expectations, to help mediate the difficulties, and to formulate learning contracts that target these behaviors.

OTHER FACTORS OR SPECIAL CONCERNS

Some factors that may need to be addressed include persistent judgmental attitudes expressed toward clients; perfectionist habits that interfere with the ability to get the job done; immaturity or naiveté that overwhelms students with the nature and complexity of client problems; or cultural or class differences that lead to misconceptions about client needs. Each of these factors indicates student learning needs; however, it is the pattern and duration of the problem behaviors that indicate whether students are marginal or failing in their field performance.

When the Field Instructor Is the Problem

Sometimes *we* are the problem. There can be a major mismatch in learning and teaching styles, or a lack of teaching skills and experiences, or we have rigid practice perspectives or exhibit personality conflicts with certain kinds of students. As we gain experience as teachers, we realize that we cannot teach in only one particular way, and that our teaching styles have to adapt to different learning styles and patterns (see chapter 4 on Adult Learning, Learning Styles, Learning Stages). Over time, we develop an understanding of our strengths and weaknesses as teachers, and this guides the continued development of our skills as field instructors.

The process of becoming a field instructor involves several stages of development (Dearnley, 1985; Blair & Peake, 1995). New field instructors may become preoccupied with technique or may "overteach" by talking too much, providing all the answers, taking over the work, and even thinking for students. A tendency toward dictating behaviors or expecting students to do things "our way" may demonstrate a lack of confidence in our abilities and may be translated by students as our lack of trust in their abilities and skills. If we fear being too dictatorial or authoritative, we may opt for more "unstructured teaching," which leads to a lack of focus in field instruction, vague directives, and unclear expectations. Equally, we may begin with flexibility in our expectations but run out of patience when students do not respond and instead seem to take advantage of this leniency. In these situations students can experience us as not concerned about the details and misinterpret our flexibility. Students may respond, *"You always accepted my reasons for my being late, I never knew it upset you or that it was a problem."*

Some of us may be ethnocentric with a narrow cultural lens and a tendency to not be receptive to different worldviews or perspectives on learning or practice. Students who experience us as culturally biased or incompetent will feel uncomfortable talking to us about diversity issues. And finally, there are field instructors who display unethical behaviors that blur the boundaries and challenge the teaching/learning relationship. Students will have various reactions to ineffective field instructors, ranging from passivity to outright hostility, and not all students will seek out their faculty liaisons for assistance. Students frequently suffer through "bad" field instruction rather than call attention to the situation.

Handling Challenges to Field Instruction

Early attention to difficulties that arise in field instruction is crucial, and seeking the support of the social work education program as soon as we recognize difficulties is essential. Most of us find it difficult to fail students, and we often extend ourselves beyond the call of duty to "save" students. When we collude with our students or fail to confront them and do not report the difficulties to faculty liaisons, we usurp our gatekeeping function. In situations where we conclude that students are not performing within defined performance expectations, due process and careful documentation are essential. A cardinal rule is to remember that *our success as field instructors is not dependent on our students' success.* Likewise, our students' failure is not necessarily a reflection of our teaching abilities. We also need to guard against evaluating students before we have taught them or identifying learning problems that we have not addressed in field instruction. Before concluding that students are "unteachable," or too resistant to learn, or that the placement is not appropriate for them, we need to do everything possible to reflect on how best to help a student learn, and how to adapt our teaching to individual student needs. We may be pleasantly surprised that students can respond to a different teaching style or approach to their learning needs. Again, consultations with the faculty liaison can be very helpful in making these determinations, in setting guidelines, and in evaluating outcomes.

Understanding Resistance to Learning

Brookfield (1990) describes factors related to the tensions and emotions of learning that underlie resistance to learning. His framework is helpful in placing this resistance in the proper context. Resistance is a response to the change inherent in new learning, and students' anxiety around their performance is expected and normal. In addition, other sources of anxiety may be present and relate to the learner's life experiences. Consider the following from Brookfield (1990, pp. 147–162):

Low opinion of oneself as a learner. Developing a self-image as a learner involves regarding oneself as someone who is able to succeed, and to acquire new skills and knowledge. This is not always easy to achieve. Equally, if students have not had necessary supports as they tackled new learning, they might assume that we will approach them in the same unsupportive and exacting manner.

Fear of the unknown. Routine, habit, and familiarity are appealing and reassuring. Therefore, it can be expected that some students approach new learning situations by seeking set rules and guidelines. Some students are uncomfortable with the uncertainty inherent in professional practice, and we may need to provide them with guidelines and a well-defined structure before they can move into less charted territory and before we can accurately assess their capacity to manage this uncertainty.

The normal ups and downs of learning. As people learn something new, they often find that a yearning to return to the comfortable certainties of the past follows their initial assumption of new ideas, attitudes, or practices. When the uncertainty or lack of structure becomes overwhelming, students naturally revert to known and comfortable ways of working or habits that have worked in the past. This return to the familiar or safer ground may be misinterpreted as resistance to adopting new methods or ideas, but it is often temporary and is the second part of "two steps forward and one step back."

Lack of clarity in field instruction. If uncertainty and ambiguity characterize field instruction, or if students are unsure of what is expected of them, or by what criteria they will be judged, they may resist and mistrust the experience. We can assume that everything discussed in field instruction is clear and understood. However, as new terms are introduced, students may not have the same reference points from which to translate these new terms. We should frequently ask students to tell us in their own words what we have just communicated to them to confirm their depth of understanding or to ascertain alternative meanings and interpretations held by students. For example, words like engagement, contracting, assessment, and use of self may have alternate meanings to students. They may understand the concepts intellectually but find these alien concepts that do not fit with their personal or professional experiences. It is also useful to give students permission not to understand and to encourage dialogue until they do.

Personal dislikes and objections. Field instructors or students may dislike each other for any number of reasons, and this can disrupt and interfere with learning. For example, a clash in personal styles—a field instructor using informality with a student who is very formal—may create a level of discomfort that interferes with daily interactions. Students do not have to like us to learn from us, and we do not have to like students to teach them. Differences can become valuable learning experiences for students as they learn to work with individuals in their professional world in different ways. We can also help students examine what aspects of their own personal styles may need to be adapted in order to use the full potential of any learning environment. Students need to sort through the most important qualities they require from us to create "good enough" learning experiences, distinguishing between what they are learning in field instruction from what they might define as characteristics of an ideal field instructor.

A clash between learning and teaching styles or levels of expectation. Sometimes the mismatch is not related to personality differences, but is related to how the content or material is presented and how students are expected to learn the new material. For example, an assignment related to the impending death of a client is "too close" to a student's personal experiences and this makes the task of dealing with the subject matter difficult. Field instruction conferences may focus on conceptual discussions about death and dying that are too abstract for a student who is struggling with a range of emotions, or the student is not allowed to express the emotional discomfort accompanying the assignment. These situations heighten the discomfort level and impede learning.

Fear of looking foolish in public. Most of us want to avoid looking foolish in public and only want to do things that we know we can do well. We will resist particular learning activities that occur in overly public forums such as presenting at staff meetings or co-leading groups with senior staff members. Fear of looking foolish can prevent students from trying new approaches or strategies with clients. Yet, trying on new roles and experimenting with new interventions are important aspects of the learning experience. Being encouraged to experiment under our guidance involves helping students sort through the new experiences to facilitate risk-taking and to eventually integrate these experiences into their professional identities.

Lack of relevance of the learning effort. If the assignments given to students are not connected to their goals and career objectives, or if they are not helped to understand the meaning of the work to these goals, students may reject or resist the new learning involved. This often becomes an issue in today's climate where students accrue high levels of debt to obtain social work education or where students are working full-time and carrying family responsibilities while carrying a full-time academic load. Students want to feel that the learning is meaningful and that their efforts are relevant to their goals.

Value conflicts. Student difficulties are often related to value conflicts arising out of clashes between personal and professional values and ethics. Adults have formed their values and interpersonal styles, and these experiences shape how they deal with authority issues, disclosure, assertiveness, communication styles, taboo subjects, and boundaries. If students are asked to perform in ways that conflict with their personal values, they will feel like their professional values challenge their allegiance to personal values. We need to be alert to these value conflicts in order to help students reconcile performance of their professional role with their personal view of themselves.

Refer to chapter 10 for more material on cultural competence and diversity or chapter 9 for discussions of professional ethics and values.

Overcoming Students' Resistance to Learning

There are many ways in which we can help students identify, evaluate, and overcome learning difficulties. Consider these suggestions offered by Brookfield (1990):

- Recognize that resistance is normal among adult learners.

- Involve students in all aspects of educational planning, including problem solving around assignments, work management, in-service training, etc.

- Identify learning problems and possible solutions, giving time and space for airing fears and confusion. Solutions evolve from an understanding of the particular factors involved and emerge over time.

- Ask yourself if the resistance is reasonable or realistic.

- Gather information on the background and culture of your students while reflecting on how these affect student/field instructor relationships. This is an ongoing process that involves helping students make connections among all of the threads in their lives that affect their work.

- Explain your intentions and expectations early in the field instruction process. Do not assume that compliance means consent or agreement. We sometimes have to explain why a learning issue is important.

- Create situations in which students can succeed, including partializing and breaking down complex practice concepts or demands into smaller, understandable components.

- Do not push students too fast or beyond their capacity at the moment. Allow for consolidation and testing of new concepts.

- Attend to building trust with students and prepare them to hear constructive criticism and to challenge learning expectations that are too high or confusing to them.

- Students and field instructors are joined together by the student's desire to learn and our desire to teach. However, it is useful to acknowledge a student's right to resist learning. Not all students will display a passion for learning while they are learning. We need to remind students about their earlier decision to enter a social work education program and what expectations and goals they set for themselves as social work professionals. We need to help students see how some change is required in achieving these goals, and how the learning opportunities that are available to them at this time will help them achieve their goals.

- Encourage peer learning and teaching by using the support of the learning community. Field instructors can help students establish peer support groups in the agency setting. This is a powerful resource for normalizing the learning process and consolidating learning. This is also a useful adjunct to individual and group field instruction.

- Finally, we can help students overcome difficulties in performance by finding ways to enable them to think differently about the work or situation or placement setting. Reframing the work from a different perspective based on our experiences in the field can shift students' perspectives to more positive outlooks.

The following excerpt from a field instruction conference taken from Shulman's *Teaching the Helping Skills* (1994) is an excellent example of how we can overcome resistance to learning, increase the demand for work, and be empathic and supportive all at the same time:

I told Frank that I was expecting to get some of his material on his first interview, so we could discuss how he began. I hadn't received it and wondered why. Frank said he had been very busy that week. I told him I realized the load was heavy, but I thought he would have had time to [write] some notes on that interview. He paused and then said that he wasn't sure why it was necessary to do that. Frank had stiffened and looked quite defensive at that point. I told him that I had sensed that there might be some reluctance on his part to do it and that perhaps this would be a good time to discuss it. I asked why he felt it wasn't necessary. He said he couldn't see the purpose, and anyway he didn't think he could remember what went on at the sessions. I said that developing the skill of recall was a difficult one. I asked if he had ever written anything like this before. He said he had not. I told him perhaps I could have been more helpful in describing what I was asking for. I asked if he understood. He said he wasn't sure, so I explained that I did not want the whole interview but rather some brief comments about the conversation in the beginning, a summary of how the interview went, some more detail about any parts he was interested in discussing, and how it ended. I told him I thought it wasn't easy as a new student to share his work with me, but I wanted to reassure him that I wasn't asking in order to snoop, or to be critical. I felt that if I had some of the detail of what he was saying and doing with his clients, I might be more helpful to him. I asked him if it was true that he had been concerned about what I would do with the records. He said he was, and that he felt that the first interview hadn't gone very well at all. He was embarrassed to present it. I told him that I didn't expect these interviews to go perfectly and that I thought by going over some of his work with clients I might be able to help him identify what he did that went well, as well as what he could do better. I then asked if he could recreate from memory some of the details of this first interview and I would try to show him what I meant. I said I was willing to work from his memory of the experience, this time, but that the next time I would be expecting a written record. (p. 35)

Mismatches Between Field Instructors and Students

Throughout this text, we have encouraged a rethinking of approaches to teaching when identifying and attempting to meet students' learning needs. Removing students from placements is disruptive for all concerned and is therefore not considered the first choice of intervention when problems in field instruction arise. However, despite all good intentions, and in spite of adjustments made, it will happen that students are not appropriately matched for the particular agency setting or field instructor. We may come to the realization that the educational plan for particular students requires a different setting that can more adequately meet their specific learning needs. A change of placement might be recommended by field instructors or faculty liaisons to evaluate student capabilities in a new and different learning environment. For instance, students who have difficulty focusing on crisis situations or whose anxiety is heightened in crisis situations may require a change to a setting that provides more of a balance between short- and longer-term contact with clients. It may also happen that students change their educational focus and career goals in the course of study. Students who initially want to work within a micro practice environment may decide that a macro practice environment is better suited to their professional development at this point in time or vice versa. Reflect on the following questions when considering if a placement mismatch truly exists.

- Identify the different styles of learning and teaching between ourselves and our students. Have these differences been discussed? Are there compromises that can be achieved? Are the differences of such a nature that a complete mismatch exists?

- How clear are students about what is expected of them? How do we know that instructions or practice content are understood? How clear have we been about methods of evaluating progress? How clear have we been in explaining the normal pattern of learning new skills? How patient have we been, or can the setting be in this process? How clear are we of what students have learned? Have we attempted to partialize tasks or skills being taught? In spite of the attempts made to clarify expectations, do students remain confused and uncertain?

- Do the content and substantive area of work present particular challenges? Are there methods of teaching that may make these challenges more acceptable? How adaptable are we in our approaches to teaching? How flexible can the agency setting be in allowing students more choices in assignments?

- How intimidating is the context of the field placement? Are students given ample support if the setting involves "high-profile" performance? How clear have we been in explaining to students the reasoning behind assignments? Do students remain frozen and unable to tackle the work assigned?

- Have attempts been made to strategize with the faculty liaison? Have learning contracts been established that set out clear objectives, strategies, and responsibilities for students and field instructors? Have realistic goals been set?

Students Who Fail to Meet Field Performance Criteria

Despite focused efforts to overcome the teaching challenges presented, we may conclude with faculty liaisons that students either will not or cannot meet expected standards for professional development. Each social work education program has a process for students in serious difficulty outlined in Field Instruction Manuals. Become aware of the social work education program's policies and procedures for dealing with difficulties in student performance. The faculty liaison is a valuable resource in these discussions and deliberations. In some circumstances, we will have to confront students to clarify the extent or seriousness of the problem. In this process, it is important to affirm what students are proficient in, but also to make clear the specifics of our concerns. Faculty liaisons can be supportive in devising alternative educational plans. Grievous and serious actions on the part of students are more easily defined than those that signal marginal performance or that may indicate a failing grade. The National Association of Social Workers Code of Ethics acts as a guide for those behaviors that signify automatic dismissal. However, learning about ethics is a learning goal, and one breech of ethics while in the process of learning may not lead to automatic dismissal from a social work education program. Again, it is the seriousness of the pattern and duration of unethical conduct that are of concern. In the long run, we may feel relieved to terminate a difficult student, but we are often left with feelings of guilt, failure, or shame at not being able to help a student succeed in the placement.

Challenges of Special Circumstances

In recent years, we have had to struggle with two particular challenges in field instruction: (1) how to provide reasonable accommodation for the special needs of students with disabilities, and (2) how to deal sensitively with allegations of sexual harassment. These situations require knowledge about legal mandates.

THE AMERICANS WITH DISABILITIES ACT (ADA)

Implementation of the ADA is being tested within all social work education programs. The information appears clear-cut, but covert discrimination and unreasonable fears about working with persons with disabilities often interfere with the placement of students and may also interfere with the evaluation of their field performance. Defining reasonable accommodations challenges the essential tasks and elements of student performance expectations. As field instructors, we are therefore at the forefront of practice in this area (Bail & Lynn, 1995; Cole, Christ, & Light, 1995; Reeser, 1992). Communication with respective social work programs must occur to best serve students who are eligible for protection under this act.

The Americans With Disabilities Act Section 504 sets forth specific considerations for: (a) individuals who have a physical or mental impairment that substantially limits a major life activity, and (b) individuals who have a record or history of such an impairment, or who are regarded as having such impairment. Some examples of disabling conditions covered under this act are: all conditions that entitle students to receive special education while attending grade school (e.g., mental retardation, learning disabilities, serious emotional disturbances), AIDS, cancer, alcohol or drug addiction (as long as students are not currently using illegal substances), attention deficit disorder, diabetes, asthma, physical disabilities, or behavior disorders. In short, all conditions that substantially limit major life activities.

Students must be registered with the social work education program's office for students with disabilities in order for them to receive accommodations. In other words, students are not entitled to reasonable accommodations for their disabilities unless they are registered at their respective university. If difficulties from disabilities arise, but the student is not registered with the university, the student is not eligible for reasonable accommodations "after the fact." Therefore, we must be informed of students' special needs at the onset of the placement in order for them to receive special treatment or accommodations. On the other hand, it is possible that some adult learners may not know that they have any special needs until field instructors bring the difficulties to their attention. In these circumstances, students can be referred to the appropriate university office so that registration and services can be offered.

Social work education programs are not allowed to identify students' disabilities or to notify a prospective field placement agency unless students give permission, as it could be construed as a violation of confidentiality. Important factors to consider include "rights of students to privacy, of clients to have their welfare protected, of agencies to make informed choices and have relevant student information, and of schools to make educationally sound student-practicum matches" (Reeser & Wertkin, 1997, pp. 347–348). The normal procedure is to acquire a release-of-information form from students. In addition, the field education office should make certain that an agency is suitable for students with certain disabilities in terms of accessibility and whether special accommodations are available. For example, if students have been granted reasonable accommodation for using personal computers for note taking or a handheld spell checker, the field education office is responsible for notifying the agencies of these requirements and asking if they can accommodate students. In most instances, the social work education program facilitates acquisition of needed special equipment. Agencies and education programs must comply with ADA requirements, but the special needs of students with disabilities have to be evaluated and responded to on a case-by-case basis.

SEXUAL HARASSMENT

Sexual harassment takes many forms, from constant joking or teasing to physical assault. It may involve threats or result in a work environment that becomes uncomfortable for students through continued sexual comments, suggestions, or pressures. Perpetrators of sexual harassment most often are persons who exert some power over students either on the job or in their academic program. This includes the harassment of students by field instructors or students by faculty or administrators. Field instructors may feel harassed by students, faculty by students, staff by co-workers, or students by fellow students. These forms of sexual harassment are also unlawful. Although the majority of incidents of sexual harassment involve a man harassing a woman, the law also covers women harassing men, women harassing women, and men harassing men. Each social work program has a policy regarding sexual harassment, and agencies have protocols and procedures that also apply to sexual harassment. Field instructors should be familiar with these policies and procedures and help students understand them as well. "Students must be explicitly trained to identify sexual harassment and to know how this situation will be handled by their institution. In addition, agency personnel, those working with the students, and those in ancillary types of association with students require training" (Fogel & Ellison, 1998, p. 27). Refer to the social work education program's Field Education Manual for guidance in these matters.

Harassment on the basis of sex is a violation of *Section 703 of Title VII of the Civil Rights Act of 1964.* Unwelcome sexual advances, requests for sexual favors, and other verbal or physical conduct of a sexual nature constitute sexual harassment when:

- Submission to such conduct is made either an explicit or implicit term or condition of an individual's employment or admission to an academic program;

- Submission to or rejection of such conduct is used as the basis for decisions affecting an individual's employment status or academic standing; or

- Such conduct has the purpose or effect of substantially interfering with an individual's performance on the job or in the classroom, or creating an intimidating, hostile, or offensive work or study environment.

Handling Reports of Sexual Harassment

When students indicate the possibility or actual incidence of sexual harassment, field instructors need to do the following:

- Determine agency and educational policies and protocols about harassment.

- Contact the field education department or faculty liaison.

- Gather specific information about the harassment by asking clarifying questions.

- Be supportive and neutral and avoid labeling anyone's behavior.

- Give students the option of writing down what actually happened.

- Do not ask students to handle the situation themselves, even if they want to.

- Speak to all parties concerned to find out what happened.

- If students ask you to do nothing, explain that you cannot "do nothing."

- Explain how you will proceed and work closely with students throughout the entire process.

- Collaborate with the student to develop a plan of action.

Frequent Mistakes in Handling Sexual Harassment

- Not seeking consultation from the social work program or field education office and viewing the allegations purely from the agency's perspective

- Trying to pretend nothing happened

- Overreacting to complaints by punishing before investigating

- Moving too fast or ahead of a student's pace

- Not telling the alleged harasser what the specific complaints are

- Not allowing the alleged harasser a chance to rebut the accusations

- Interfering with an investigation because an alleged harasser is a friend or someone powerful in management

- Having preconceived ideas about perpetrators or complainants

- Not giving students adequate hearing of the complaints

- Not educating students about possible opinions and legal responses to complaints

Sexual Harassment Scenario

What constitutes an appropriate response to the following allegation of sexual harassment by a student?

A 27-year-old female student alleges that a 32-year-old male student accosted her against her will in the agency elevator. The male student asked the female student for a kiss, and when the female student said she did not want to kiss him, the male student kissed her anyway. She felt embarrassed and frightened by the situation. In addition, she recounted several other incidents in which the male student pushed himself onto her. She is angry with the male student and is frightened to be alone with him. She talks to her field instructor for advice about what to do.

1. What are the first steps to be taken?

2. What information does the field instructor need to know in order to proceed?

3. What "advice" should the field instructor give the student?

4. Should the faculty liaison be informed of this incident?

5. What action, if any, should occur regarding the male student?

6. Do the actions considered in this situation alter if the student accuses another staff member in the placement? If so, specify in what way.

At the end of chapter 10, Cultural Competence and Diversity, on page 193, there is a Diversity Scenario that deals with the different abilities of a student. Refer to this scenario, which provides an opportunity to consider a range of issues that arise in the accommodation of special needs.

Chapter 12

TRANSITIONS AND TERMINATION

*T*he process of termination is like finishing a knitting project. A knitter needs to bind off and secure the yarn so the piece doesn't unravel and come undone—to prevent the planning, work, and effort from being lost. If it is the knitter's first piece, the finished project may have a few bumps and uneven corners, but the next project will likely show improvement. If it is an advanced project, the piece is likely more complex and has fewer obvious mistakes. As in knitting, ending...involves attention to small details and to the larger, completed work. (Cochrane & Hanley, 1999, p. 150)

Termination is a crucial component of the helping and teaching relationships. As crucial and complex as endings are, this phase of relationships is often neglected, whether it is helping students end well with clients or dealing with the end phase of field instruction (Fox, Nelson, & Bolman, 1969; Grossman, Levine-Jordano, & Shearer, 1990; Shulman, 1994; Wall, 1994). Preparing students for termination involves anticipation of the inevitable responses to transitions and termination with clients, agencies, and field instructors. It also involves careful monitoring of our reactions and responses. We model the termination process for our students who, through a parallel process, use these same methods and techniques with their clients during the transition and termination phases of their work (Wall, 1994).

In a study of client responses to separation from social work trainees (Brill & Nahmani, 1993, pp. 99–100), six assumptions about termination are posed by the authors:

- The separation process is in the background of the treatment relationship from the initial phase through to the final phase.

- The separation process generates intense emotional involvement on the part of both the worker and client.

- The current experience of separation at the end of treatment is influenced by past experiences of separation.

- The quality and depth of the treatment relationship affect the degree of intensity with which separation is experienced and the time that is devoted to the process (six weeks minimum).

- The separation process has universal characteristics as well as cultural and ethnic features.

- The development of self-consciousness is of enormous significance on both the personal and the professional plane during the phase of separation and the termination of treatment.

Transitions and Termination

We know that transitions and terminations involve loss and change and all of the complex and individual emotions and responses that endings raise for us. These reactions are further complicated when the ending is unplanned or unanticipated. Even the achievement of a planned transition or the identification of a new goal or stage of development involves some loss of comfort and increased anxiety associated with beginning something new or ending a phase of work that facilitated the attainment of this new plateau. Providing an educationally constructive termination experience involves addressing the major tasks and issues associated with all of these facets while at the same time enabling students to deal with their own feelings about the process. In this respect, teaching during the termination phase is coupled with supporting students in anticipation of these complex reactions to change from the client systems they have been working with, and of course, with understanding their own reactions to this process.

Social work literature has historically focused on negative or difficult client reactions to termination such as denial, indirect or direct anger, regression, avoidance, bargaining, mourning, and depression (Garland, Jones, & Kolodny,

1973; Northern, 1988; Palombo, 1982). However, more recent strengths-based theoretical considerations have pointed to the positive reactions associated with achieving growth and maturity, positive advancement, increased self-reliance, and hope for the future (Corey, 2004; Fortune, 1987; Shulman, 1994). The expressions of sadness and regret that a valued relationship will not continue are viewed as positive and healthy responses to connections that have personal meaning rather than as problematic or regressive emotions that forecast unhealthy responses to endings (Walsh, 2003). Each ending experience presents challenges and opportunities for growth and learning—for us, our students, and the client systems served through field placements.

Termination begins with the choice of assignments for our students and their first contacts with client systems. It involves the implications of their student status that delineate a time frame for their working relationships. We help our students work within a time-limited contract in which termination is part of the initial contracting phase, and the rhythm of the work must be kept within this reality and context (Feiner & Couch, 1985; Wall, 1994). It is through the ongoing work of review, summation, and evaluation that this context is kept in the forefront of the work and new levels of growth and achievement are monitored and accomplished. The examination of working relationships developed over time provides another opportunity for integration of practice and increased self-awareness.

Teaching Tasks Associated With Termination

The steps involved in teaching termination and preparing students for transitions from one academic year to another and eventual graduation include ongoing evaluation and assessment, anticipation of the many forms that ending takes, enabling students to identify their own feelings regarding endings and planning for the future. The following section looks at each of these tasks individually.

ONGOING EVALUATION AND ASSESSMENT

This ongoing process involves the review and reflection of students' work, the goals achieved and accomplishments attained, and identified unfinished business. The period of time leading up to the ending phase pays attention to the following:

- How students began the year and how they will begin the next phase of the work ahead

- Identification of the characteristics students rely on from us during supervision

- A review of written and oral evaluations as well as process recordings, logs, or journals that provide evidence regarding professional growth and development and areas for future work

- Recalling and sharing of experiences that triggered strong emotional reactions and ultimately resulted in professional growth and self-awareness (Grossman, Levine-Jordan, & Shearer, 1990)

- Involving students in a review of similar growth patterns with their client systems and assignments and identifying gains achieved and goals still unrealized

- Paying special attention to termination with groups and macro assignments

On the last point, sometimes a group may have been unsuccessful in achieving its major objectives but with closer review, students "will usually discover some positive elements overlooked in the group that can be reinforced" (Garvin, 1996, p. 218). Members of groups may have to deal with the concurrent ending of three different relationships: with the group leader, with the group as a whole, and with each other. Peer group experiences for students can be particularly powerful experiences. The support that one receives as part of a membership in a group is unique:

> Because groups are small "communities," their endings sometimes merit a different type of attention than endings with either individuals or families. The practitioner needs to consider not only the needs of individual members but also their attachment to the dissolving community of supportive others. When groups have been successful, members have formed ties that may not be easily replicated in the outside society. (Walsh, 2003, p. 152)

ANTICIPATING THE MANY WAYS OF ENDING

BSW and first-year students will be ending their roles as students within a particular placement site. They are in transition to their 2nd year or Advanced Standing Program and to a new focus and new placement experience.

Second-year students are involved in totaling up the experiences of their education and ending their role as students and social work interns, their relationships with classroom peers and professors while also ending their specific relationship to this second placement, field instructor, agency staff, and clients. For some students, this may be the end of financial impoverishment, an end to nonprofessional jobs, and an entry into the professional workforce. Both levels of students must acquire understanding of the progress and process of their learning achievements as well as what learning goals they have identified for the next stage of their professional development. Students also need to focus on differential assessments of their clients and begin to anticipate the range of termination reactions they will have to the student leaving the agency.

GETTING IN TOUCH WITH OUR FEELINGS ABOUT ENDINGS

Reflecting on the range of emotions, reactions, and behaviors—negative as well as positive—involved in ending reduces the anxiety and helps students prepare for the work of this phase of the helping process (Kahn, 1979). Whether the assignment being terminated involves work on the micro, mezzo, or macro level, reactions to the work of ending will emerge, and processing these reactions is part of the development of a professional stance to the task of terminating well. The following is a guide to this work:

- Review previous experiences with endings (Cochrane & Hanley, 1999).

- Promote reflection on students' personal needs as they relate to the work (for example, to be needed, liked, or in control) and anticipate how these may affect the termination process (Walsh, 2003).

- Enable a discussion of the meaning of endings to students as derived from their own cultural backgrounds and ethnic identifications. Discuss "culturally defined good-bye markers" (Fortune, 2002, p. 462) and help students anticipate similarities and/or dissimilarities from their field instructors and client systems. How will these markers affect the termination process? The cultural context of gift giving, hugging, and shaking hands, etc., is useful material for discussion.

- Review process recordings as a foundation for discussions of termination with clients. Check for omissions, missed opportunities to address the issue, insufficient time spent on issues, and a lack of depth or evidence of conflict and discomfort. Use this material to access students' feelings about termination and to resolve blocks so that students will be able to do the same with their clients (Kahn, 1979).

• Teach students how to introduce activities and interventions that help clients deal with their feelings about endings and make connections between past endings and future plans. Some examples within the context of group work include:

> a "toast" to each person about what members learned from them . . . exchanges of mementos with special meaning, such as group photos or certificates of completion...a potluck supper with each person contributing his/her ethnic specialty. (Fortune, 2002, p. 462)

• Share our own feelings regarding termination with students in order to help students discuss similar feelings with clients (Shulman, 1994).

PLANNING FOR THE FUTURE

Terminations mark the end of a phase of work and the beginning of another phase. Planning for the future includes processing information and experiences that inform our anticipation of what is ahead and provides foresight on how to proceed. In the way that we prepare our clients for future problem solving, we prepare our students to be a bridge from one learning experience to the next. This work includes the following elements:

• Discuss details regarding the transfer or termination of assignments. Sometimes ambivalence or insecurity around termination prompts our students to suggest transfer rather than termination when it is in the client's best interests to terminate.

• Help students to own their achievements while also identifying what they still need to work on in supervision. This aids in understanding how much they have learned and what they will need to continue to work on and clarifies what misconceptions may exist regarding the work they actually accomplished. We assist and facilitate the learning effort, but students actually do the work.

• Clarify the parameters of post-termination relationships between us and students and between students and their clients. (Refer to the Termination Scenarios at the end of this chapter.)

- Provide some rituals to mark the ending of student placements. They serve to acknowledge the importance of the experience for all involved—students, staff, and us. We are responsible for making sure that the agency acknowledges our student's last day. Rituals also highlight the importance of closure to our student's experiences in the agency.

- Even if agency-wide formal "good-bye" rituals are planned, encourage students to take an even more active role in their termination from the agency by scheduling private "final" conversations with those staff who have been important to their field placement experience (Sweitzer, Frederick, & King, 1999). This prepares students for their eventual entry into the professional arena and the reality that on graduation, relationships with staff may evolve into colleagues and collaborators around service delivery.

As we prepare for termination with our students, consider the following:

- Was the match between you and the student a good one? If so, in what ways was this a good match? If not, what made it a difficult match?

- How did the student's cultural similarities or differences influence your experience? The student's experience?

- How clear have you been with the student to delineate the progress he or she has made?

- How clear have you been with the student in identifying what made this experience a positive one? If learning goals were not achieved, how clear have you been in identifying the factors involved?

- What were some of the rewards of your experience as a field instructor? What would you like to have changed?

- How did the nature of field instruction change as you became more familiar with your role?

- Have your ideas about field instruction or social work education changed? If so, in what ways?

- How could your role be better supported by the educational program? By your agency?

• Will you be a field instructor again?

• What can the program or agency do to retain field instructors? To whom can you communicate your thoughts about this?

The following scenarios are provided to prompt dialogue between field instructors and students regarding different perspectives on termination.

Termination Scenarios

SCENARIO #1
The Field Instructor's Perspective

Two weeks ago you told your student to begin terminating with clients and the projects he has been working with, but to date he has not raised the issue in any of these forums. The process recordings and logs submitted this week show no mention of the topic. In a field instruction conference, your student has asked you to keep several client cases open and active, but you feel they are appropriate for termination. He has not begun to prepare the work committee on a project he is involved in for a transition to another worker. This student has also applied for a job in the agency. While he has done adequately as a student, you and your director think you can find a better candidate for the job. You don't plan to hire him, but you have not told him so yet.

The Student's Perspective

Two weeks ago your field instructor told you to begin terminating with the project committee you have been working with, but you have not begun to do this yet. It's a difficult topic to discuss, especially in relation to one particular group task that you feel very attached to. Besides, you have applied for a job in the agency, and you hope you'll get the job and you won't have to terminate with this project at all.

SCENARIO #2

The Field Instructor's Perspective

Two weeks ago you told your student to begin termination with Mrs. Jones, her favorite client, who, unfortunately, still has many unresolved problems. The student's process recordings show no evidence that she has yet raised the issue of termination with the client.

The Student's Perspective

Two weeks ago your field instructor told you to begin termination with Mrs. Jones, your favorite client, who, unfortunately, still has many unresolved problems. You meant to discuss termination both last week and this week, but both times Mrs. Jones raised very important issues before you could get to it. This week she learned that her mother has a life-threatening illness and she is very upset about it. You are tempted to give Mrs. Jones your home phone number since she seems so upset. How can you possibly tell her you are leaving? What are you going to tell your field instructor?

Chapter 13

CONCLUDING THOUGHTS

*T*his book serves as both a primer for new field instructors in the development of their knowledge and skills and a guide for experienced field instructors as they continue their professional growth and development. It is also a useful text for students and faculty liaisons. Although comprehensive, this book does not cover everything you want to know about field instruction, but rather it is a work in progress. The challenge for all of us who are field instructors is to continue to train the social workers of the future while responding effectively to the realities of social work practice in the present day. We need to continually advocate for ourselves, improvise, and in so doing, contribute to the knowledge base of the profession.

Summary of Major Themes Emphasized in This Text

Field instruction serves as a parallel process for everything that goes on in the field placement. Everything we say and do in field instruction in some way parallels student experiences with clients and agency staff. We model the importance of establishing sound professional relationships, contracting for goals and objectives, recognizing diversity in social work practice, upholding professional values and ethics, working through solutions, breaking through resistance, and assessing, evaluating, and ending working relationships. The way in which we give feedback to students parallels the way students give feedback to their clients. The manner in which we respect students and their learning struggles parallels the way in which they approach their clients and their struggles.

Field instructors need to be supported by their agencies in order for them to be supportive to students. Agencies need to see themselves as partners in field instruction and not expect us to be on our own in this role and function. Ultimately, the agency is responsible for the teaching and learning that takes place in its setting. We need to receive release time for taking on the responsibilities of teaching students or we will feel pressed for time and stressed in fulfilling job expectations along with training students. Social work education programs also have a responsibility to assist and support us, as we are partners in the education of their students. Faculty liaisons play a major role by providing us with essential consultation and validation of our important educational role.

Field instructors are gatekeepers for the profession. Every social work education program has a procedure for evaluating students, their academic and field performance, and their abilities to enter the profession. We are often the first persons to raise concerns about individual field performances. It is our responsibility to let faculty liaisons and social work education programs know how students are doing, and whether they have the necessary knowledge, skills, and values to become professional social workers.

Excellent social workers often make excellent teachers of practice. We need to realize that our skills as field instructors are sometimes limited for a variety of reasons. Students do not live up to our expectations, or we do not live up to theirs. We may find that we are better practitioners than we are teachers of practice. On the other hand, we may find true enjoyment from teaching others about social work, and we may feel that we can teach well. Thus we have found a new career for ourselves and can continue to hone our skills as field instructors and even become adjunct faculty liaisons or adjunct classroom instructors. Post-master's education or a doctoral degree can lead to a career in academia, where we can contribute to the scholarship and research of the profession.

Field instructors teach the realities of social work practice. Social workers are not just helpers. We act as advocates, counselors, organizers, managers, and activists for social change, and we need to teach and model these roles for students. We need to discuss with students the importance of active participation in professional organizations to help promote social change and innovation in the profession. We need to teach, and students need to be willing to learn, skills and knowledge in more than one method of practice. This is a reality and necessity of current practice demands that often stretch the abilities of both students and field instructors. We also need to see the agency of social work practice through the eyes of students who have a fresh perspective on how best to help people with complex problems and concerns.

Field instruction is a challenging and important part of social work that deserves enormous respect and recognition. We train our own, and each and every one of us has a hand in preparing the future workforce in the profession by passing on the history and philosophy of social work. We do this in social agencies that range far and wide, across a region or state, or around a large metropolitan city. We teach in myriad fields of practice, each with a unique mandate and organizational culture. Social workers teaching social workers is the primary means by which new members are inducted into professional roles and functions. We all need to recognize each other for our unique and invaluable contribution to social work education and the profession.

The authors hope that this book lends a vision and conceptualization of field instruction that embraces the diversity of social problems, service settings, and methods, but has at its core:

- A unifying ethic, purpose, and integrity;

- Substantial breadth and diversity of learning experiences across client populations, problem areas, methods, and services structures;

- Ample opportunities for students to learn conceptual problem solving, direct service skills with individuals, families, groups, and communities, and larger system interventions in policy, programs, and administration;

- An instructional emphasis on the integration of learning that seeks to interrelate classroom and field learning experiences and to incorporate personal and life experience;

- An active and complementary instructional team of field educators, including faculty, field instructors, educational coordinators, faculty liaisons; and

- A planful use of tutorial, tandem, team, and group learning methods, activities, and structures (Schneck, 1995, pp. 7–8).

This field instruction text has been designed to promote excellence in field education. The authors wish to acknowledge that this work builds on the significant knowledge base of field education. It is a testament to field instructors everywhere. It serves to recognize the central role that field instructors play in social work education and the profession and the invaluable contributions they make to student education and professional development. It is meant as a thank you to all field instructors and students past, present, and future.

Appendix A

SEMINARS IN FIELD INSTRUCTION (SIFI)

*F*ield instructors who attended SIFI provided students with a more structured learning experience, particularly regarding aspects of the student's role, responsibilities, and learning needs. Furthermore, the trained field instructors were more conceptual in their teaching methods when using process recordings. (Abramson & Fortune, 1990, p. 284)

This text could be used in Seminars in Field Instruction (SIFIs) designed for new field instructors as they adapt to the demands of their new role, or in advanced seminars that highlight particularly problematic or challenging aspects of field instruction like teaching about cultural competence or professional ethics. As stated in the acknowledgments of this book, Naomi Pines Gitterman led the New York area's efforts in developing the first SIFIs almost 30 years ago. SIFIs are now commonplace in most parts of the United States and abroad. From the beginning, SIFIs were designed to support field instructors in acquiring the necessary knowledge, skills, and values in field teaching (Bogo, 1981; Rogers, 1996; Saari, 1989). SIFIs are usually led by experienced field instructors or faculty with a special interest in field instruction. Fishbein and Glassman (1991) stated that a well-designed SIFI is a "gift to the new field instructor." The following section includes guidelines for the management, content areas, and teaching principles shaping the seminars.

Purpose of SIFIs

The main goal of SIFIs is to help new field instructors educate students on how to practice social work within specific agencies and according to the expectations of a social work education program and the profession. Field instructors are generally required to have a few years of post-master's experience in social work, an interest in broadening their professional expertise, and the general support of their agencies to undertake this new and important responsibility. All SIFI participants are new field instructors who are currently assigned social work students. Advanced SIFIs for experienced field instructors are generally viewed as contributing to the conceptualization of the art and science of field teaching.

SIFIs emphasize the following goals and objectives:

- To help new field instructors develop familiarity with a social work program and its educational objectives

- To parallel students' experiences in a new agency-based field placement from orientation through to evaluation of their field performance and the ending of the field placement

- To present a "goodness of fit" with the beginning, middle, and end phase of field instructor/student relationships

- To provide mutual support and assistance among peers. SIFIs are meant to be a safe place to discuss teaching problems and concerns, to discuss the learning needs of individual students, and to problem-solve special circumstances and situations.

- To help field instructors develop professional, generic knowledge, skills, and values rather than technical, vocational skills relating to specific agency practice

Structure of SIFIs

SIFIs have a fairly long history in the profession, and in some areas there is a collaborative or consortium of social work education programs that develops and maintains a uniform SIFI curriculum with set standards and requirements. This allows the programs to exchange affiliations and establish reciprocity.

Once certified as a field instructor, an individual can be a field educator for any social work education program in the area.

As SIFIs are developed across the country, Canada, and internationally, a variety of models are emerging. One way to deliver an SIFI is to offer 10 to 12 2-hour sessions on a weekly or every-other-week basis in 1 semester. SIFIs can also be offered in daylong sessions, just a few times a semester, or spread out over 2 semesters. However the SIFI is delivered, it generally begins by reviewing the structure and format of the SIFI, including the time commitment, specific dates, locations and length of sessions, and methods used for teaching and learning, e.g., active participation, readings, videotapes, and small-group exercises.

Early in the SIFI, there should be discussion about policies around confidentiality for seminar participants as well as between field instructors and students. Confidentiality extends to all SIFI participants regarding any oral or written material shared about students, agencies, clients, or faculty. Field instructors need to be free to raise confidential or ethical issues and to discuss any field education experiences and concerns. As such, SIFIs are professional forums bound by rules of confidentiality and mutual respect. In the best of circumstances, the first session of the SIFI takes place prior to the arrival of students in field agencies. This allows SIFI participants the opportunity to discuss preparations for orientation programs and developing assignments while examining the demands of their new roles as field educators. SIFI teachers should be prepared to discuss the specific requirements established by each social work education program represented by participants in the SIFI. And last, there should be a review of what the requirements are for certification as a field educator, i.e., attendance, participation, and written assignments.

An important theme in the seminar is how SIFIs model everything taking place in field instruction. As field educators engage in a teacher/learner relationship with students, they model or parallel students' engagement of clients in a professional working relationship. As they engage with each other in the SIFI, they model how they engage with their students. As they evaluate students in the field placement, they will find themselves evaluating themselves as educators. SIFI teachers emphasize the collegial and mutual support possible among participants as particularly important as field educators learn together how to teach others about what they do as social workers (Bertrand, Finch, & Feigelman, 2003). Assignments are designed to help field educators identify teaching issues and areas to work on as well as to parallel student experiences. Assignments are focused and brief so as not to overburden field instructors. A sample SIFI course outline (Appendix B) and assignments (Appendices C, D, and E) can be found following this discussion.

Distance-Learning SIFIs

SIFIs can be delivered via distance learning or through online Internet formats that can be accessed more locally, on the job, or even from home. This relieves some of the added pressure on field instructors traveling to the social work education program location for a SIFI. Technology can also be viewed as adding a new learning dimension to traditional field instruction and SIFI formats with such opportunities as online curricula, discussion boards, and individual and group assignments in between face-to-face sessions. Whether to enhance or to provide ready access, technology can become an important tool for SIFI teachers. SIFI teachers can conduct SIFIs at several different locations and with several cohorts of field instructors synchronously, simultaneously, and live. This technology requires rather elaborate television studio-like equipment that can be located in either a school or agency, and the sites need to be wired for accessibility. The major advantage of such technology is that field instructors can go to a nearby site from which they can see and interact with the SIFI teacher and other field instructors simultaneously across several sites and miles. With the right equipment and training, participants can have real, live interactions with each other and the instructor, just as if they were face-to-face in the same location. Some of the seminar quality of collegiality may get lost in transmission; however, participants at different sites tend to bond quite well with each other. The major disadvantage of distance-learning SIFIs is that some spontaneity is sacrificed. In addition, the technology does not always work perfectly, and glitches can delay the smooth running of an SIFI session. There are pros and cons to distance learning, but it can without a doubt provide easier access to SIFIs across large areas and will likely alter the ways in which SIFI content is delivered in the future.

Online SIFIs

Another technological advance allows field instructors to access SIFI materials, SIFI teachers, and other field instructors entirely or at least partially through the Internet. By logging on to the SIFI's Web page, field instructors can review a lecture, a small-group discussion topic, a vignette, or an assignment and respond instantly or at their leisure to a discussion occurring online with other field instructors. They can also have access to the SIFI instructor directly and privately for consultation. Discussions can take place anytime and anywhere field instructors or SIFI teachers have access to the Internet (late at night from home or early in the morning from the agency). Individual choice has many advantages, chief among which is instant access to consultation with colleagues when and if it is needed in the course of field instruction.

Online courses can be taught entirely via the Internet, or SIFI teachers can use a combination or hybrid of live seminars and online chat sessions to enhance the delivery of the SIFI content. In between SIFI sessions, field instructors can collaborate with each other and SIFI teachers on particular aspects of their field instruction experience, including questions about the social work education program's requirements, dealing with field instruction problems in the agency or difficult student issues, exchanging best teaching practices, or consulting with each other on field evaluations. When used properly, this online consultation can be extremely beneficial and can act as an extension of the seminar as SIFI teachers filter out the discussions and bring them to the seminar for additional collaboration. Full-text articles are also becoming more available online and can facilitate the exchange of professional literature on field instruction.

Appendix B

SEMINAR IN FIELD INSTRUCTION: SAMPLE COURSE OUTLINE

*T*his Seminar in Field Instruction (SIFI) is a 12-week post-master's certificate program for field instructors who are about to teach graduate social work students for the first time. All of the area social work education programs require the SIFI and have worked together to develop a standard and comprehensive curriculum. Field instructors are required to attend a minimum of 10 sessions, submit required assignments, and share their evolving teaching styles and approaches as part of the seminar format. Upon completion of the SIFI requirements, field instructors will receive a "Certificate in Field Instruction."

Seminar Objectives

1. To help experienced social work practitioners acquire competence as field instructors in relation to relevant educational principles and methodology, the social work education program's curriculum and expectations for field instruction, and the criteria for evaluation of field education performances.

2. To provide a forum for learning and the mutual exchange of ideas and concerns related to acquiring the role, knowledge, and skills of teaching.

Content Areas

INTRODUCTION TO THE SEMINAR IN FIELD INSTRUCTION

1. Introductions of participants and instructor

2. Seminar expectations and requirements

BEGINNING PROCESSES IN FIELD INSTRUCTION

1. Orientation of students to field instruction, the agency, and the client group/community

2. Setting the climate for field instruction

3. Roles and responsibilities of field instructors, students, faculty advisors/liaisons

4. Beginning field instructor/student relationships

TEACHING PROFESSIONAL ETHICS IN FIELD INSTRUCTION

1. NASW Code of Ethics

2. Conflicts of interests, confidentiality, dual relationships/boundaries

TEACHING CULTURAL COMPETENCE IN FIELD INSTRUCTION

1. Diversity as integral to learning/teaching

2. Discussion of the range of diversity factors

3. NASW *Standards for Cultural Competence in Social Work Practice*

THE RANGE OF STUDENTS' ASSIGNMENTS: MICRO TO MACRO

1. Developing and beginning student assignments

2. Selecting casework assignments (individuals, pairs, families), group, community, organizational, management, community organizing, research, and policy assignments

PROCESS RECORDINGS, LOGS, AND JOURNALS AND THEIR USE IN FIELD INSTRUCTION

1. Teaching and learning from student recordings

2. Different formats for recording

TEACHING ADULT LEARNERS

1. Different styles and approaches to adult learning

2. Stages of adult learning

EDUCATIONAL ASSESSMENTS AND LEARNING CONTRACTS

1. Formulation of educational assessments

2. Mutuality and collaboration

3. Parallel process and learning contracts

FIELD PERFORMANCE EVALUATIONS

1. Different ways of evaluating field performance

2. Mid-semester oral evaluations

3. End-of-semester written evaluations

TEACHING CHALLENGES IN FIELD INSTRUCTION

1. Field instructors as gatekeepers

2. Resistance to learning

2. Special circumstances (students with disabilities, allegations of sexual harassment)

TEACHING METHODS IN FIELD INSTRUCTION

DIFFERENT TEACHING METHODOLOGIES AND STYLES

TEACHING TERMINATION IN FIELD INSTRUCTION

1. Examination of end process in field instruction between student and agency, student and clients, and student and field instructor, and ending the SIFI

Appendix C

SEMINAR IN FIELD INSTRUCTION: SAMPLE ASSIGNMENT—TEACHING FROM STUDENT RECORDINGS

$\mathcal{S}$ubmit a student's recording of an individual, group, community organizing, or administrative assignment. Attach your process recording of the field instruction conference in which the specific assignment and recording are reviewed. Include your assessment or impressions of the conference, especially the teaching and learning that takes place around the discussion of the recording. List at least three questions or issues generated by this field instruction session. Identify the student by program (1st year, 2nd year, advanced standing) and by foundation or advanced practice method. Selected parts of field instructors' process recordings will be used in the SIFI with the field instructors' permission.

- Briefly describe the agency's programs and services and the client populations served.

- Briefly describe the student's assignment and the educational rationale for the assignment.

- Include objectives for the field instruction conference.

- Cite word-for-word content on important "teaching moments."

- Assess the teaching that takes place as the focus of this assignment. What was effective and why? What might the field instructor have done differently and why?

•Be certain to maintain *confidentiality* of both the student's recording and the field instructor's recording.

Appendix D

SEMINAR IN FIELD INSTRUCTION: SAMPLE ASSIGNMENT—EDUCATIONAL ASSESSMENT AND TEACHING PLAN

*P*resent an educational assessment for your student using the outline provided below. Be sure to include the student's demonstrated learning patterns and styles. Also discuss the specific learning/teaching goals developed, timing and sequencing of assignments and goals, teaching methods chosen, discussions of diversity, and learning goals and priorities set.

Field instructor:

Agency and placement site:

Student's status in social work program
   (e.g., 1st year, 2nd year, advanced standing etc.):

Student's major method:

Student's 2nd method:

STUDENT'S LIFE EXPERIENCES, SKILLS, AND PROFESSIONAL ATTRIBUTES

Describe student's prior educational and employment history as well as other experiences relevant to learning in the field. Highlight the student's strengths for further professional development.

LEARNING GOALS AND OBJECTIVES

What does the student need to learn in order to meet the criteria established by the educational program for his or her particular practice method and level of professional education? Identify specific areas that need attention. (Refer to the Field Education Manual for educational guidelines and competencies.)

DEMOGRAPHIC CHARACTERISTICS OF STUDENT, FIELD INSTRUCTOR, AND CLIENTS

Describe similarities and differences in culture, ethnicity, race, gender, class, age, sexual orientation, religion, and abilities and their implications for the teacher/learner relationship. How do you teach students to deal with the diversity encountered in the agency and with their clients? What are the student's strengths and learning needs in the area of cultural competence?

STUDENT'S CHARACTERISTIC LEARNING PATTERNS AND PROBLEMS

Evaluate the student's pattern of responses to the learning situation, including understanding of the learner role. Identify the type of learner and implications for teaching. What are the student's strengths as well as any obstacles to learning that impede his or her performance at this time? Give one or two examples to support your point of view.

LEARNING OPPORTUNITIES

Describe the range and nature of learning opportunities in the agency, including available assignments and other resources for learning. Describe a major assignment for the student and how this responds to the student's learning needs.

Educational Plan

The teaching plan evolves from all the data provided above and in consultation with the student. The plan should identify essential elements of the student's learning needs, indicating both short- and long-term objectives, major teaching methods employed, and types of assignments planned to advance learning. Be as specific as possible when discussing future goals and how these translate into assignments. Remember to include goals for the development of cultural competence knowledge and skills.

SEMINAR IN FIELD INSTRUCTION: TWO MORE SAMPLE ASSIGNMENTS

Critique of Written Field Performance Evaluation

Submit a copy of an end-of-semester evaluation of a student's field performance. Critique the evaluation process as well as the written evaluation. There should have been several discussions and significant interchanges between field instructor and student around evaluation of student performance. Reflect on student's efforts to grasp an identified learning issue and your teaching methods to deal with sensitive or difficult content areas in the evaluation.

Self-Evaluation of My Evolution as a Field Instructor

Review your first experience as a field instructor to date and how it felt to teach social work practice. Give particular attention to your initial expectations, anxieties, and concerns. What major transitions occurred in your field instruction role, and what goals have you set for your future development as a field instructor?

REFERENCES

Abramson, J. S., & Fortune, A. E. (1990). Improving field instruction: An evaluation of a seminar of new field instructors. *Journal of Social Work Education, 26*, 273–286.

Akin, G., & Weil, M. (1981). The prior question: How do supervisors learn to supervise? *Social Casework*, October, 472–479.

Americans With Disabilities Act of 1990, Pub. L. No. 101-336, §2, 104 Stat. 328 (1991).

Ames, N. (1999). Social work recording: A new look at an old issue. *Journal of Social Work Education, 35*, 227–237.

Aptekar H. H. (1966). Education for social responsibility. *Journal of Education for Social Work, 2*(2), 5–11.

Barker, R. L. (1999). *The social work dictionary* (3rd ed.). Washington, DC: NASW Press.

Bial, M., & Lynn, M. (1995). Field education for students with disabilities: Front door/back door: Negotiation/accommodation/mediation. In G. Rogers (ed.), *Social work field education: Views and visions* (pp. 437–451), Dubuque, IA: Kendall/Hunt.

Belenky, M. F., Clinchy, B. M., Goldberger, N. R., & Tarule, J. M. (1986). *Women's ways of knowing: The development of self, voice, and mind.* New York: Basic Books.

Berengarten, S. (1957). Identifying learning patterns of individual students: An exploratory study. *Social Service Review, 31*, 407–417.

Berger, B., Thornton, S., & Cochrane, S. (1993, Feb. 29–March 2). *Communicating a standard of professional behavior: A model for graduate and undergraduate field education.* Presentation at the 39th Annual Program Meeting, Council on Social Work Education, New York.

Berg-Weger, N. & Birkenmaier, J. (2000). *The practicum companion for social work: Integrating class and field work*. Boston: Allyn & Bacon.

Berman-Rossi, T. (1992). Empowering groups through understanding stages of group development. *Social Work With Groups, 15*(2/3), 239–255.

Bertrand Finch, J., Bacon, J., Klassen, D., & Wrase, B.J. (2003). Critical issues in field instruction: Empowerment principles and issues of power and control. In W. Shera (ed.), *Emerging perspectives on anti-oppressive practice* (pp. 431–446), Toronto: Canadian Scholars' Press.

Bertrand Finch, J., & Feigelman, B. (2003). *Training new field instructors: The power of mutual aid in the educational process*. Paper presented at the 24th Association for the Advancement of Social Work with Groups, Brooklyn, New York, Oct. 16–19.

Bertrand Finch, J., Lurie, A., & Wrase, B. J. (1997). Student and staff training: empowerment principles and parallels. *The Clinical Supervisor, 15* (1), 129–143.

Birnbaum, M. L., Middleman, R., & Huber, R. (1989, November). *Where social workers obtain their knowledge base in group work*. Unpublished paper presented at the Annual Meeting of the National Association of Social Workers, Washington, DC.

Black, P., Hartley, E., Whelley, J., & Kirk-Sharp, C. (1989). Ethics curricula: A national survey of graduate schools of social work. *Social Thought, 15* (3/4), 141–148.

Blair, K. L., & Peake, T. H. (1995). Stages of supervisor development. *The Clinical Supervisor, 13*(2), 119–126.

Bogo, M. (1981). An educationally focused faculty/field liaison program for first-time field instructors. *Journal of Education for Social Work, 17*(3), 59–65.

Bogo, M., Globerman, J., & Sussman, T. (2004). The field instructor as group worker: Managing trust and competition in group supervision. *Journal of Social Work Education, 40*, 13–26.

Bogo, M., & Power, R. (1992). New field instructors' perceptions of institutional supports for their roles. *Journal of Social Work Education, 28*, 178–189.

Bogo, M., & Vayda, E. (1987). *The practice of field instruction in social work: Theory and process.* Toronto: University of Toronto Press.

Bogo, M. & Vayda, E. (1991). Developing a process model for field instruction. In D. Schneck, B. Grossman, & U. Glassman (eds.), *Field education in social work: Contemporary issues and trends* (pp. 59–66). Dubuque, IA: Kendall/Hunt.

Bogo, M. & Vayda, E. (1993). *The practice of field instruction in social work: A teaching guide.* Toronto: University of Toronto Press.

Bonosky, N. (1995). Boundary violations in social work supervision: Clinical, educational, and legal implications. *The Clinical Supervisor, 13*(2), 79–95.

Bowser, B. P., & Hunt, R. G. (eds.). (1996). *Impacts of racism on white Americans* (2nd ed.). Thousand Oaks, CA: Sage.

Boyd Webb, N. (1988). The role of the field instructor in the socialization of students. *Social Casework, 69,* 35–40.

Brill, M., & Nahmani, N. (1993). Clients' responses to separation from social work trainees. *Journal of Teaching in Social Work, 7*(2), 97–111.

Brookfield, S. (1995). *Adult learning: An overview.* In A. Tuinjman (ed.), *International encyclopedia of education.* Oxford: Pergamon Press.

Brookfield, S. D. (1990). *The skillful teacher: On technique, trust, and responsiveness in the classroom.* San Francisco, CA: Jossey Bass.

Brooks, D., & Riley, P. (1996). The impact of managed health care policy on student field training. *Smith College Studies in Social Work, 66,* 307–316.

Burack-Weiss, A., & Brennan, F. C. (1991). *Gerontological social work supervision.* New York: Haworth Press.

Burrill, G. C. (1976). The problem-oriented log in social casework. *Social Work, 21,* 67–68.

Carlson, S., Delgado, M., Hagerty, L., Jarman-Rohde, L., Kolar, P., McFall, J., Navarre, J., Pace, F., Palya. K., Resser, L., Strom. G., & Sykes, D. (2000, March). *The canary in the mine: Crisis in field education, danger or opportunity.* Position paper of the North Central Field Education Director's Consortium, presented at the Council on Social Work Education, Annual Program Meeting, New York.

Carter, B., & McGoldrick, M. (1999). *The expanded family life cycle: Individual, family and social perspectives* (3rd ed.). Boston: Allyn & Bacon.

Cartney, P. (2000). Adult learning styles: Implications for practice teaching in social work. *Social Work in Education, 19*, 609–629.

Carter, R. T. (1995). *The influence of race and racial identity in psychotherapy: Toward a racially inclusive model.* New York: Wiley.

Caspi, J., & Reid, W. (1998). The task-centered model for field instructors: An innovative approach. *Journal of Social Work Education, 34*, 55–70.

Civil Rights Act of 1964, Pub. L. No. 88-352, 88th Congress, H. R. 7152.

Cobb, N. H. & Jordan, C. (1989). Students with questionable values or threatening behavior: Precedent and policy from discipline to dismissal. *Journal of Social Work Education, 25*, 87–97.

Cochrane, S. F., & Hanley, M. M. (1999). *Learning through field: A developmental approach.* Boston: Allyn & Bacon.

Cohen, M. B., & Garrett, K. J. (1995). Helping field instructors become more effective group work educators. *Social Work with Groups, 18*(2/3), 135–48.

Cohen, R. I. (2004). *Clinical supervision: What to do and how to do it.* Belmont, CA: Brooks/Cole.

Cole, B. S., Christ, C. C., & Light, T. R. (1995). Social work education and students with disabilities: Implications of Section 504 and the ADA. *Journal of Social Work Education, 31*(2), 261–268.

Cole, B. S., & Lewis, R. G. (1993). Gatekeeping through termination of unsuitable social work students: Legal issues and guidelines. *Journal of Social Work Education, 29*, 150–159.

Coleman, H., Collins, D., & Aikins, D. (1995). The student at risk in the practicum. In G. Rogers (ed.), *Social work field education: View and visions* (pp. 256–269), Dubuque, IA: Kendall/Hunt.

Collins, D., Thomlison, B., & Grinnell, R. M. (1992). *The social work practicum: A student guide.* Itasca, IL: F. E. Peacock.

Congress, E. P. (1993). Teaching ethical decision-making to a diverse community of students: Bringing practice into the classroom. *Journal of Teaching in Social Work, 7*(2), 23–36.

Congress, E. P. (1994, September). Dilemmas of dual relationships. *Currents*, Newsletter of the New York City Chapter of NASW.

Congress, E. P. (1996). Dual relationships in academia: Dilemmas for social work educators. *Journal of Social Work Education, 32*, 315–328.

Congress, E. P. (1999). *Social work values and ethics: Identifying and resolving professional dilemmas.* Chicago: Nelson-Hall.

Congress, E. P. (2000, Feb. 23–27, 2002). *Dual relationships in academia: Results of a national survey.* Presentation at the Annual Program Meeting, Council on Social Work Education, Nashville, TN, Feb. 23–27.

Congress, E. P. (2002). Social work ethics for educators: Navigating ethical change in the classroom and in the field. *Journal of Teaching in Social Work, 22*(1/2), 151–166.

Corey, G. (2004). *Theory & practice of group counseling* (6th ed.). Belmont, CA: Brooks/Cole.

Coulshed, V. (1993). Adult learning: Implications for teaching social work education. *British Journal of Social Work, 23*(1), 1–13.

Council on Social Work Education. (2001). *Educational policy and accreditation standards.* Alexandria, VA: Author.

Dearnley, B. (1985). A plain man's guide to supervision—or new clothes for the emperor? *Journal of Social Work Practice, 2*(1), 52–65.

Dettlaff, A. J. (2003). *From mission to evaluation: A field instructor training program.* Alexandria, VA: Council on Social Work Education.

Donner, S. (1996). Field work crisis: Dilemmas, dangers, and opportunities. *Smith College Studies in Social Work, 66*, 317–331.

Dore, M. (1993). The practice-teaching parallel in educating the micro practitioner. *Journal of Social Work Education, 29*, 181–190.

Dore, M. M., Epstein, B. N., Herrerias, C. (1992). Evaluating students' micropractice field performance: Do universal learning objectives exist? *Journal of Social Work Education, 28*, 353–362.

Drisko, J. W. (2000). Play in clinical learning, supervision and field advising. *The Clinical Supervisor, 19*(1), 153–165.

Dwyer, M., & Urbanowski, M. (1965). Student process recording: A plea for structure. *Social Casework, 46*, 283–286.

Fauri, D. P., Wernet, S. P., & Netting, F. E. (2000). *Cases in macro social work practice*. Boston: Allyn & Bacon.

Feiner, H. A., & Couch, E. H. (1985). I've got a secret: The student in the agency. *Social Casework, 66*, 268–274.

Fishbein, H., & Glassman, U. (1991). The advanced seminar for field instructors: Content and process. In D. Schneck, B. Grossman, & U. Glassman (eds.), *Field education in social work: Contemporary issues and trends*. Dubuque, IA: Kendall/Hunt.

Foeckler, M. M., & Boynton, G. (1976). Creative adult learning-teaching: Who's the engineer of this train? *Journal of Education for Social Work, 12*(3), 37–43.

Fogel, S. J., & Ellison, M. L. (1998). Sexual harassment of BSW field placement students: Is it a problem? *Journal of Baccalaureate Social Work, 39*(2), 17–29.

Fortune, A. E. (1987). Grief only? Client and social worker reactions to termination. *Clinical Social Work Journal, 15*(2).

Fortune, A. E. (2002). Terminating with clients. In A. R. Roberts & G. J. Greene (Eds.), *Social worker's desk reference*. Oxford University Press.

Fox, E., Nelson, M. & Bolman, W. (1969). The termination process: A neglected dimension in social work. *Social Work, 14*, 53–63.

Fox, R. (1989). Relationship: The cornerstone of clinical supervision. *Social Casework, 70*, 146–152.

Fox, R., & Gutheil, I. A. (2000). Process recording: A means for conceptualizing and evaluation practice. *Journal of Teaching in Social Working 20*(2), 39–55.

Fox, R., & Zischka, P. C. (1989). The field instruction contract: A paradigm for effective learning. *Journal of Teaching in Social Work, 3*(1), 103–116.

Franks, C., Hess, M., Sheiman, E., Walters, K., & Wheeler, D. (1999). *Self-awareness for professional practice: A multicultural orientation curriculum for graduate social work students*. Unpublished manuscript.

Freire, P. (1993). *Pedagogy of the oppressed*. New York: Continuum.

Ganzer, C., & Ornstein, E. D. (2004). Regression, self-disclosure, and the teach or treat dilemma: Implications of a relational approach for social work supervision. *Clinical Social Work Journal, 32*(4), 431–449.

Garfield, G., & Irizarry, C. R. (1971). The record of service: Describing social work practice. In W. Schwartz & S. R. Zaiba (eds.), *The practice of group work* (pp. 241–265). New York: Columbia University Press.

Garland, J., Jones, H., & Kolodny, R. (1976). A model of stages of group development in social work groups. In S. Bernstein (ed.), *Explorations in group work: Essays in theory & practice* (pp. 17–71). Boston: Charles River Books.

Garrett, K. (1993). *Controlling for group process in group work research.* Unpublished paper presented at the 15th Annual Symposium, Association for the Advancement of Social Work with Groups.

Garvin, C. D. (1996). *Contemporary group work* (3rd ed.). Boston: Allyn & Bacon.

Garvin, C. D., Gutierrez, L. M., & Galinsky, M. J. (2004). *Handbook of social work with groups.* New York: Guilford Press.

Gelman, C. R. (2004). Anxiety experienced by foundation-year MSW students entering field placement: Implications for admissions, curriculum and field education. *Journal of Social Work Education, 40,* 39–54.

Gitterman, A. (1988). Teaching students to connect theory and practice. *Social Work with Groups, 11,* 33–41.

Gitterman, A., & Gitterman, N. P. (1979). Social work student evaluation: Format and content. *Journal of Social Work Education, 15*(3), 103–108.

Gitterman, A., & Miller, I. (1977). Supervisors as educators. In F. Kaslow (ed.), *Supervision, consultation and staff training in the helping professions* (pp. 100–114). San Francisco: Jossey Bass.

Glassman, U., & Kates, L. (1988). Strategies for group work field instruction. *Social Work with Groups, 11*(1/2), 111–124.

Globerman, J., & Bogo, M. (2003). Changing times: Understanding social workers' motivation to be field instructors. *Social Work, 48,* 65–73.

Goldenberg, I., & Goldenberg, H. (2000). *Family therapy: An overview* (5th ed.). Belmont, CA: Brooks/Cole.

Goldstein, E. (1989, December). *The field instructor as master teacher.* Keynote speech at the 7th Annual Symposium sponsored by the Greater New York Area Schools of Social Work.

Goldstein, H. (1993). Field education for reflective practice: A re-constructive proposal. *Journal of Teaching in Social Work, 8*(1/2), 165–182.

Goldstein, H. (2001). *Experiential learning: A foundation for social work education and practice.* Alexandria, VA: Council on Social Work Education.

Granello, D. H. (1996). Gender and power in the supervisory dyad. *The Clinical Supervisor, 14*(2), 53–67.

Graybeal, C. T., & Ruff, E. (1995). Process recording: It's more than you think. *Journal of Social Work Education, 31*, 169–181.

Grossman, B., Levine-Jordano, N., & Shearer, P. (1990). Working with students' emotional reactions in the field: An educational framework. *The Clinical Supervisor, 8*(1), 23–39.

Hamilton, N., & Else, J. (1983). *Designing field education: Philosophy, structure and process.* Springfield, IL: Charles C. Thomas.

Harry, B. (1992). Developing cultural self-awareness: The first step in values clarification for early interventionists. *Topics in Early Childhood Special Education, 12*, 333–350.

Hart, G. M., & Falvey, E. (1987). Field supervision of counselors in training: A survey of the North Atlantic region. *Counselor Education and Supervision, 26*(3), 204–212.

Hartman, A. (1995). Family Therapy. In *Encyclopedia of social work* (19th ed.), (pp. 983–991). Washington, DC: NASW Press.

Hartman, A. (1997). Power issues in social work practice. In A. Katz, A. Lurie, & C. Vidal (eds.), *Critical social welfare issues* (pp. 215–226). New York: Haworth.

Hartman, A., & Laird, J. (1983). *Family-centered social work practice.* New York: Free Press.

Hartman, B. L., & Wickey, J. M. (1978). The person-oriented record in treatment. *Social Work, 23*, 296–299.

Hartung, R. J. (1982). The practicum instructor: A study of role expectations. *Journal of Sociology and Social Welfare, 9*, 662–670.

Hawthorne, L. (1975). Games supervisors play. *Social Work, 20*, 137–144.

Hawthorne, L. (1987). Teaching from recordings in field instruction. *The Clinical Supervisor, 5*(2), 7–22.

Health Insurance Portability and Accountability Act of 1996, Pub. L. No. 104-191, 104th Congress.

Helms, J. E. (1990). *Black and White racial identity: Theory, research and practice*. Westport, CT: Greenwood Press.

Hickcox, L. K. (1995). Learning styles: A survey of adult learning style inventory models. In R. R. Sims & S. J. Sims (eds.), *The importance of learning styles* (pp. 79–88). Westport, CT: Greenwood Press.

Horejsi, C. R., & Garthwaite, C. L. (2002). *The social work practicum: A guide and workbook for students* (2nd ed.). Boston: Allyn & Bacon.

Huang, C.A., & Lynch, J. (1995). *Mentoring: The Tao of giving and receiving wisdom*. San Francisco: Harper Collins.

Jacobs, C. (1991). Violations of the supervisory relationship: An ethical and educational blind spot. *Social Work, 36*, 130–135.

Jarman-Rohde, L., McFall, J., Kolar, P., & Strom, G. (1997). The changing context of social work practice: Implications and recommendations for social work educators. *Journal of Social Work Education, 33*, 29–46.

Jarvis, P. (1999). *Adult & continuing education: Theory and practice* (2nd ed.). New York: Routledge.

Jones, J. M. (1997). *Prejudice and racism* (2nd ed.). New York: McGraw-Hill.

Kadushin, A. (1968). Games people play in supervision. *Social Work, 13*, 23–32.

Kadushin, A. (1991). Field education in social work: Contemporary issues and trends. In D. Schneck, B. Grossman, & U. Glassman (eds.), *Field education in social work: Contemporary issues and trends* (pp. 59–66). Dubuque, IA: Kendall/Hunt.

Kadushin, A. (1992). *Supervision in social work* (3rd ed.). New York: Columbia University Press.

Kadushin, A., & Harkness, D. (2002). *Supervision in social work* (4th ed.). New York: Columbia University Press.

Kagle, J. D. (1991). Teaching social work students about privileged communication. *Journal of Teaching in Social Work, 4*(2), 49–65.

Kagle, J., & Giebelhausen, P. (1994). Dual relationships and professional boundaries. *Social Work, 39*, 213–220.

Kahn, E. M. (1979). The parallel process in social work treatment and supervision. *Social Casework, 60*, 520–528.

Kilpatrick, A. C., & Holland, T. P. (1995). *Working with families: An integrative model by level of functioning*. Boston, MA: Allyn & Bacon.

Kilpatrick, A. C., Turner, J. B., & Holland, T. P. (1994). Quality control in field education: Monitoring students' performance. *Journal of Teaching in Social Work, 9*(2), 107–120.

Kirst-Ashman, K. K., & Hull, G. H., Jr. (2001). *Generalist practice with organizations and communities* (2nd ed.). Belmont, CA: Brooks/Cole.

Knight, C. (1996). A study of MSW and BSW students' perceptions of their field instructors. *Journal of Social Work Education, 32*, 399–414.

Knight, C. (2000). Engaging the student in the field instruction relationship: BSW and MSW students' views. *Journal of Teaching in Social Work, 20*(3/4), 173–201.

Knowles, M. (1975). *Self-directed learning: A guide for learners and teachers*. Glenwood Cliffs: Prentice Hall/Cambridge.

Knowles, M. (1984). *Androgyny in action: Applying modern principles of adult education*. San Francisco: Jossey Bass.

Knowles, M. S. (1972). Innovations in teaching styles and approaches: Based upon adult learning. *Journal of Education for Social Work, 8*(2), 32–39.

Knowles, M., Holton, E. F., & Swanson, R. A. (1998). *The adult learner: The definitive classic in adult education and human resource development* (5th ed.). Woburn, MA: Butterworth-Heinemann.

Kolb, D. (1984). *Experiential learning: Experience as the source of learning and development*. Englewood Cliffs, NJ: Prentice Hall.

Kurland, P. (1989). Viewpoint/process recording: An anachronism. *Social Casework, 70*, 312–314.

Lager, P. B., & Robbins, V. C. (2004). Guest editorial–Field education: Exploring the future, expanding the vision. *Journal of Social Work Education, 40*, 3–11.

Landon, P. S., & Feit, M. (1999). *Generalist social work practice.* Dubuque, IA: Eddie Bowers.

Latting, J. K. (1990). Identifying the "isms": Enabling social work students to confront their biases. *Journal of Social Work Education, 26*(1) 36–44.

Lazar, A., & Eisikovits, Z. (1997). Social work students' preferences regarding supervisory styles and supervisors' behavior. *The Clinical Supervisor, 16*(1), 25–37.

Lemberger, J., & Marshack, E. F. (1991). Educational assessment in the field: An opportunity for teacher-learner mutuality. In D. Schneck, B. Grossman, & U. Glassman (eds.), *Field education in social work: Contemporary issues and trends* (pp. 187–197). Dubuque, IA: Kendall/Hunt.

Linzer, N. (1999). *Resolving ethical dilemmas in social work practice.* Boston: Allyn & Bacon.

Lowenberg, F. M., Dolgoff, R., & Harrington, D. (2000). *Ethical decisions for social work practice.* Itasca, IL: Peacock.

Marino, G. (2004, February 20). Before teaching ethics, stop kidding yourself. *The Chronicle of Higher Education*, B4–B5.

Marshack, E. F., Ortiz Hendricks, C., & Gladstein, M. (1994). The commonality of difference: Teaching about diversity in field instruction. *Journal of Multicultural Social Work, 3*(1), 77–89.

Marshack, E. F., & Rosenfeld, D. (1986, February). *Agency perspectives on current practice implications for education.* Paper presented at the Annual Program Meeting, Council on Social Work Education, Miami, FL.

Martens, W. M., & Holomstrup, E. (1974). Problem-oriented recording. *Social Casework, 55* 554–561.

Mathews, G., Weinger, S., & Wijnberg, M. (1997). Ethics in field education: Promise, pretension, or practice? *Journal of Sociology and Social Welfare, 24*, 103–116.

Mattinson, J. (1975). *The reflection process in casework supervision.* London: Tavistock Institute of Marital Studies.

McRoy, R. G., Freeman, E. M., Logan, S. L., & Blackmon, B. (1986). Cross-cultural field supervision implications for social work education. *Journal of Social Work Education, 22,* 50–56.

McRoy, R. G., Freeman, E. M., & Logan, S. (1986). Strategies for teaching students about termination. *The Clinical Supervisor, 4*(4), 45–56.

Miller, J., Kovacs, P. J., Wright, L., Corcoran, J., & Rosenblum, A. (2004). Field education: Student and field instructor perceptions of the learning process. *Journal of Social Work Education, 41,* 131–146.

Miller, J., & Rodwell, M. K. (1997). Disclosure of student status in agencies: Do we still have a secret? *Families in Society, 78,* 72–83.

Minuchin, S. (1974). *Families and family therapy.* Cambridge, MA: Harvard University Press.

Munson, C. (2001). *Handbook of clinical supervision* (3rd ed.). New York: Haworth Press.

National Association of Social Workers. (1984). *Standards for the practice of clinical social work.* Washington, DC: Author.

National Association of Social Workers. (1999). *Code of ethics.* Washington, DC: Author.

National Association of Social Workers. (2000). *Standards for cultural competence in social work practice.* Washington, DC: Author.

Navari, S. (1993, February 29–March 2). *The essence of a field educator.* Paper presented at the Annual Program Meeting, Council on Social Work Education, New York.

Nelsen, J. (1974). Teaching content of early fieldwork conferences. *Social Casework, 55,* 147–153.

Netting, F. E., Kettner, P. M., & McMurtry, S. L. (1998). *Social work macro practice* (2nd ed.) New York: Longman.

Neuman, K. M., & Friedman, B. D. (1997). Process recordings: Fine-tuning an old instrument. *Journal of Social Work Education, 33,* 237–243.

Nichols, W. C., Nichols, D. P., & Hardy, K. V. (1990). Supervision in family therapy: A decade of restudy. *Journal of Marital and Family Therapy, 16,* 275–286.

Nisivoccia, D. (1990). Teaching and learning tasks in the beginning phase of field instruction. *The Clinical Supervisor, 8*(1), 7–22.

Northern, H. (1988) *Social work with groups* (2nd ed.). New York: Columbia University Press.

Northern, H., & Kurland, R. (2001). *Social work with groups* (3rd ed.). New York: Columbia University Press.

Okundave, J. N., Gray, C., & Gray, L. B. (1999). Reimaging field instruction from a spiritually sensitive perspective: An alternative approach. *Social Work, 44*(4), 371–383.

Ortiz Hendricks, C. (2003). Learning and teaching cultural competence in the practice of social work. *Journal of Teaching in Social Work, 23*(1/2), 73–86.

Palombo, J. (1982). The psychology of the self and the termination of treatment. *Clinical Social Work Journal, 10*, 15–27.

Papell, C. P. (1980). *A study of styles of learning for direct social work practice.* Doctoral dissertation, Wurzweiler School of Social Work, Yeshiva University.

Papell, C. P., & Skolnik, L. (1992). The reflective practitioner: A contemporary paradigm's relevance for social work education. *Journal of Social Work Education, 28*, 18–26.

Paul, R. (1992). *Critical thinking: What every person needs to survive in a rapidly changing world.* Sonoma, CA: Foundation for Critical Thinking.

Pinderhughes, E. (1989). *Understanding race, ethnicity and power: The key to efficacy in clinical practice.* New York: Free Press.

Pippard, J. L., & Bjorklund, R. W. (2003). Identifying essential techniques for social work community practice. *Journal of Community Practice, 11*(4), 101–116.

Plaut, S. M. (1993). Boundary issues in teacher student relationships. *Journal of Sex and Marital Therapy, 19*(3), 210–219.

Raphael, B. F., & Rosenblum, A. F. (1987). An operational guide to the faculty field liaison role. *Social Casework, 68*, 156–163.

Raphael, B. F., & Rosenblum, A. F. (1989). The open expression of difference in the field practicum: Report of a pilot study. *Journal of Social Work Education, 25,* 109–116.

Raschick, M., Maypole, D., & Day, P. (1998). Improving field education through Kolb learning theory. *Journal of Social Work Education, 34,* 31–42.

Raskin, M. S., & Bloome, W. W. (1998). The impact of managed care on field instruction. *Journal of Social Work Education, 34,* 365–374.

Reeser, L. C. (1992). Students with disabilities in practicum: What is reasonable accommodation? *Journal of Social Work Education, 28,* 98–109.

Reeser, L. C., & Wertkin, R. A. (1997). Sharing sensitive student information with field instructors: Responses of students, liaisons, and field instructors. *Journal of Social Work Education, 33,* 347–362.

Regehr, C., Regehr, G., Leeson, J., & Fusco, L. (2002). Setting priorities for learning in the field practicum: A comparative study of students and field instructors. *Journal of Social Work Education, 38,* 55–65.

Reisch, M., & Jarman-Rohde, L. (2000). The future of social work in the United States: Implications for field education. *Journal of Social Work Education, 36,* 201–214.

Reynolds, B. C. (1985). *Learning and teaching in the practice of social work.* New York: Russell & Russell.

Rhodes, R., Ward, J., Ligon, J., & Priddy, W. (1999). Fighting for field: Seven threats to an important component of social work education. *Journal of Baccalaureate Social Work, 5*(1), 15–25.

Richan, W. C. (1989). Empowering students to empower others: A community-based field practicum. *Journal of Social Work Education, 25,* 276–283.

Roche, S. E., Dewees, M., Trailweaver, R., Alexander, S., Cuddy, C., & Handy, M. (1999). *Contesting boundaries in social work education: A liberatory approach to cooperative learning and teaching.* Alexandria, VA: Council on Social Work Education.

Rogers, G. (ed.). (1995). *Social work field education: Views and visions.* Dubuque, IA: Kendall/Hunt.

Rogers, G. (1996). Training field instructors British style. *Journal of Social Work Education, 32,* 365–276.

Rogers, G., & McDonald, L. (1992). Thinking critically: An approach to field instructor training. *Journal of Social Work Education, 28*, 166–177.

Rosenblatt, A., & Mayer, J. E. (1975). Objectionable supervisory styles: Students views. *Social Work, 20*.

Rosenblum, A. F. & Raphael, F. B. (1983). The role and function of the faculty field liaison. *Journal of Education for Social Work, 19*, 67–73.

Rosenfeld, D. J. (1989). Field instructor turnover. *Journal of Teaching in Social Work, 2*(2), 49–65.

Sarri, C. (1989). The process of learning in clinical social work. *Smith College Studies in Social Work, 60*, 35–49.

Searles, H. (1955). The informational value of the supervisor's emotional experiences. *Psychiatry, 18*, 135–146.

Schneck, D. (1995, April). *Realizing the vision: The enduring mission and challenge of field education.* Paper presented at a Field Education Conference Celebrating the 25th Anniversary of the Queens Field Instruction Center, New York.

Schneck, D., Grossman, B., & Glassman U. (eds.). (1991). *Field education in social work: Contemporary issues and trends.* Dubuque, IA: Kendall/Hunt.

Schon, D. A. (1983). *The reflective practitioner: How professionals think in action.* New York: Basic Books.

Schon, D. A. (1987). *Educating the reflective practitioner.* San Francisco, CA: Jossey Bass.

Sheafor, B. W., & Jenkins, L. E. (eds.). (1982). *Quality field instruction in social work: Program development and maintenance.* New York: Longman.

Shen Ryan, A. (1981). Training Chinese-American social workers. *Social Casework, 62*, 95–105.

Shen Ryan, A., & Ortiz Hendricks, C. (1989). Culture and communication: Supervising the Asian and Hispanic social worker. *The Clinical Supervisor, 7*(1), 27–40.

Shulman, L. (1983). *Teaching the helping skills: A field instructor's guide* (1st ed.). Alexandria, VA: Council on Social Work Education.

Shulman, L. (1984). *Skills of supervision and staff management.* Itasca, IL Peacock.

Shulman, L. (1994). *Teaching the helping skills: A field instructor's guide* (2nd ed.). Alexandria, VA: Council on Social Work Education.

Shulman, L. (1999). *The skills of helping individuals, families, groups, and communities* (4th ed.). Itasca, IL: Peacock.

Shulman, L. (2004, December). *Teaching about group work in the child welfare context: A field instructor's guide.* Keynote address, Field Instructors' Recognition Day Conference, The NYC Social Work Education Consortium and the Administration for Children's Services' James Satterwhite Academy for Child Welfare Training, Professional Development Program, Hunter College School of Social Work.

Sikkema, M. (1966). A proposal for an innovation in field learning and teaching. In *Field Instruction in Graduate Social Work Education: Old Problems and New Proposals* (pp. 1–7). New York: Council on Social Work Education.

Siporin, M. (1982). The process of field instruction. In B. W. Sheafor & L. E. Jenkins, *Quality field instruction in social work: Program development and maintenance* (pp. 175–197). New York: Longman.

Smith, M. K. (2002). Malcolm Knowles, informal adult education, self-direction and andragogy. *Informal education encyclopedia.* Retrieved on April 15, 2005, from http://www.infed.org/thinkers/et-knowl.htm

Solas, J. (1990). Effective teaching as construed by social work students. *Journal of Social Work Education, 26,* 145–154.

Solomon, B. (1982). Power: The troublesome factor in cross-cultural supervision. *Smith College School of Social Work, 10,* 27–32.

Steinberg, D. M. (1993). Some findings from a study on the impact of group work education on social work practitioners' work with groups. *Social Work With Groups, 16*(3), 23–39.

Strom-Gottfried, K., & Corcoran, K. (1998). Confronting ethical dilemmas in managed care: Guidelines for students and faculty. *Journal of Social Work Education, 34,* 109–119.

Sue, D. W., & Sue, D. (2003). *Counseling the culturally different: Theory and practice* (4th. ed.) New York: Wiley.

Sweitzer, H., Frederick, R., & King, M. A. (1999) *The successful internship: Transformation and empowerment*. Belmont, CA: Brooks/Cole.

Swenson, C. R. (1988). The professional log: Techniques for self-directed learning. *Social Casework, 69*, 307–311.

Toseland, R. W., & Rivas, R. F. (1984), *An introduction to group work practice*. New York: Macmillan.

Tourse, R. W. C. (1994). Completing the process tapestry. *Journal of Teaching in Social Work, 9*(1/2), 155–167.

Towle, C. (1954). *The learner in education for the professions as seen in education for social work*. Chicago: University of Chicago Press.

Tropman, E. J. (1977). Agency constraints affecting links between practice and education. *Journal of Education for Social Work, 13*(1), 8–14.

Tully, C. T., Kroff, N. P., & Prick, J. L. (1993). Is the field a hard hat area? A study of violence in field placements. *Journal of Social Work Education, 29*, 191–199.

Urbanowski, M. L., & Dwyer, M. M. (1988). *Learning through field instruction: A guide for teachers and students*. Milwaukee, WI: Family Service of America.

Urbanowski, M. L., & Dwyer, M. M. (1989). Counterpoint/In defense of process recording. *Social Casework, 70*, 312–314.

Urdang, E. (1979). In defense of process recording. *Smith College Studies in Social Work, 50*, 1–15.

Van Soest, D., & Kruzich, J. (1994). The influence of learning styles on student and field instructor perceptions of field placement success. *Journal of Teaching in Social Work, 9*(1/2), 49–69.

Videka-Sherman, L., & Reid, W. (1985). The structured record: A clinical educational tool. *The Clinical Supervisor, 3*(1), 45–62.

Wall, J. C. (1994). Teaching termination to trainees through parallel processes in supervision. *The Clinical Supervisor, 12*(2), 27–36.

Walsh, J. (2003). *Endings in clinical practice: Effective closure in diverse settings*. Chicago: Lyceum.

Walter, C. A., & Young, T. M. (1999). Combining individual and group supervision in educating for the social work profession. *The Clinical Supervisor, 18*(2), 73–89.

Wayne, J., & Cohen, C. S. (2001). *Group work education in the field.* Alexandria, VA: Council on Social Work Education.

Wilson, J., & Moore, D. (1989). Developing and using evaluation guidelines for final practicum. *Australian Social Work, 42*(1), 21–27.

Wilson, S. J. (1980). *Recording guidelines for social workers.* New York: Free Press.

Wolk, J. L., Pray, J. E., Weismiller, T., & Dempsey, D. (1996). Political pratica: Educating social work students for policymaking. *Journal of Social Work Education, 32,* 91–100.

Yutrzenka, B. A. (1995). Making a case for training in ethnic and cultural diversity in increasing treatment efficacy. *Journal of Consulting and Clinical Psychology, 63*(2), 197–207.

Zemke, R., & Zemke, S. (June). Adult learning: What do we know for sure? *Learning.* Minneapolis: Lakewood Publications.

ABOUT THE AUTHORS

*T*he authors have worked together as members of the Seminar in Field Instruction (SIFI) Subcommittee of the Greater New York Area Directors of Field Instruction. The subcommittee was established over 30 years ago to maintain and monitor the quality and breadth of field instruction seminars in New York City and throughout the tri-state area. SIFI Subcommittee members represent schools of social work at Adelphi University, Columbia University, Fordham University, Hunter College/City University of New York, New York University, Rutgers University, Southern Connecticut State University, Stony Brook University/State University of New York, and Yeshiva University/ Wurzweiler School of Social Work.

The impetus for this text emerged over a number of years of collaboration on the development of a uniform curriculum for the delivery of seminars for new field instructors. Although the three primary authors have taken leadership in the writing and preparation of this text, the work is the result of a group collaboration that has integrated each member's expertise in teaching SIFI. The authors have made numerous presentations at the field work symposia and annual program meetings of the Council on Social Work Education to advance knowledge of the SIFI and the importance of preparing field instructors for their roles as teachers, evaluators, and gatekeepers for the profession.

Carmen Ortiz Hendricks, DSW, LCSW, is associate dean and professor at Yeshiva University Wurzweiler School of Social Work and was formerly on the faculty of Hunter College School of Social Work of the City University of New York. She is best known for her expertise in culturally competent social work practice and education. She was a major contributor to the development of the National Association of Social Workers' *Standards for Cultural Competence in Social Work Practice*. Hendricks has been a field instructor, field coordinator, director of field education, faculty liaison, and SIFI teacher.

Jeanne Bertrand Finch, DSW, LCSW-R, is assistant dean for field instruction and director of the Student-Community Development Specialization at the School of Social Welfare, Stony Brook University/State University of New York. She has worked in the field of child welfare in both the United States and England. She teaches Foundation and Advanced Social Work Micro Practice, Student-Community Development Seminar and Colloquia, and Social Work with Children. In addition to being a director of field education, she has been a field instructor, faculty liaison, and SIFI teacher.

Cheryl Franks, PhD, is the executive director of diversity, human rights, and social justice at Columbia University School of Social Work. Formerly the associate director of field education, she managed the World of Work and the International Social Welfare Fields of Practice, and coordinated the SIFI program at Columbia. She teaches Advanced Generalist Practice and Programming, Issues of Diversity, and International Immersion at the School of Social Work, and Rethinking Human Rights at the School of International and Public Affairs. Franks is best know for her expertise in race and racial identity theory. She has been a field instructor, faculty liaison, and SIFI teacher and has developed advanced SIFIs in macro practice.

INDEX